Praise for
The World's Stronges

"Hanagarne, kind and uncomplaining, is ... ...
ity throughout, a proponent of the importance of curiosity ... ...
learning. He's a born storyteller, unpretentious and irreverent. . . . The
whole of this delightfully rich and unconventional gem of a book is even
greater than the sum of its parts. Read it and laugh and learn."
—The Washington Post

"Fearless and funny." —NewYorker.com

"An inspiring, often funny tale about the power of persistence."
—People

"Hilarious. . . . You'll be moved by [Hanagarne's] resilience and his family's unflagging love." —Parade

"Unique and engaging. . . . There's real humanity and humility to this
memoir." —The Boston Globe

"Told with antic humor, unself-conscious candor, and a humble, deep
love for the family that held him up."—The Atlanta Journal Constitution

"Rollicking but also poignant." —The Salt Lake Tribune

"Josh Hanagarne has somehow managed to fit a small collection of
books into his memoir, *The World's Strongest Librarian*. There's the story
of a boy who fell in love with books early and never let go. The drama of
a youth with an extreme case of Tourette Syndrome who fights back
through power lifting and other feats of strength. The tale of a 'mildly
religious,' questioning man figuring out what it means to live in a Mormon community. Hanagarne is the self-deprecating hero of all these
stories. If his engaging narrative voice is an accurate reflection of his
physical presence, he's a truly rare gentle giant."
—Milwaukee Journal Sentinel

"[Hanagarne's] book is a poignant story of hope, wrapped in a born-
librarian's delight over books, and witty observations about life. . . . He's
not just lifting weights, he's lifting spirits. And, sometimes, that can take
some pretty heavy lifting." —Deseret News (Utah)

"Enlightening and very funny." —The Hartford Courant

"Josh Hanagarne's *The World's Strongest Librarian* is one of the rare greats and paints an intricate portrait of a Salt Lake City original."
—SaltLakeMagazine.com

"*The World's Strongest Librarian* . . . joyfully celebrates books and reading and illuminates an unlikely hero who will be remembered long after the final page is turned. I couldn't put this book down." —*BookPage*

"Wildly quirky memoir of facing down his ferocious Tourette's tics . . . Hanagarne's account manages to be very gag-full and tongue-in-cheek . . . highly engaging." —*Publishers Weekly*

"A jaunty memoir covering both the influence of the Church of Jesus Christ of Latter-day Saints and the torments of Tourette Syndrome. . . . A clever, affable story of one Mormon, his family, his vocation, and his implacable ailment." —*Kirkus Reviews*

"Witty and upbeat voice . . . fun (and inspiring) reading."
—*Library Journal*

"An excellent and uplifting story." —*Booklist*

"Will cause any librarian's chest to bloom a bit with pride. . . . Thanks to Hanagarne's gift of humor, good writing, and honesty, this book is full of tears and laughs to last many a library book group discussion."
—*Public Libraries Online*

"*The World's Strongest Librarian* is witty and wry but also generous and full of heart. Hanagarne's book reads less like a memoir than a story told by a good friend." —Jennifer Miller, author of *The Year of the Gadfly*

"A sumptuous read, as funny, erudite, and energizing as a chat with a conversational intellectual, as engrossing and moving as a medical detective drama . . . the book leaves all of us who've read it feeling a little stronger and brighter ourselves."
—Martha Beck, author of *Expecting Adam*,
Leaving the Saints, and *Finding Your Way in a Wild New World*

"Just like the library has every funny, beautiful, moving, wise story you'd ever need in it, so too does this book. This is not just your ordinary memoir: It is a soaring, inspiring elegy to the small and big miracles of parenthood and friendship and marriage and how they triumph over the not-so-small challenges of life. It is a perfect, perfect gem of a read, unputdownable, unforgettable, unmatchable."
—Pam Allyn, author of *What to Read When*

"Josh Hanagarne inspires in his pursuit to break the shackles of Tourette Syndrome and live his life to the fullest as a husband, a father, and a librarian. Insightful, heart-wrenching, and delightfully humorous, *The World's Strongest Librarian* is a triumph!"
—Cory MacLauchlin, author of *Butterfly in the Typewriter: The Tragic Life of John Kennedy Toole and the Remarkable Story of* A Confederacy of Dunces

"As a gym rat myself, I can attest to the power of hurling one's sinews against heavy stuff that keeps wanting to slam you back into the floor. The difference with Josh Hanagarne is he has lifted much weightier impediments—Tourette's, loneliness, geekitude, and the calling to be a writer. That he is—and a talent to savor, to emulate, and to be inspired by."
—Steven Pressfield, bestselling author of *The War of Art* and *Turning Pro*

"Josh Hanagarne has an astonishing story to tell, and he does so with insight, humor, grace, and wonder. All human beings suffer and struggle. Through the lens of his own miraculous experiences, Mr. Hanagarne illuminates the path to joy and the infinite possibilities of transcendence."
—Melanie Rae Thon, author of *Sweet Hearts*

"A truly interesting, engaging, and fascinating memoir."
—Joe R. Lansdale, author of *Edge of Dark Water*

"Josh's special struggles to deal with his own doubts, Tourette's, and society give his journey a patina of honesty, resilience, and a flavor of humanity that truly inspires. Josh has a unique voice, and I was privileged to read and be empowered by his story."
—Stephen Abram, vice president of Gale Cengage Learning

"A funny, profound, emotionally generous, and wonderfully human story."
—Lou Schuler, coauthor of *The New Rules of Lifting*

"Everything about this book is big: Certainly it is the story of a 6' 7" librarian with Tourette's, but it is also the quest for how we know, how we feel, and how we love . . . without reservation. I found it impossible to put down; save a day to read this." —Dan John, author of *Intervention*

"Josh Hanagarne is a giant of a man and a giant of a writer. . . . This guy is the real freaking deal in a very fresh and exciting way."
—Larry Brooks, author of *Story Engineering*

Josh Hanagarne believes in curiosity, questions, and strength, and that things are never so bad that they can't improve. He is a librarian at the Salt Lake City Public Library. He lives with his wife, Janette, and their son, Max, in Salt Lake City, Utah.

www.worldsstrongestlibrarian.com

To arrange a speaking engagement for Josh Hanagarne, please contact the Penguin Speakers Bureau at speakersbureau@us.penguingroup.com.

THE
WORLD'S
STRONGEST
LIBRARIAN

A Book Lover's Adventures

JOSH HANAGARNE

GOTHAM BOOKS

GOTHAM BOOKS
Published by the Penguin Group
Penguin Group (USA) LLC
375 Hudson Street
New York, New York 10014, USA

USA | Canada / UK | Ireland | Australia | New Zealand | India | South Africa | China
penguin.com

Previously published as a Gotham Books hardcover

First trade paperback printing, May 2014

10   9   8   7   6   5   4   3   2   1

Gotham Books and the skyscraper logo are trademarks of Penguin Group (USA) LLC

The Library of Congress has catalogued the hardcover edition as follows:

Hanagarne, Joshua, 1977–
    The world's strongest librarian : a memoir of Tourette's, faith, strength, and the power
of family / Joshua Hanagarne.
        pages cm
    ISBN 978-1-59240-787-3 (HC)   978-1-59240-877-1 (PBK)
    1. Hanagarne, Joshua, 1977– 2. Librarians—Utah—Salt Lake City—Biography.
3. Public libraries—Utah—Salt Lake City. 4. Tourette syndrome. I. Title.
    Z720.H24H36 2013
    020.92—dc23   2012037713

Printed in the United States of America
Set in Adobe Garamond • Designed by Spring Hoteling

This is a work of nonfiction. I've re-created the majority of the dialogue, but it's all faithful to the substance of the conversations. When writing scenes, I interviewed the other people involved to see whose memory was the best. This led to some spectacular posturing about the health of our respective brains. Whenever we had different memories of how something happened, I tried to give the tiebreaker to my dear old mom. I'm sure I'll still find mistakes in here, probably the second after the book is published, but I doubt they'll be of much consequence.

—Josh Hanagarne

For Janette, who waited

CONTENTS

INTRODUCTION

Today the library was hot, humid, and smelly. It was like work-ing inside a giant pair of glass underpants without any leg holes to escape through. The building moved. It breathed. It seethed with bodies and thoughts moving in and out of people's heads. Mostly out.

"You tall bigot!"

I stopped and wondered if these two words had ever been put next to each other. The odds were astronomical; even some-one with my primitive math skills knew this. I laughed, which didn't help the situation, which was this: A guy wearing a jaunty red neckerchief had walked by the reference desk, yelling about the "motherfucking Jews and lesbians on the Supreme Court." I had asked him to lower his voice and voilà! Now I was a tall bigot . . . the worst kind of all.

"What are you, some kind of *Jew*?" he sputtered. I've never seen someone so enraged. I wondered what he'd do if he knew I'd been raised Mormon.

Maybe he was mad because he couldn't find the anti-Semitism section. The library has a robust collection of what I call non-cuddly hate lit. This is one of my favorite things about working here: If you believe censorship is poison, here lies paradise. We have sections on anti-Mormonism, anti-Semitism, anti-anti-Semitism, anti-atheism, anti-God, anti-feminism, pro-gay . . . there's something to offend everyone.

Moshe Safdie, the architect who designed the Salt Lake City Public Library, won numerous awards for his vision and technical derring-do. He thought big, appropriately, because a building that can hold 500,000 books is enormous. The number of items circulating each hour is rivaled only by the number of people napping in the corners. But nothing is as impressive as the way the building *looks.* I work in a beautiful building made almost entirely of glass. Seen from the air, it looks like the Nike Swoosh if it got frightened and began to cower.

An older librarian—one of the few other males—once said to me, "Whatever we deal with, coming here is always a visual reward." This statement is poetic, accurate, and maddening. Because most of the time it feels like people show up just to fight about something with total strangers like me. Which is fine. I'm not here for the good company.

One of the reasons I work here is because I have extreme Tourette Syndrome.* The kind with verbal tics, sometimes loud ones; the kind that draws warning looks. Working in this library is the ultimate test for someone who literally can't sit still. Who can't shush himself. A test of willpower, of patience, and occasionally, of the limits of human absurdity.

A patron recently took exception to a series of throat clearings I couldn't suppress. As he approached, I put on my customer service smile and readied myself for one of those rare, mind-blowing reference transactions that I hear about from

---

* I've had neurologists who write "Tourette Syndrome" without the apostrophe *s* and others who write "Tourette's Syndrome." I'm going to use Tourette's when I only use one word, and Tourette Syndrome when I use two. That seems to be the most common.

other librarians. Instead this man said, "If you're going to walk around honking like a royal swan, you don't belong in the library. I'm going to call security. Somebody needs to teach you a lesson."

I stood up. I'm six feet seven inches tall, and I weigh 260 pounds. "Is it you?" I'm not confrontational, but I don't lose many staring contests. I'm good at looming when it's helpful. He walked away.

I also work here because I love books, because I'm inveterately curious, and because, like most librarians, I'm not well suited to anything else. As a breed, we're the ultimate generalists. I'll never know everything about anything, but I'll know something about almost everything and that's how I like to live.

Earlier today a young woman asked me to help her find a book about how to knit lingerie. This is the sort of question library school recruiters should feature in their dreary PowerPoint presentations, not claptrap about how we're the "stewards of democracy." They would definitely attract more males to the profession. When I arrived in my library department two years ago, the alpha male was a sixty-six-year-old woman.

On our way to the lingerie section—yes, the official subject heading is Lingerie, call number 646.42—I tripped over another young woman who was lying on the floor beneath a blanket, nestled between two rows of law books. I'm thirty-five years old and it both relieves and elates me to know I can still be surprised.

"I'm sleeping here!" she yelled.

I'm rarely at a loss for words outside the library. But within its walls I'm required to form sentences that no logical person should ever have to utter, for instance, "You can't sleep on the floor at the library under your blanket."

"I don't snore!" she said, gripping her blanket with both hands, as if I might snatch it away.

"I'm sure you don't," I said. "That's not the point."

"Well, there's no other point!"

This was an occasion when my need to be right didn't feel that important. I made a phone call. Security interrupted her derailed slumber and led her out of the building. *And stay out,* I pictured them yelling, tossing the blanket after her, where it would be swept into traffic by a sudden gust of wind.

I felt a twinge of envy. I couldn't remember the last time I'd taken a nap. I'll admit to often feeling sleepy in the library. Most of the time, in fact. The building was constructed with the ability to save power and warm itself, so the glass walls make it difficult to find an area that isn't bathed by soporific sunbeams. I briefly considered lying down on the floor between *Black's Law Dictionary* and the Morningstar investment guides. Someone would probably report me, but I might be imposing enough to buy myself a power nap. Then someone came to the desk for help and the plan ended before it began.

I really want someone to ask me a question that is not "How many times can I fall asleep in here before I get kicked out?" I really want this building to serve the purpose for which it was intended—as a breeding ground for curiosity.

I work on Level 3. If you're on my floor you're probably looking for information about Bigfoot or the healing powers of crystals, self-help, or psychology; you're trying to expunge something from your record and need the law section; you need to lose weight; you heard that people make money on the Internet; you need to summon some pixies; you want to get into hat-making; you can't sight your rifle; you're sick of the Jews; you're sick of the people who won't shut up about being sick of the Jews; you're looking for a Bible; or you're cramming for the SAT. Unless you're just looking for a place to sleep, in which case I'd direct you to any of the comfortable chairs laid out around the perimeter, out of my direct line of sight. And if you're hooking up with your drug dealer, that's usually conducted in the restrooms.

Later this morning, something actually happened that didn't require me to wake someone up or tell him to watch porn at home. An African American man asked me if the Hutu tribe in Rwanda had any Jewish ancestry. What a fascinating question. We started hunting through the library's incredibly expensive, underpromoted, and underused research databases. After an hour we realized that the question was bigger than we could complete during one session, but he had enough leads to pursue on his own. We'd forgotten that the rest of the world existed as we leaned over my computer and hurried to and fro in the stacks grabbing books.

As always, many patrons wanted to research their genealogy. I always wonder why. Were they trying to discover whether they might have an inheritance coming to them? Being kept from them? Researching the people who led to their own genetic impairments? I have Tourette Syndrome because of some combination of my parents' crazy innards. His genes met hers and said, "Hey, let's get stupid!" I can't blame them for not knowing any better. If there's a memo out there that says Never cross a Navajo and a Mormon or you'll create a twitchy baby who will be a burden forever, they never got it.

At lunch, many of the librarians lurched up to the staff room and fell onto chairs and couches with their books and magazines. Librarians as a rule move about as well as the Tin Man did before Dorothy brought him the oilcan. Their heads often sit so far forward on their necks that they look like woodpeckers frozen in mid-peck. Their shoulders are rounded from answering the phone, typing, eating, and reading. Their hands at rest inevitably rotate into the typing position. They spend so much time looking down at computers and into books and talking down to people from their tall desks that it's become an unnatural effort to raise their eyes to make eye contact during conversation.

I move quite well, partly because during my lunch break, I go downstairs to the library's diminutive fitness room, wrap my hands in thin, well-seasoned leather strips to protect them, and bend horseshoes. I'm also working on the goal of deadlifting six hundred pounds, but I do that outside the library walls. The sound of six hundred pounds hitting the ground is serious. Dropping that much weight in the basement of the library would echo up to the top floor and wake everyone up. When I hit a snag, I call my coach, a man named Adam.

Adam is a former air force tech sergeant, an expert in hand-to-hand combat, and the sort of hard-ass who describes poor haircuts as "a lack of personal excellence," even though his hair is currently poufy and awful and makes him look like a Dragon Ball Z character.

He has the entire poem, all sixteen lines, of "Invictus" by William Henley tattooed on his left arm.

> Out of the night that covers me,
> Black as the Pit from pole to pole,
> I thank whatever gods may be
> For my unconquerable soul.
>
> In the fell clutch of circumstance
> I have not winced nor cried aloud.
> Under the bludgeonings of chance
> My head is bloody, but unbowed.
>
> Beyond this place of wrath and tears
> Looms but the Horror of the shade,
> And yet the menace of the years
> Finds, and shall find, me unafraid.
>
> It matters not how strait the gate,
> How charged with punishments the scroll.
> I am the master of my fate:
> I am the captain of my soul.

More on him later.

After lunch a teenage boy with chains crisscrossing his pants slumped into the library, limping as if he'd stepped into a bear trap. He needed some books for school, he told me, "Books that aren't all gay and shit." I'd love to have a sign demarcating that section. We probably need another one for the child abuse books. The teenagers love that stuff. One of our most popular books is a memoir about child abuse: *A Child Called "It"* by Dave Pelzer. I tried to read it once and was too unsettled by the second chapter to ever pick it up again. But the teens can't seem to get enough of it.

I can always tell the kids who've been sent to the library to find a book from some teacher's boring reading list. They trudge in with their eyes on the carpet, breathing hard with annoyance. Many of these kids will do anything to avoid talking to us. Many of these kids have never said anything to me besides, "Yeah, I have to read this book called *Johnny Tremain*." Kids who want to read Pelzer's book practically jump on top of my desk in their eagerness to read about a child being mistreated. We should probably just give up and order a hundred more copies of *A Child Called "It."*

After helping the kid find the not-gay section, I watched another patron vomit into a garbage can.

"Pardon me, sir," I said. "Could you make it to the restroom?"

"I'm fine here," he said.

I did lots of dusting. I focused on the tops of shelves that only the very tall can see. I helped a delightful elderly woman with an unidentifiable accent create an e-mail account on the public computers. When I asked her what she liked to read—I can't figure out how to quit asking this question of total strangers—she said, "I enjoy the nakedest of romances."

There was some excitement in the afternoon. We had a break in a two-year-old mystery. Someone has been waging a war against the harmless 133s. Occultism. Crystals. Sylvia Browne. Summoning pixies safely—yes, there is apparently a wrong way to do it. Energy fields. Enneagrams. Aleister Crowley and Anton LaVey. Angels. Satan. These books have been vanishing.

One day a shelver spotted a shelf that was wrenched open at the bottom. In the hollow underneath it was a bunch of Wicca books and the timeless classic *Witch in the Bedroom: Proven Sensual Magic*. When we looked under the other shelves, we found a couple hundred books that had been hidden. We pretended to be outraged—this was censorship!—but it was hilarious. I wanted to know who was doing it, and how.

When we put the books back on the shelves, they vanished again. Replacement copies disappeared as well, sometimes within an hour. I'd taken to patrolling the perimeter every ten minutes, determined to apprehend the crooks and thank them for entertaining me so well—and to remind them that there were a few Sylvia Browne books on the shelves that they'd missed. We found no one.

But today a shelver saw two men raising the bottom shelves! They escaped. We investigated and found dozens of missing books. Now we're trying to figure out how to entice the shelf-secreters back and trap them. I suggested leaving some books about Stonehenge and the Mayan calendar strewn about as bait. I long to shake the hand of the man or woman who scuttled *Accepting the Psychic Torch* out of sight, out of mind, out of reach, in the dust below the bookshelves.

I can't imagine the monks in the libraries of yore dealing with this nonsense. Waking people up, encouraging them to view porn, vomit, and procure drugs elsewhere. Sure, those monks had to condemn Jews and lesbians, but they didn't attend patron education workshops because there were no patrons, only themselves. Beyond the occasional visit from a grand inquisitor, they were left alone to use the libraries as they were meant to be used.

The purpose of libraries—to organize and provide information—hasn't changed. They're billed as the Poor Man's University. (Many librarians also bill them as the Poor Man's Day Care or the Poor Man's Urinal.) I love working here because the reasons behind libraries are important to me.

The public library contains multitudes. And each person who visits contains multitudes as well. Each of us is a library of thoughts, memories, experiences, and odors. We adapt to one another to produce the human condition.

Libraries have shaped and linked all the disparate threads of my life. The books. The weights. The tics. The harm I've caused myself and others. Even the very fact that I'm alive. How I handle my Tourette's. Everything I know about my identity can be traced back to the boy whose parents took him to a library in New Mexico even before he was born.

The library taught me that I could ask any questions I wanted and pursue them to their conclusions without judgment or embarrassment.

And it's where I learned that not all questions have answers.

CHAPTER 1

808.543—Storytelling
011.62—Children—Books and Reading

I don't like to see children cry, but I couldn't feel much sympathy for the little guy. I told his mom there was no need to apologize as he sniffled and wept and wiped his nose on his Pokémon T-shirt. The problem? Our library system's Expanded Card lets a patron borrow a hundred items. But this boy's mother was playing the Evil Queen and would only let him take fifty.

It was hard to feel much sympathy for him, but empathy? Oh, yes, I've been there. When I was his age, and even today, when it comes to books and libraries, too much is never enough.

I love to witness kids' unvarnished curiosity. They're willing to ask questions because they still understand that that's how to find answers. Most of the younger kids I see in the library would rather put the question out there and run the risk of sounding silly than go without an answer. Another evening, a six-year-old girl approached my desk with a piece of paper. "Can you tell me how to spell 'princess'?" she asked.

"I'll tell you what," I said. "Why don't you write down the first letter, and I'll tell you if you make a mistake, okay? Then you can write the second. We'll keep going until the word is spelled out." She got it and was very proud. I wondered why she thought she couldn't spell. When put on the spot like this, most kids were better spellers than they thought they were, although there were exceptions. When Oprah was giving away free Kentucky Fried Chicken dinners, a five-year-old asked me how to spell "KFC." I didn't laugh. I was happy that she felt like she could ask. She reminded me of myself at that age—whatever I didn't know, I could ask, and if my parents didn't know the answer, the librarians would.

For its first few years, my life was divided by a lightning strike into two distinct chapters: Before Fern and After Fern. Fern, my first romantic love, from E. B. White's book *Charlotte's Web*.

It was during the Before Fern years that I entered my first library in Moab, Utah, carried by my mom.

Inside the library was order. Information cataloged into rows, authors, titles, columns, shelves, and librarian's preferences. Everything had its place. Everything proceeded according to patterns established even before the current crop of ancient librarians began working there. The lights were dim and the atmosphere was the opposite of the manic landscape outside. I slobbered and drooled as she wandered through the aisles.

"How old is he?" a librarian asked.

"Thirteen months."

"Hmm . . . looks like somebody's been forgetting to feed him."

They laughed. I was as cube-shaped as it's possible for a human to be. My grandfather actually told my mom that she should put me on a diet. My mom said that she'd put me on a diet if he'd go on one as well.

Mom walked away from the desk and began browsing. After finding books for herself, she put me on the floor in the children's section. According to her, I put a book in my mouth and chewed. When I fell asleep, she picked me up and checked out her books.

She walked three blocks to our big yellow house, which lay nestled at the base of a red sandstone hill. The house was two stories tall and included a terrifying unfinished basement. My mom pushed a playpen onto the porch, laid me inside of it, and read until my dad got home.

"How was your day?" she asked him. He told her. Familiar patterns repeated themselves. Cleaning up. Dinner. Diapers. Bottles. Laughter. When it was my bedtime, my dad put me into my crib. He lifted one of the cardboard books that my mom had borrowed from the library and read it to me before kissing my forehead and turning out the light. When he turned and saw my mom watching, he smiled. "I never get tired of this." He'd begun reading to me about eight months before I was born.

My dad was twenty years old, my mom a year older, when I was born. They'd met at a uranium mine in Moab the previous summer. He was trying to figure out what to do with his life and decided that shoveling mud was the best way to do it. She was home from college for the summer and was working in the mine's assay lab.

When approaching from the north, the hundred miles leading into Moab are lonely and desolate and abrasive to the eyes. The traveler experiences the visual equivalent of a tumbleweed rubbing across his face. The landscape is featureless except for the unbecoming oceans of sagebrush that spread to the horizon in all directions. Mild bumps masquerading as hills are the only visual distraction. It's so dreary that the highway can't even work up the ambition to turn once in a while. It just plods straight ahead, as bored by its surroundings as the travelers on its surface. But when the salmon-colored walls begin shooting up from the horizon, the sudden shift is like being smacked over the head with a lovely watercolor.

An exquisite red bowl of sandstone cradles the road, guiding it along a highway that has at last begun to twist and turn again. Sand dunes roll between and around the rock formations and seek shade at the base of the cliffs. Sheer walls of rock veer off at crazy angles, and the fractured sandstone cliffs give the impression that the whole structure—the mesas, peaks, bluffs, and plateaus—was assembled by a giant toddler with a limited attention span. From a massive block of red stone, the toddler carved out the bowl and threw a handful of houses down into the basin. Then he pounded the rocks with a giant hammer, creating the jagged splinters and pillars that jut out in every direction. In other places, stones without edges have been sanded down until they appear soft as a blanket.

The town of Moab itself is hidden until the traveler turns and crosses a bridge that divides the canyon walls. The Colorado River winds under that bridge, wrapping the town in its coils. The water is dark, with sandbars peeking up from the shallow spots.

The uranium mill sits at the northern edge of Moab. There's no pit, but piles from the tailings of mined earth make a lofty ring like a radioactive Bundt cake or a toxic anthill. Leach pads the color of airplane lavatory water fan out from the ring. Looking down from the air, the surrounding red walls, the ponds, and the crater caused by the ring become an ugly bloodshot eye, glaring from the ground.

That's where Frank Hanagarne, Jr., worked during the summer of 1976. He was the strongest, tallest, funniest, roughest guy in the universe. Frank stood north of six feet four (he

would top out at six-five), with thick glasses that could double
as blast doors. The left side of his mouth sneered constantly, as
if someone had slipped a fishhook through it and was tugging
it from an invisible scaffold above his head. He could throw
anyone over the moon with one finger.

Linda Dalton was over six feet tall and had a bust and legs
that generated intense interest from the town's boys, not that
many of them were brave enough to talk to her. She had blond
hair that fell to just above her ears, as if someone had melted a
yellow Frisbee and set it on her head. She was an athlete and
looked it. Her squared shoulders were built for climbing trees
and fighting with seven siblings. Her legs were long and strong,
and she had a reputation for being able to start any motorcycle
in town. She referred to men who couldn't start her dirt bike as
"weenie legs." The moment my dad saw her exiting the assay lab
at the uranium mill, her hips drawing a figure eight as they hurried to the parking lot, his mouth flew open and he thought,
I'm going to marry her.

He did, just before the year ended. Little changed in the
next few months besides the fact that they lived together and
were sufficiently married to get it on with the Lord's approval.
My parents say they got married because they're soul mates. It's
a nice thought, but if they're soul mates, they're made for each
other in the same way as cotton candy and cooked carrots are.
Here's my simple theory about their union: Teenagers are horny
and Mormons don't have sex before marriage. For all my mom's
good intentions and lofty spirituality, she was tooling around in
a hot nineteen-year-old body set ablaze by hormones. My dad
didn't have the spiritual or moral restraint she possessed, especially before they met, and he was even younger and less mature
than she was. They can talk about soul mates and logic and love
all they want, but I think agitated hormones won the debate
and spirituality tagged along behind. Soon, my mom's womb
was toting a twitchy little embryo around Moab while they

made preparations to become a family. On December 1, 1977, they gave the world their first contribution to the Hanagarne race of giants.

By the time I was born, Mom had decided that she'd stay home with me. My dad supported her decision. For all his flaws, then and now, he could work anyone into the ground and was happy to prove that he could support his fledgling family. And he did, while she stayed home and tried to create an intelligent, courteous, kind, morally upright, and insatiable bookworm.

Sometimes I think a cliché is best: My parents were my heroes. In my eyes, my mom was nicer than anyone in the world. She could also sing more sweetly, cook better; she was smarter, and was certainly the most beautiful woman. More than anything, she liked to play games. This would only become truer as the years passed. She'd pretend to fall asleep while walking across the living room, stopping, mouth agape, and beginning to snore while we all screamed, "Mom! Mom! Wake up!" She'd take my He-Man action figures and make them marry my sister's Rainbow Brite toys. Sometimes if we disagreed with her, she'd turn her hands into blades and chase us around, rapidly karate chopping our backs and stomachs until we admitted she was right. One of her favorite pranks was to wait until my dad was showering, fill up a paper Dixie cup full of ice water, and then throw it over the shower curtain. We'd all laugh while he screamed and vowed to take revenge, half hoping that he'd storm out in a rage, naked and dripping. Once, during one cold February, she was trying to get my picky brother to eat stroganoff. "Will you do it if Dad runs around the house naked?" she asked him.

"Ha!" My dad knew he would never eat it. But then my dad was naïve enough to go and use the restroom. My mom quickly divided up Kyle's stroganoff onto my sibling's plates. When my suspicious but defeated dad stepped out onto the porch in nothing but his fraying slippers, he said, "Only once, right?" And then he ran. My mom quickly locked the door and turned on the porch lights. "Let me in!" he yelled, pounding on the door.

"You have to run!" she said. "Then we'll see!"

We lived at the top of a long cul-de-sac, so it wasn't like anyone was going to see his pale, shivering body hoofing it through the crunchy snow, but he sure was mad when she finally let him in. Until he saw that we all had tears of glee rolling down our cheeks. Then he laughed and demanded that someone bring him a robe. This just made us all laugh harder and he stalked off to cover himself.

Most people would agree that there's only one word to describe my dad. But I don't think any two would choose the same word. When my wife was my fiancée, she described him as a "great tethered bear." That's pretty accurate. But she has reason to jab at him. During a spirited discussion (that he started) about which animals we each wanted to claim as our spirit animals (he insisted), he named her *Gaagi bechant*—which is Navajo for "bird shit on head." A malevolent bird once gave her an undistinguished gift from above, and she had foolishly told my dad.

If pressed—and pressing a tethered bear is unwise—my dad would probably describe himself as "Navajo." It's how he has portrayed himself—shrilly and defensively—for decades, despite being a white guy. It's his shtick and it's funny when it works. He's got a good tan, but that's about as far as it goes. The Navajo meaning of Hanagarne is, depending on my dad's mood, "Leader of People" or "Those whom God has saved." My own half-hearted attempts to research the origins of my name have only revealed one interesting fact: I have a great-uncle named Cigarette. A couple of generations back, the Hanagarnes were indeed full-blood Navajos, but today we're so white you can go snow-blind if you stare at us for too long. Most of Dad's family lives on a reservation in Shiprock, New Mexico. But by the time my dad was born, the proud blood of the People made up only a quarter of his DNA.

This itty-bitty heritage never stopped Dad from attributing one hundred percent of his failures and successes to twenty-five percent of his bloodline. Navajo fierceness. Navajo boldness. Glossy Navajo hair that looks like a horse's mane and is the stuff of shampoo commercials. Navajo thirst. Navajo diabetes. Good or bad, anything he can attribute to his Navajo roots is a win for him. His dream is that my siblings and I will bring our families to Shiprock one day to live in the mansion he'll build. Picture the landscape from *Mad Max*. Now picture the rain from the movie *Seven*. Dip a paintbrush in a bucket of gray, the shade of the Modern Library covers, and paint the entire city. Now open the book *The Noonday Demon: An Atlas of Depression* and upend it over the citizens. Now throw in lots of turquoise jewelry. And really good fry bread. That's Shiprock. It always feels like it's raining there, even when it isn't. But to Dad, what matters is that the Hanagarne clan will be reunited on native soil and his children will embrace their heritage.

Dad calls me *awee*, which he says is the Navajo word for the layer of congealed fat that sits atop Navajo stews. It actually means baby. But semi-fluency in Navajo is only one of my dad's superpowers. His lineage gives him abilities that the X-Men would envy: "I can sneak up on a deer," he says. "Not only am I beautiful, but I sing like a bird." "I'm the only Navajo who can grow a beard." "My advice is always right."

My parents didn't really fight, but reading was a continual point of good-natured disagreement. Mom adored fiction. My dad couldn't understand why someone would read a book about things that weren't real. "Isn't the real world interesting enough for you? I mean, the world we live in?" Dad would retort when Mom teased him about not reading.

"I read," he said. That was true. He just didn't like the books my mom and I did. He was studying engineering at a local college and was more interested in practical titles like *F-16 Tactical Maneuvers*. When the two of them went to bed, they'd spend some time reading together—she lost in the fictional world of a popular novel, and he reading about something useful by the light of her halo.

Whatever their mild disagreements about literature, they were united in their adoration of me. They spent the majority of their free time teaching me, usually under the guise of playing games. My dad had less free time, so he couldn't play as many games with me, but Mom was so fun that I didn't notice the disparity.

One day Mom and I were sitting on the living room floor practicing the fine art of recognizing shapes. My goldfish, Jaws, watched from his bowl atop the television. At age four, I was already wearing glasses, which were constantly bent. My mom liked to say that my three greatest talents were making librarians happy, sitting on my glasses, and reading. "Josh," she said. She pressed a paper heart to her chest. "I love you with all my heart."

"Mom," I said, peering through my thick, bent glasses and holding up a paper circle, "I love you with all my circle."

Most days included a trip to the library. I never had a chance not to love the place. My mom and I usually sat in the kids' section, shoulder to shoulder on the couch while I turned the pages and read aloud from books like *Tawny Scrawny Lion* and *Are You My Mother?*

I owned lots of books, but I usually had nearly as many checked out from the library. My mom often made this deal with me: "Josh, go outside and play for an hour and then we can go to the library." I'd go outside and read stories to my dog, Topaz, and then we'd go to the library, where the librarians knew me by name. One morning after fifteen minutes of me shuffling my feet and sighing loudly as I followed her around the house, Mom cut me a better-than-usual deal: "All right! If you'll go play outside for thirty minutes, I'll take you to the library."

I grabbed the first book I saw, ran outside, and read it in the front yard. *Mr. Gopher.** My mom had gotten this book for me a week earlier and we'd read it several times already.

As I read I had a wonderful idea. Mr. Gopher lived in a hole. He came out occasionally to eat marigolds, his favorite breakfast. I'd already eaten breakfast, but that didn't mean I couldn't have some more. While my mom busied herself in the house, I ate a bunch of marigolds from her garden. She gardened for many of the same reasons that she practiced devout Mormonism: Her parents did it, it gave her a sense of purpose, and it allowed her a source of reliable beauty, no matter how ugly the rest of the world might get.

Now, if you were to design something that a person shouldn't swallow, you couldn't do any better than the marigold's pointy, curved seeds. This indelicate second breakfast lodged painfully in my throat. My eyes started to water. I ran inside, hands around my neck, and tried to convey that I was dying. I could breathe, but I couldn't swallow.

Like her mother, Mom was good at folksy remedies. She got me to eat some bread to push the seeds down. "This always works," she said. The bread mixed with the seeds and formed a doughy, prickly, unmovable lattice below my uvula.

"All right, we're going to the doctor," she said, shooing me outside. During the drive to the clinic, she kept telling me to breathe. This is my first memory of true panic. My mom couldn't fix this. The question had been asked for which she had no answer.

Soon I was sitting on a table sheathed in flimsy paper. The doctor asked me to tilt my head back. I sat rigid, hands bunched

---

* I can't find any record of this book, but my mom swears that's what it was called. She then wondered if maybe it was called *Mr. Mole*, but I can't find any record of a fictional mole eating marigolds either.

into fists. He asked again. When I didn't respond, he put his hand on my forehead and tipped my head back. A pair of long clamps came into view. I sat still. I opened my mouth. I tried not to gag when the cold metal hit the back of my throat.

The doctor grabbed the tips of the seeds and withdrew them from my throat, one by one. "What happened?" he asked my mom as he worked.

"A story went to his head," Mom said. She told him about Mr. Gopher. He nodded at her swelling stomach and said, "Are you ready for another one?"

"He likes books," she said. "They give him ideas, though."

"That's the point, right?" said the doctor.

I wasn't yet in kindergarten when *The Cat in the Hat* gave way to, with some help from my parents, more advanced fare like the Encyclopedia Brown books.

"Where do we keep our magnifying glass?" I asked my dad.

"We don't have one. Why?"

I didn't tell him that I was trying to solve a mystery I'd invented: "Who stomped on this anthill?" I'd stomped it an hour before that. Days earlier I'd stumbled and fallen into an enormous anthill in the hills behind our house. I raced down to our backyard, sprinting and falling, covered in ants, screaming and slapping at myself, interrupting the lunch my mom and some friends were having on the back lawn. She stripped me down and they all helped slap the ants off me. My dad reminded me of this humiliating experience, which he'd gotten quite a laugh out of. "Are you sure it wasn't you? Seems like you've got the motive."

"No, Dad."

"He's going to drive his teachers crazy in the fall," Dad told my mom.

"No, he won't," she said. "There are worse problems for a teacher than a kid who loves to read. They'll love him."

"I love him too. But just because they'll love him doesn't mean he won't drive them crazy. Can't we just get him some books about airplanes or something?"

"He can read what he wants. He's nervous enough about school without you fussing. It's going to be however it's going to be."

After reading *Harriet the Spy*, I started keeping spy notebooks. *The Great Brain* convinced me that I'd make my fortune as a genius, while *Where the Wild Things Are* confused me—when I threw a tantrum I got sent to bed and that was that; I was never transported to a faraway land of giant beasts who made me king. And yet, for all my book lust, I didn't know what true mania was until we brought home *Charlotte's Web* and the After Fern era began.

Charlotte's Web looked like other books. It had a cover, a title, and pages. I sat on the couch and started leafing. My mom asked if I wanted her to read it to me. "I'll try it first by myself," I said. In the early pages, a farm girl named Fern saves a piglet named Wilbur from being killed and decides to raise him herself. I stopped on page 11 and stared at the picture. The book drifted toward me as the walls of our house dissolved. My face got hot. And then the sound of my mom's laughter snapped me back into reality.

I looked up. Mom stood in the doorway with mirthful tears in her eyes. "Can you show me which picture you were kissing?" she asked when she could talk again.

It was the picture of Fern pushing Wilbur in a stroller that first caught my eye. And then there was a picture of her sitting on a milking stool, watching Wilbur in his sty with a love in her eyes that lit my head on fire. She was so beautiful that I forgot where I was and wound up kissing a dusty page in a library book. But so what? I wasn't embarrassed. I wanted to be that pig. I would even have worn the bonnet. Later, I practiced making faces at myself in the mirror, looking up at myself under my long eyelashes, just like Wilbur.

"I'm in love with Fern," I told my mom the next day. She laughed harder than I thought was possible. That is, until my dad came home and she told him. Her laughing was nothing compared to his. He still thought fiction—other than Tony Hillerman's detective tales set on the Navajo reservation—was a waste of time, but he was giddy at this sign that I'd be interested in girls.

On the first day of kindergarten, I put my copy of *Charlotte's Web* in my new plastic crayon box. After the first hour of school, I wasn't nervous anymore. When I opened my lunch that day, there was a note on top of my sandwich: *I'm glad you're my son.* That was the first of the many messages Mom would write.

I'm proud of you.

And just as often—*Your dad and I love you so much.*

At the end of the first week of school, my mom wasn't there to pick me up on time. It was an early-dismissal day and she'd forgotten. It took only thirty minutes for my teacher to get her on the phone and down to the school. I hadn't given her much thought in the interim. I was in the middle of my first book club meeting. To teach us the alphabet, our teacher used inflatable cartoon characters that each held a letter. When my mom rushed in full of apologies for the teacher and for her oblivious son, I was seated at a table with some letter people. They each had a book, which I'd selected from the shelves that ringed the class. I'd asked each of them to read a page, and then tell me what it said, so that I could absorb more books in less time. I don't think there was anything special about my reading ability—if I read better at that age than other kids it was because I didn't spend much time doing anything else. I didn't understand that that wasn't the norm for boys my age. After that day my teacher, who'd helped me arrange the book party, started letting me take books from the class onto the playground for recess if I wanted them. I usually did.

After the initial uneasiness of something as new as spending half the day in a classroom, I loved school. How could I not? My parents had a knack for making *everything* into a game. Learning was a reward. And when I came home from school, instead of asking, "How was school today?" they'd ask, "What did you ask today?"

My memories of those teachers are about how kind they were. I certainly didn't cause them as many headaches as the kids who couldn't sit still or pay attention, or who didn't like books, numbers, or anything not involving recess. And I was perhaps pathologically respectful of my elders. Despite my dad's rough edges, my mom molded me into a perfect little gentleman, and she taught me that nobody was as worthy of respect as a teacher.

So it was with great reluctance that I disagreed, ever so politely, with Ms. Poindexter, my first-grade teacher, as she cast the Thanksgiving program. But I had to. I wanted to score a big role, and not just any role. I wanted to be a pig, and not just any pig.

"What is it, Josh?"

"I'll be a pig. My name is Wilbur. I'm from *Charlotte's Web.*"

Ms. Poindexter sighed. The Thanksgiving play didn't call for a pig named Wilbur. She sized me up, which wasn't hard; I was already the tallest kid in class. "No, you're a tree," she said.

"I don't want to be a tree," I said.

"You're tall and we have enough animals, Josh."

"Okay. I'll be a tree that oinks."

"Please go sit down, Josh."

After a month of rehearsals in which I tried my best to look arboreal, it was time. We shuffled onto the stage in the gymnasium at Farmington Elementary and divided into Indians, pilgrims, some animals, and one tree. As the show progressed, it became apparent that the tree was alive and was possibly fighting a stiff breeze.

My parents squinted at me in the dark auditorium. "Why's he doing that?" whispered my dad.

Under the bright lights, my nose, eyes, lips, and tongue contorted as if they'd seceded from my face and were involved in a game of one-upmanship.

"I don't know," said my mom.

Not only did my tics last the entire performance, they got worse the longer I was onstage.

"Josh, honey, are you okay?" my mom asked after the show.

"What do you mean?" I asked.

My parents didn't tell me what had happened. I didn't know anything was wrong.

After the play, Mom and Dad started a surveillance operation at home. Mom observed me while I watched TV, while I played with my friends, while I read, and while I wrestled with my dad. After a week of mental note-taking, she asked me why I was doing it.

"Doing what?"

She explained what they'd seen the night of the play and told me that I was still "doing it."

"What do you mean?"

Mom curled her upper lip and touched her nose with it. She blinked her eyes rapidly, at the same time, then in intervals of forceful winking with either eye. She jerked her head back and forth as if trying to toss away some hair that had fallen over her eyes. She stretched her neck to its limit like a turtle, then bobbed her head backward and forward like a chicken. "Like that. Do you think you could stop?"

"Do I really look like that?"

She made a deal with me. "If you quit doing that for five minutes I'll buy you a new book," she said.

"Mom, I'm sorry," I said, after lasting only one minute before the tics returned. Lips and nose and tongue and eyes. Up and down. Up and down. Over and over and back again. Now that Mom had pointed it out, I was more aware of "doing it." Not always, but often. I didn't like it that she wanted me to stop. If it were a good thing, she wouldn't care.

"It feels weird if I don't do it. Am I really doing it all the time?"

Mom became convinced that what I was doing wasn't a deliberate behavior. She felt so bad about this that she took me to the library that night after dinner.

I brought home some books about sharks. I'd probably read as many books about shark attacks that year as I did fictional stories about gallant horses and child sleuths.

Dad sat by me while I opened the first book. Certain sharks, I discovered, can't breathe if they stop swimming. They have to move or they can't breathe.

"That's like me!" I said.

"What do you mean?" he asked.

"I can't stop moving either."

Dad thought about it and then said, "Well, you like sharks, right?"

I did.

"Sharks are the toughest things ever!" he said. "What do you want, to be a little dolphin? Would you rather be a kitten? No way! Sharks get whatever they want. A shark can punch the whole world in the face and then just swim away. That's going to be you."

A couple of weeks later, Dad came home from work agitated. "Josh has Tourette Syndrome," he told my mom during dinner. My little sister Megan babbled away in her high chair. She was two, chubby, and her head was as round and seamless as a bowling ball. A messy bowling ball.

"What?"

"I was talking to a guy at work and he said his boy's doing some of the same things Josh is doing."

"And?"

"And his boy has Tourette Syndrome."

"And?" said my mom.

"What do you mean, 'and'?"

"What's Tourette Syndrome?" I asked, twirling a bunch of spaghetti on my fork and flying it over my plate.

My mom said, "What are you talking about? Isn't that that thing where people just yell and swear all the time? Josh doesn't have that." She looked at me. "You have to eat your salad, Josh."

"Swearing is bad," I said.

My dad pushed food around his plate in a circle. "Well, I was talking to the guy, and it sounds a lot like . . . you know." The ticking clock was the only noise until my mom drummed her fingernails on the table and then tapped the pitcher of water with her fork. *Ding.*

Megan giggled.

"Well . . . ," Mom said. "Maybe we could investigate it a little more. But don't make your mind up yet." She poured herself a glass of water and held it for a while, not drinking.

My dad nodded and turned to me. "What do you think about all this, buddy?" he asked.

I stood up on my chair. "I don't care. I'm a shark."

My mom watched me through the glass of water, then put it down. She walked over, picked me up, and sat me back down in my seat. "Even sharks don't get to stand on the chair at dinner."

"Leave him alone," said my dad. "He's a Great White."

I felt like I'd grown a foot taller. My dad always knew just what to say.

My parents tucked me into bed together and Mom read to me. Dad returned to say prayers. After we prayed, Mom squeezed my hand and said, "You'll be fine."

I heard them talking in their bed. The rhythms changed and the volume rose and fell.

The next day Mom and I went to the library again. While I looked for books about talking animals, she found a book about Tourette's. When we got home, I went into my room with *Charlotte's Web* and she sat on the couch with her neurology book.

She learned that, in the broadest sense, Tourette Syndrome affects people in three ways. It either makes them move involuntarily, vocalize involuntarily, or both. These movements or sounds are called "tics." Motor and vocal tics both have a continuum that can swing pretty freaking far. Mom was both unnerved and incredulous. The book made it sound like Tourette Syndrome was a life sentence of perversion. Study after study talked about poor little boys who kept getting suspended from school because they couldn't quit displaying their weenies in public. The author discussed famous people who may or may not have had Tourette's; Mozart, for example. Oh, and there was speculation that some of the poor women who were burned at the Salem witch trials might not have been possessed by the devil, but may have had Tourette's.

But most of the book focused on the disorder itself. Even less was known about it then, but the symptoms mentioned were so different from what my mom saw me doing that she couldn't convince herself that it was Tourette's.

I didn't know about the book. She told me all of this later. This is something I give my parents a lot of credit for: After their initial rounds of questioning, they didn't bring up the subject anymore. I wasn't asked to talk about the tics, or asked to fight them. Once they decided I wasn't in danger, they kept their worries to themselves and let me get back to being a relatively carefree kid. They didn't see the point of having Tourette's, if that's what it was, on my mind, even if I was having frequent tics.

They didn't take me to a doctor. My father had a deep suspicion of them. "Doctors are idiots," he said after I'd been diagnosed with asthma; the prescribed inhaler did nothing for my symptoms. Mom took me to a specialist when I asked why I wasn't getting better. "A specialist is like a super-doctor," she said. "A super-idiot," said Dad. When the super-doctor misdiagnosed me with an allergy to dairy products, my dad crowed.

I learned that doctors could be wrong. Doctors have the opportunity and the credibility to really screw up someone's life. Doctors' calm detachment and reassurances could help my parents, but they might not help my symptoms. My parents didn't feel the need to put them on the case yet.

"Hold still," said Ms. Poindexter, pressing the now-red cloth to my forehead. "I don't know how many times I have to tell you all, but you need to slow down out on that playground."

"I tripped," I said. It made me sick to lie.

I could've told Ms. Poindexter what had happened, but I thought it would sound stupid. My long arms and endless energy made me a menace during games of tag. I had the longest reach, the longest legs, and I could run forever. I'd been running down another victim when I started shaking my head from side to side, like the hair-shaking tic my mom had shown me, but with the ferocity of a T. rex who had just caught its prey. This violent motion altered my trajectory and I plowed face-first into a brick wall.

I'd been a happy little airplane, soaring above the clouds. Now there was a kamikaze pilot in the cockpit of my skull, scowling at the horizon, trying to find a battleship to crash into.

I started crying when my mom asked me what had happened.

"I lied to Ms. Poindexter."

Faced with my strange tics, Mom did what she always did—she went merrily along her way, seeing beauty in all things. She's part caterpillar, weaving a lovely cocoon of euphemisms around herself, giving purpose to life and seeing the best in things.

Not my dad. He probably wouldn't admit it, but I suspect that he wondered how the circus would treat me in the freak show. I picture him watching me pick at my carrots at dinner and thinking, *Eat up, boy. It beats those fish heads they'll be serving you out of buckets.*

But for now, safe in my mother's cocoon, the circus would have to do without me.

CHAPTER 2

Forty-five small faces watched me as story time began. The fidgeting kids teetered on the verge of chaos. They waited for a crack in my composure, any sign that I couldn't hold or didn't deserve their attention.

But I'm too big, too loud, too *fun* for this pack of three- to five-year-olds. Especially armed with a book like *No! That's Wrong!* by Zhaohua Ji and Cui Xu. What child could resist the allure of a well-illustrated story featuring a rabbit that puts a red pair of underwear on its head? I waved my arms while I talked and stomped around the library's meeting room.

When a small face wandered away, I raised my storytelling voice until it was pointed at me again.

They were mine until a ratty-looking German shepherd burst into the room, barking like Cerberus himself. The kids exploded into motion. Some cried, some recoiled. Most stood and chased the dog around the room chanting, "Doggy doggy doggy!" The dog was too fast for me to grab, not that I would have tried to grab a strange dog. Mothers locked in conversation dotted the room's perimeter. I tried to get their attention and failed.

In ten seconds, story time had ended. I walked into the library and asked, "Whose dog is that?"

A woman in a blue sweat suit glanced up from her computer. "It's mine," she said, before returning her eyes to the screen. She was playing Farmville on Facebook.

"Your dog is not allowed in the library."

"He's okay." *Type type type.*

"Your dog is in there screwing up story time."

Typeity typeity type.

I turned off her computer. "Get that dog out of here."

She squawked and hissed, but she did it.

I'm not a children's librarian; I was filling in. But I wanted these kids to understand that books are wonderful and that learning is worthwhile. I didn't want to lose them to a dog.

Later, as I patrolled, I heard the sound. Only one thing sounds like paper being ripped—but my mind refused to acknowledge it as I walked through the stacks, looking for the source of the noise.

I walked around the young adult shelves and stopped. A boy and a girl, perhaps four and three years old, were kneeling on the floor, tearing pages out of a large, colorful picture book, and throwing them into the air, creating an illustrated mess that fluttered back to earth in tatters. "Hey!" I said, louder than I meant to. "Where's your mom?"

The boy pointed toward the computers. "Can you show me who she is?" I asked. The boy nodded and stood up. The girl returned to the book and took the corner of a page in her hand. "Don't!" I said. Her arm dropped. I watched her until she stepped away from the book.

The boy led me to the computers and pointed to a woman who was squinting into the depths of MySpace. I cleared my throat. She looked at me. "Yeah?"

"Is this your son?"

"Why?" Her eyes flicked back toward the screen, where a picture of a kitten called for her attention.

"Because he was tearing pictures out of a book while you were here on the computer."

"Oh." Her eyes moved to the computer again. Her lips moved a bit as she read something on the screen.

"And you'll have to pay for the book," I said. She jumped like someone had poured cold water down her pants. "I can't! I don't have the money!"

"Ma'am, those kids are your responsibility. If you bring them here, whatever they do is your responsibility." Her eyes narrowed and I wondered if she might bite me. "I'm not telling you how to parent," I said. "But you'll have to pay for the book."

She turned to her son and slapped his hand. He flinched and cowered. "Why you gotta do things like this, stupid? This is my last computer session and now I've got to quit it!" I envisioned myself lifting her over my head and spinning around a few times WWE-style before tossing her into the ceiling fan. Instead, I went to the desk and told my assistant manager that I was going for a walk. What the woman had said (and done) to her child shocked me more than seeing those kids tear the pages out of that book. And the library's fan doesn't rotate at a high enough RPM to shred someone to pieces.

Had we lost another kid? I'd seen it before. The sight of that boy tearing up that book suggested that books were simply objects for him, not worlds between covers. Just things that made a pleasant noise when rent and scattered. And now I imagined that boy had a negative association to hinder him—read and get hit. Read and it hurts. Books are bad. Mom gets mad when I look at books. This was a reach, but it didn't feel like it because the whole incident had echoes of every other child I'd seen whose tenuous perceptions of the library could shift instantly.

Kids like Javier.

Javier was friendly when he was alone. He was at ease with any librarian in the branch. He asked lots of questions and he asked for lots of books. When he was alone.

Accompanied by his older brothers or friends, however, he was aloof and uninterested. If he spoke to us within earshot of his peers, it was to mock us. "Oh, please don't tell me you *like* doing this job!" he said to me one day while walking through the doors with his brothers.

"You know I like it," I said. "I told you yesterday when you came in. You *asked*. Remember?"

"Oh, man, whatever," he said, turning to his brothers for approval. "Like I'd—" They'd stopped in the lobby to make phone calls; he was alone. I could almost feel the confusion and embarrassment pouring off him. But he said nothing. Then his brothers returned and Javier hardened his face and strutted into the library, bumping me with his shoulder. "Oops," he said.

We usually lose the boys first. They're excited about reading at first, but once they get tight with someone who looks down on reading, knowledge, or librarians, their opinions change. Some, like Javier, are torn, at least for a while. Most get swept up in how good it feels to belong to a group, and our group rarely gets chosen. This is frustrating but understandable. It doesn't mean we quit trying to reach them, but it's hard.

I was walking to my fourth grade class at Helen M. Knight Elementary. I counted the falling autumn leaves. A rock skittered away under my foot and planted me on my butt in the road. From this vantage point I saw a culvert in the curb.

A baby chick sat in the mouth of the pipe. Besides its muddy feet it was perfect, the kind of yellow, downy chick whose image greeted me on Easter mornings from various foil candy wrappers.

I scooped the chick up and ran home, four blocks' distance. Mom wasn't pleased to see me rushing back in the door, and wasn't thrilled when the chick hopped from my crayon box onto the floor. She shooed it outside.

The chick stood motionless on the lawn. Four-year-old Megan toddled onto the porch and squealed and pointed. The chick fell on its side and was still.

"Oh," said my mom.

I cried so hard that she almost let me stay home. That night Mom said that she'd given the bird a nice funeral and that now it was in Heaven.

This was a new idea, this Heaven for birds. As far as Heaven for humans, like the other kids in my Sunday school classes, I had a vague idea of a place full of clouds, harps, and singing. But what would Bird Heaven be like? Bottomless bird feeders full of the choicest seeds? Birdhouses with fireplaces in them so they wouldn't have to fly south for the winter? A world without predators? I pestered my mom with these questions and she humored me as long as she could. But most of these discussions ended with her saying, "You'll have to ask your teachers." I did. My teachers eventually responded with "You'll have to ask your mother."

My dad didn't admit that he didn't know things; he invented answers as needed. "Buddy, Bird Heaven is basically just one long worm that birds can eat forever and ever, amen," he said with all the gravitas of a Supreme Court justice. "And even better, the birds never get full—they can eat and eat and every bite or peck is just as enjoyable as the one before it."

Dad had converted to the LDS Church—the Church of Jesus Christ of Latter Day Saints—shortly after his nineteenth birthday so he could marry my mom. He took the lessons from the local missionaries and quit drinking, smoking, and swearing. The elders taught him the missionary discussions at Mom's parents' house. He learned about the angel Moroni and the prophet Joseph Smith and committed to read and pray about the truthfulness of the Book of Mormon. He got baptized on Halloween day, 1976. The mask of belief that he donned kept him going to church, pleasing my mom, and he would become a devout member of the Mormon Church. Eventually.

But he could never compete with Mom on that front. Few people could. It's hard to talk about my mom without making her sound fanatical, because she weighs all decisions against her faith, but nothing is further from the truth. Nobody laughs more than my mom. Nobody is more playful. Or humble. She's no grim True Believer. There's a verse in the Book of Mormon that sums her up perfectly: *Men* (and women) *are that they might have joy.*

Mom didn't believe that her purpose was to be grave and dour and disapproving of every little thing. Her purpose was to have joy, and nothing was more joyful to her than raising her kids righteously. If a Jehovah's Witness has ever knocked on your door and demanded that you admit that the world was going to Hell and maybe, just maybe, you could save yourself if you let them in—she was the opposite of that.

Mom obeyed church doctrine more from a sense of not wanting to disappoint God than from fear of damnation. It was that simple: We obey our parents, and He was the parent of everything. She loved Him. She served a loving being that was as real to her as the chick in the drain was to me. This God provided everything we had, and brought our happy family together, so going against His wishes was either carelessness or ingratitude. Christianity hinges on the struggle to repay an Unpayable Debt, a constant wondering whether you've done enough to earn salvation, but this didn't weigh her down.

My mom lived and died by the maxims "If you can't say anything nice, don't say anything at all" and "It's humiliating to be lied to, so we don't do it." She could say this, and live it, with total conviction, because we were made in God's image.

God wasn't some punk who belittled people for laughs, and He didn't lie. So neither would she, and neither would we. Or if we did, she wanted us to acknowledge our mistakes and correct them by asking forgiveness.

My dad was willing to bend or ignore certain maxims if it meant he could have a laugh, make his kids laugh, or have a good story to tell.

I'd gone to church every Sunday for the previous eight years. I didn't love it, I didn't hate it; it was just the way it was. I'd be lying if I said that it was exciting. Of course, being exhilarated wasn't the point of church. The point was to worship with quiet reflection—the opposite of what an eight-year-old boy wants.

Church was just part of life, like june bugs in the summer or books on our shelves. I'd rather have been reading my books than spending my time pretending to adore the Bible and the Book of Mormon, which were dull. The stories *behind* the doctrine weren't dull. The *stories* in the scriptures weren't dull. There was nothing dull about virgin births and Joseph Smith translating the Book of Mormon with magic glasses and Ammon cutting off everyone's arms, Schwarzenegger-style, when a bunch of grubby crooks tried to steal the king's flocks.

The teacher stood before us during Sunday school. "Ammon was a Nephite. Do you know who the Nephites were?"

I raised my hand. "The Nephites were the good people in the Book of Mormon. Except when they were being bad and stupid."

"That's right, but it's not nice to say 'stupid.' And the king put Ammon in charge of his flocks of sheep. His job was to guard them from robbers and other people who wanted to make trouble for the king. One day while Ammon was in the field, a group of Lamanites came and started scattering the flocks, and the animals were running away. Do you know who the Lamanites were?"

"They were the bad people in the Book of Mormon. Except when they were being good."

"Right, Josh, but remember, when they were bothering the king's flocks, they were being wicked. But Ammon told his friends that they should go find all the sheep and that God would help them."

"And then he cut off—"

"Not yet, Josh. When they had gathered the flocks up again, the Lamanites came again and made more trouble. So Ammon, because he wanted to make the king happy, started throwing stones at them with his sling. It wasn't a slingshot like you might be thinking of—it was a little piece of cloth with strings on it. You could put a rock in the bag, twirl it around, and throw the rocks out of it, really hard. In fact, he threw some of the stones so hard that he killed some of the Lamanite robbers."

"Yeah, and then he cut—"

"This made the Lamanites angry. So they took their weapons and tried to kill Ammon. But Ammon was full of the power of God, and even though there were so many of them, he took out his sword and started smiting off the arms of the robbers. Do you know what 'smiting' means?"

Everyone joined in. "He cut off all of their arms!" Noises of disgust and delight filled the air as we swung imaginary swords and recoiled from the imaginary pile of arms that grew with each savage smite.

"Yes, but he did it because the flocks belonged to the king, and the Lord had plans for him. They were the Lord's flocks, and Ammon couldn't let anything bad happen to them. And to show the king what a good servant Ammon was, some shepherds took the arms and dumped them out at the king's feet. And the king was impressed with Ammon's righteousness and glad that he still had his flocks. So what do you think the lesson is here?"

"What did the king do with all the arms?" I asked.

The teacher's shoulders slumped. "I don't know, Josh."

The lesson was that we spent the rest of the day having feverish, high-stakes sword battles at home with our exasperated parents.

But these exciting stories didn't work on the page. I didn't like the *thee*s and *thou*s and the stories ended before they began. You could skim a verse and miss a civil war. Reading the scriptures was the opposite of hearing or reading a story and watching it unfold, and that felt like some perverse, literary, alchemical reversal. That a book could be transmuted into something boring. Borrrrrrring.

This was most evident during family scripture study. Here's how it was supposed to work: My mom would select a passage for one of us to read aloud, or maybe we'd take turns reading it. And we'd discuss the story and the doctrine in reverent tones and exclaim about how wonderful it all was and say, "Oh, oh, aren't we so blessed and lucky to have a map as fine as the Holy Scriptures!" We, the children, would thank our parents for showing us the way, and they'd beam with pride at their children's insatiable curiosity for the good word of God. And then we'd set goals and talk about how good we'd be tomorrow, and then the next day, and the family would be knit ever tighter with the bonds of love and scriptural fellowshipping. You couldn't listen to someone speak at church for five minutes without hearing about how essential it was that families read and pray together. And so we did. Then we'd close with a song and a prayer and be better for it all. Ideally.

When we actually had family scripture study, it went like this: Megan and I would groan and throw ourselves on the floor while Mom got the books. Kyle drooled nearby. My dad would wink at me over the cover of his scriptures. He was as bored as I was, but wouldn't admit it unless he wanted to tease my mom.

"Can't we just tell the story?" I asked one night when we were going to read a section that contained a juicy, thrilling war.

"Yeah, let's do that," said my dad.

My mom started reading:

And it came to pass that after this tenth year had passed away, making, in the whole, three hundred and sixty years from the coming of Christ, the king of the Lamanites sent an epistle unto me, which gave unto me to know that they were preparing to come again to battle against us.

Blech.

This style made it impossible to picture the massive battle that took place verses later, or that the victorious Nephites got so arrogant that their brilliant war chief/prophet, Mormon, renounced them and said, "Okay, suckers, fend for yourselves, I won't lead you." And this started a chain of events that led to the Nephites being wiped off the face of the earth. Gone! But we got *none* of that by reading the scriptures word for word. When she quit reading, my mom wanted to talk about the spiritual responsibilities we had, and my dad said, "Can you guys imagine what it would be like to fight all day with a sword that weighed as much as you do?"

We couldn't, but we liked to try. It wasn't that we didn't believe that what we read was true. But knowing it was true didn't make it feel like it mattered more. My mom might close with a solemn line like "And that is why it is very, very important that we do what we know is right." To which we would respond, "Okay, can we have Otter Pops now?" To which she would respond, "Okay, fine, but think about what you— I'm not finished! Get back in here!"

"Yeah, guys, come back," my dad would say, hunting for the remote in the couch cushions. "Do we really have Otter Pops?"

When you join the Mormon Church, you can expect to receive a calling soon. Callings are assignments, ranging from the bishop of the ward to the person who leads the music to the person who greets you at the door (yes, there are divinely ordained greeters). A ward is the name for a geographically delineated congregation. If you live in this zip code or neighborhood, you go to this building for services. In larger locations a stake comprises several wards. Your calling depends on your age and on the inspiration of the person leading the church group you're part of. For instance, the Young Men's Organization comprises the male members of a ward from age twelve to eighteen. Suppose the bishop calls you to be the Young Men's president. You accept, and now you oversee the teachers of the Young Men's classes, activities, and more. Now suppose that one of your teachers moves away. You have to call a new one. You do this by praying for guidance and listening for inspiration.

Not everyone has a calling, because the decision to call someone rests on the answers that a church leader receives during prayer. So maybe you'd make a great teacher, but if you never flash into someone's head while he's trying to figure out the best person to fill that slot in Sunday school, your number might never come up.

You can probably see how this could be exploited. Even an organization with God at the helm is still run by people. Fallible people bring their personalities and foibles and flaws with them when they agree to serve. If you get a calling that puts you in close and frequent proximity to someone who you find about as enjoyable to be around as an outhouse, it doesn't mean that you now love that person. And if you were in a position to assign callings to ward members, a weaker (read: normal) person might be hesitant to give someone they didn't like a calling that meant seeing that person more often.

You can always say no when you're called, although if you believe your selection is inspired, it's hard to say, "Sorry, tell omniscient God I just can't right now. I don't think he knows." When it's time for you to be released from a calling—because your circumstances make it impossible to continue, or someone receives inspiration that you're done—you're done. That calling goes to someone else and becomes his responsibility.

As a retention tool, callings make sense. A calling helps new converts stay active. After the euphoric intensity of spiritual conversion—not unlike what the ancient Greeks called "being consumed by a ball of fire"—begins to fade, they have a reason to be there. They're not just a face in the crowd; they're people without whom *those specific, necessary* tasks will not get done.

Immediately post-conversion, my dad was called to teach the Sunbeams class, which is ages three to four. On his second Sunday in his new calling, the person monitoring the halls during classes (another calling) heard a ruckus coming from his room. Upon entering, he found my dad asleep on the floor. The children had removed a screen from the window. Half of them were playing in the parking lot.

The bishop quickly released Dad from his calling.

My mom was always serving, often by sitting in more meetings than she wanted to, although she might not have admitted it. She almost always had multiple callings, despite having young children and despite having assignments that were time-intensive, such as leading the Young Women's organization. When the calls came, she accepted them.

My dad was faithful enough so that my mom wouldn't regret marrying him, but if the Sunbeam incident was any indicator, his priorities swung more toward naps than pious service. My siblings and I had enough faith in our parents to obey them and accept what they said about the grand scheme of things, meaning the Plan of Salvation.

The Plan was the doctrine of Everything Happens for a

Reason. We came to earth because we sided with Jesus in the preexistence, unlike the poor bastards who chose Satan and landed in Hell before they even got to visit earth. Once here, we were tempted and tried and given opportunities to prove that we could be faithful and worthy of returning to Heaven. When something bad happened, it was so that we could show that we could react wisely to difficulties. If something good happened, it was so that we could have a chance to express our gratitude to a benevolent God. There was no guesswork for us, no questions about the Meaning of Life, no existential dread, etc. The Plan boiled down to "do more good things than bad things, repent of the bad things, you'll be rewarded." We liked my dad's definition better: "This is the church of Don't Be a Dick."

Now pass the Otter Pops.

My mom was so faithful it was like she was playing a different sport. She knew that we were walking the path back to glory. But we all felt like we were heading in the same direction, together. The church put us together constantly, and this is still miraculous to me: Whether or not following the doctrine meant that we'd be together in Heaven, the family-centric aspects of the gospel led to a family that I *wanted* to spend eternity with.

Every Monday night we had family home evening. This was exactly what it sounds like: time set aside to be together. We played games, told jokes, went to the movies, occasionally had scripture study . . . we did what we wanted and we did it together. I'd guess that I spent more time sitting with my family, laughing and talking and being *together* than any kid I knew. And if we *didn't* spend time together, at least before we all became teenagers and had our own social circles, it was weird. A day without us laughing at the dinner table was abnormal.

Megan is four years younger than I am, Kyle came four years after Megan, and Lindsey three years after that. I didn't understand that not everyone loved to be with their siblings, or their parents, or God forbid, even their children. Hell, my dad didn't even always know where his family members lived, let alone when he'd see them next.

I remember a weekend when my dad was going to take us all fishing and he told us that we could each bring one friend. We chose each other. At Hidden Lake we fished and played and swam and, when the sun set, we said a blessing over the fish we'd caught. It was the most natural thing in the world.

We always blessed the food when we ate and my dad snuck jokes into the prayers. His love for fly-fishing was profound, and without fail, every time we'd sit down to eat the fish he'd caught, he'd ask God to please make "the bounty provided by my fly-rod expertise to be even more delicious because of the skilled hands that caught it."

We always had family prayer before we slept. In private, I struggled. I knelt and did my best to feel pious and connected to the God who watched me, knew my name, saw everything I did, and knew my thoughts. My Sunday school teachers said, "Just talk to him like you would to a friend. Saying your prayers is just checking in and telling someone about your day."

So I chatted it up with this all-powerful deity. *I cut the fingers off my mom's Isotoner glove so that I could start an arm wrestling club. I read two Beverly Cleary books today. I ate some candy. I put a frog on a big leaf and watched it float away down at the creek.* Was this interesting to anyone but me? The thought of *not* being the center of my own universe was impossible, but the thought that it mattered to anyone not living in my house didn't resonate.

My teachers taught me to tell God the sins I'd committed during the day and ask for forgiveness. *Dear God, I ate some grapes out of the produce section at the supermarket. When Mom dropped me and Greg off to go swimming, he asked me if I wanted to swear and we yelled "Shit!" every time we went off the diving board. Oh, and I ate a bunch of candy bars out of Aunt Sue's Snack*

Shack business, the one she drives over to the high school during lunch period. During a game of Four Square I kicked the ball and it hit Kelly in the butt. She kicked me and threw me down and while we were wrestling I decided that I wanted to spend more time wrestling with girls. P.S. I'm sorry and I'll never, ever do any of it again.

At night I made the gravest promises while praying; the conviction dissolved before breakfast.

I was also supposed to ask God questions. This was more interesting. I had plenty of questions, and answers were like candy. I'd been taught that prayers were answered by a feeling of a "burning in the bosom," "hearing the still, small voice," or feelings of clarity and assurance. But my emotions got tugged around by everything. It was easy to "feel" the answers I wanted as a distractible kid.

I remember my parents taking me to the first *Land Before Time* movie, and especially the scene where the shrill little dinosaurs made it to the Great Valley. The music swelled; they'd come so far and the hair on my neck stood on end and my eyes watered. It was how I felt when Luke Skywalker was trying to save Darth Vader after he threw the emperor off the walkway and the saddest music ever played in the background. I cried at the end of *Terminator 2* when Arnold gave the thumbs-up while lowering himself into the molten metal (Come on! A machine learned the value of human life!). I felt something similar when I finished Super Mario Bros. 2 on the original Nintendo. Good grief, if my mom bought Pop-Tarts it felt like a sacred experience. But prayer didn't give me that undeniable, visceral reaction. I never experienced anything unequivocally divine or had sensations that I couldn't associate with anything else. If I felt something during prayer, it was as likely because I was humming the soundtrack to *The Land Before Time* as it was because a Supreme Being was bridging the gaps in my understanding.

I never found answers in silence. Of course, sitting still and

listening for inspiration was challenging with the constant in-
terruptions of my blinking eyes and facial contortions.

Halfway through my fourth-grade year my parents told us we
were moving to Spring Creek, Nevada. My dad had taken a job
at a Nevada gold mine.

When I asked why we were moving, they said it was a great
opportunity for my dad and that they "felt good about it" after
praying on it. If they thought they had divine support behind
the move, how could I argue? I tried, though. Oh, I tried.

I didn't want to leave my friends. I didn't want to go to a
new school full of kids who didn't know me.

So I asked God if we should move. I tried to stay very still.
I squinted and listened and frowned and sent my mind into the
cosmos to plead with whoever was there. After a couple of minutes I knew I'd received an answer. I felt better when I was done
praying than before I'd started. If that wasn't a sign, what was?
What a relief!

"Mom, Dad, I prayed and we aren't supposed to move," I
said. Stalemate! Two parties ask the same question; each receives a different answer. Who is right? Who can prove that
they received enlightenment? The child's prayer is worth as
much as anyone's, yes?

No.

We moved to Spring Creek, an ugly little clump of brown
nothing with sagebrush for hair, lurking eight miles outside of
Elko. We moved, I started school, and I was miserable . . . for
about twenty-four hours.

On my first day at school I was walking the perimeter of
the playground at recess. A couple of hours earlier I'd been introduced to the class, who didn't seem interested in me. That
was a relief. But then a girl named Heather, sitting behind me,

had tapped me on the shoulder. I turned, half hoping for a smile or some other sign that I was more than a wretched sub-creature. Instead, she blinked her eyes and touched her nose with her upper lip. "Your head is too big," she said. In fairness, she was probably right. Until I was about twenty-five, I was rail thin and had a big head. She probably thought I looked like a big toddler.

Moab was a million miles away. I couldn't keep my face still. The wind blew just to bother me and the happy sounds of the recess-in-progress were excruciating.

Oh please oh please, please help me! my mind cried.

"Hey!"

I kept walking.

"Hey, Josh!"

I'd read enough books to know about mirages, but I didn't know if one could occur in the winter on snow-covered asphalt. Walking toward me was a boy named Keith—he'd been a good friend in Moab before moving a couple of years earlier. Until this moment I didn't know where he'd gone.

Thank you, I whispered.

The first day of fifth grade at Spring Creek Elementary began with an assembly. We were the first students in a brand-new school. I wasn't impressed. Sure, the walls were white with new paint and the desks sparkled, but it was just a building. Then my teacher took our class into the school's library. New desks were one thing—a room full of new books was something else.

These books haven't been read. A virgin landscape of pages and paragraphs and dust jackets that gleamed so brightly under the fluorescent lights that they deserved a choir of singing angels to announce their advent.

"How many can I check *out*?" I asked.

The school librarian laughed. She was the only one.

My teacher had fifth *and* sixth graders in the same class. This meant that 1) the class was huge; 2) each grade got half of the teacher's time and attention; 3) I could read as much as I wanted after I did my work. Our teacher didn't have time to check on me. I'd never been so excited. Now I'd have daily, uninterrupted hours of reading time.

One day as I sat reading *Are You There God? It's Me, Margaret*, I realized that someone was calling my name.

I looked up and noticed that the class was quiet. I looked to the left into Jason Lawson's eyes. Jason was a cross between a gargoyle and a demon, a blond mixture of torment and confidence. He breathed cruelty and ate nice kids. He held up a book and started blinking his eyes and making noises that signaled to everyone that he was someone stupid.

He was me.

Everyone laughed, except me. The teacher wasn't in the room and I didn't know how to deflect the attention away from myself.

I returned to my book, but the page was no longer written in English. The laughter burned my face. It finally stopped when Mr. Maderis returned and class resumed. I blinked, over and over. I couldn't stop.

I was no longer anonymous; I'd become That Kid. That Kid who does That Thing. I was already as tall as my teacher so I couldn't exactly hide.

Around my parents and siblings, I had tics, but if my siblings noticed, they didn't mention it. That might have been my mom's doing, or maybe they'd never known me without tics, so that me *not* having tics would've been what caught their attention. My parents never asked me about it unless I mentioned it. I was safe with my family.

My other refuge was the bookmobile, a big, fat RV full of books. A library on wheels that came to school once a week.

The driver looked at me like I stank when I asked her how I could become a bookmobile driver.

The first time the bookmobile came I grabbed the biggest book I saw: *The Tommyknockers* by Stephen King. Thus began a beautiful partnership. The deal was that King would write gigantic books and I'd drown in the obscene word counts, lost to the world until the book was closed. *The Tommyknockers* was full of swearing and I was uneasy during a section in which a woman's picture of Jesus began talking. People had sex, lost their skin, murdered one another, and wrecked their town. And there were aliens. I couldn't get enough of it.

I followed *Tommyknockers* with *Pet Sematary,* a book that frightened the bejabbers out of me. Then came *Misery.* That's when I learned that my deal with Stephen King included one small contract rider: My mom couldn't know about it.

The day after I checked out *Misery* I came into the living room to find my mom with a serious look on her face. "Honey, sit down."

I sat.

"Can you tell me why you'd want to read this?" she asked, waving the book at me.

Because it's a book, I thought. "It's a good story," I said.

"How far have you read?" she asked.

"About a hundred pages."

"And what's it about?"

"It's about a writer who gets in a wreck. He gets saved by a nurse, but it turns out that she's crazy, but he's hurt so he can't get away."

She nodded. "I want to tell you a couple of things so you'll know why I ask. I read the whole book this morning. It made me feel sick. I'm not saying it's good or it's bad, I just want you to know how it made me feel. Did you know that she ends up cutting off his foot with an ax?"

"Really! Why?"

She shook her head. She hadn't intended to pique my interest. "Did you read about why she couldn't be a nurse anymore?"

"No."

"Because she was killing kids in the hospital."

"Really? How did they catch her? Did she go to jail?"

She smiled. "Do you think the author escapes?"

I nodded. "He has to."

"Well, you're right about that. But first she runs over a police officer with a lawnmower, and she cuts off the writer's thumb with an electric knife, and at the end he has to kill her to get away, and I—" My eyes were so wide and excited that she stopped. "Honey, do you really think that's a good story for you to be reading? Oh, no, you don't!" I was reaching for the book.

"I've got to see how it ends!"

"I just told you how," she said. "If you want to read it when you're older, that's your choice, but it's not an appropriate book for a fifth grader. And no more Stephen King in this house for now. Please."

When I complained to my dad, he said, "Your mom's right, don't read fiction." But the only way I could've quit reading King's books was to "not be there." "There" being the bookmobile. But it didn't stop pulling up to the curb just because my mom didn't want me reading about crazy nurses chopping people up with axes. So I formed a brilliant plan. I checked out two books whose covers were the same size: *It* by Stephen King, and *The Color of Her Panties* by Piers Anthony.

It was about a monster who murders children. A terrifying book full of blood, scares, and sharp teeth. *The Color of Her Panties* was a harmless, pun-riddled volume in the Xanth fantasy series. I removed their dust jackets and switched them. I was so cunning that I even taped the dust jackets down so they wouldn't fall off accidentally. The Great Brain would have approved.

And yet, to brilliant young Josh, he of the big forehead,

bent glasses, and darkening literary appetites, it never occurred that a mother who didn't like blood and mayhem in her young son's books might also frown on a book that proudly purports to be about panties.

When Mom saw the book I was reading—*It* wrapped in panties—she asked to see it. She removed the dust jacket and saw what I'd done. We looked at each other for a long time without saying anything.

I've read every book King has written since. A contract is a contract. If she saw no issues with binding herself to a God she'd never seen, I didn't see why I couldn't bind myself to a guy out in Maine who wrote horror stories.

But man doesn't live by mayhem alone. The darkness, and the illicit thrill of reading King, had to be tempered with books that didn't cause nightmares. Ideally, with books that caused other, warmer sorts of dreams altogether. My girl Fern had competition. Lots of it. When I wasn't reading horror I was spending time with the sassy new brunette and a pair of gorgeous blond twins.

Beverly Cleary created the brunette, Ramona Quimby. My favorite was *Ramona the Brave*, and there was one scene in that book where I knew I was hers.

During an argument over dinner, Ramona announces that she's going to say a "bad word" to shut everyone up and get some respect. Her family goes quiet with anticipation. "Guts!" she yells. *"Guts! Guts! Guts!"* And of course they all burst out laughing. I vowed to marry Ramona.

The public library was twelve miles away from our house, and my mom couldn't always take me. One Friday she was sick and my dad was out of town. This was the worst possible scenario; "I will not be taking you into town this weekend," she said before retiring to bed on Friday evening. I fought the withdrawal as long as I could, but finally decided to raid Megan's shelves, which were filled with girls' books.

And that's how I met the Wakefield Twins from Sweet Valley High. I read about ten of them that weekend. I was hooked. Boys' books, girls' books, it didn't matter. They were stories (with lots of kissing) that progressed from point A to point B, and once I'd started reading, I couldn't abide the unresolved stress that came with not finishing them. But that wasn't something I could explain to the bookmobile driver the following week when I checked out a Special Double Issue!!! of Elizabeth and Jessica's trip to Europe.

"Are you sure *this* is what you want?" she said, holding it up for everyone to see. Jason Lawson snorted behind me. I couldn't tell him about point A and point B and the narcotic of long-arc narrative. I couldn't explain how worried I'd been after Enid got in the plane crash and thought she'd be in a wheelchair forever. I couldn't tell him that the snotty rich kids Lila Fowler and Bruce Patton weren't as bad as they seemed. I couldn't tell him about how annoyed I was that Elizabeth stopped dating basketball player Todd, but was now with soccer-playing weenie Jeffrey French. Soccer!

But maybe I could appeal to his sense of lust. "I think they're cute," I said, pointing to the book's cover, where Elizabeth and Jessica were laughing at something in Europe. *Huh? Huh? Anyone?*

Oh, boy. Wrong thing to say.

That night I asked God to melt Jason Lawson's head.

It "felt" like I'd asked for the right thing.

The next morning I was shocked to find Jason's ugly face glaring at me. He still had his eyes, ears, teeth, and tongue, and all were functioning adequately enough for him to catch my eye and call me "sperm head" in front of the whole class. We'd had sex ed a week earlier and being called sperm head was now a hideous and trendy insult. I went home after school in a haze of embarrassment, but before going inside I got into the back of the family van and whispered, *I hate God. I love the Devil.*

CHAPTER 3

616.89075—Diagnosis, Differential
302.3—Bullying

During the school year at the Day-Riverside library—a branch of the Salt Lake City Public Library System—at about three in the afternoon, the doors would open and a flood of kids would spill into the stacks and over the computers. Most of them got beached on the PCs. The rest of them would wash up on the chairs, or sometimes the floor. And then, in accordance with some occult signal, they would all start jabbering like seagulls.

While this was going on, I'd patrol and do some looming. After fifteen minutes there was always new graffiti. Most tags were what I saw in the nearby neighborhoods—Rose Park Kids, Inner City Souljas, and one prolific enigma with horrible penmanship who advertised himself as Sir Snowflake. But sometimes I'd find an act of vandalism so exceptional that I couldn't bear to clean it up. Sometimes I didn't even share it with anyone in the hopes that it would go unnoticed.

Carved into a desk: *I love math!*

Written on the edge of a bookshelf in permanent black

It was out. It was out and I couldn't take it back. I waited to be smited, as if by Ammon's avenging sword, exploded, imploded, burned, struck by lightning, or for the skies to open up and say, "I heard that, sperm head!"

Instead . . . silence. Nothing but the sounds of wind and dogs barking and faint voices from the nearby golf course. The silence didn't disturb me. Or encourage me. It made me wonder. Was this a test? Had I damned myself? Was Someone waiting to see if I'd have the courage to say it again? I didn't.

Silence and stillness were in short supply in my life. There were only three times when I could count on them: when I slept, when I read, and apparently when I blasphemed.

By uttering those words, I'd taken a risk and stepped toward the limits. A friend would later tell me that the best way to expand your limits is to work within them. I'd put my hand out and tried to find the wall but there was nothing there.

magic marker: *I am a shelf. I am alive!!!* I liked that one so much that I almost took the shelf home.

MC Hammer fever was at its zenith when I was in eighth grade, and so were the huge baggy pants he wore onstage. MC Hammer danced like a maniac and the sight of the students trying to mimic his athleticism in the junior high hallways must have been annoying for the teachers. Suddenly every kid was dressing like him and cutting steps into their hair. I knew kids who wanted glasses just because Hammer had them.

I wore my best pair of Hammer pants to school one day—they were purple with enormous yellow dots. The pants hid my skinny legs, although my feet were enormous and getting bigger by the day.

But the pants couldn't hide a bigger problem. Ever since I'd turned thirteen, my body had betrayed me in myriad ways. From the second I opened my eyes to the time I closed them at night, I was humming with desire. I wanted every girl I saw. I was a gawky highlight reel of fantasies that I barely understood but couldn't turn off. And it was getting worse.

I'd fallen asleep in science class with my head on the desk. I woke to the laughter of my eighth-grade classmates. My favorite Hammer pants showcased an unfortunate erection that had reared up majestically during my nap. Everyone was looking at it.

Wow.

I ran—well, shuffled quickly—out of the room and hid in the restroom down the hall. I sat in a stall until my legs fell asleep. The next few weeks were predictably awful. But I learned a great truth in the last half of that school term: Kids can forget anything. Even you. Two months later they were picking on someone else.

I fought competing impulses. I wanted to be seen—and not seen. And I wanted both on my own terms. I wanted the females to giggle and ask to feel my muscles (I was six-three and my muscles were virtually nonexistent). I wanted the males to part when I walked down the hall.

Too bad.

Ms. Henderson passed out the math tests. The room was quiet. To my horror, I started clearing my throat. "Hmm-*hmm! Huh.*" With each noise, my feet stomped the ground. "Huh! *Huh!*" I had never concentrated on a math test so hard. But maybe it wasn't as bad as I thought. Maybe nobody could hear me.

We'd been working on our tests for about five minutes when Steven, who sat in front of me, turned around and yelled, "Shut up!" into my face. Somehow the class got even quieter. Everyone looked at him, then at me.

"Are you okay?" I asked.

"Am *I* okay?" he said, eyes wide. But I didn't know what else to say. I looked down at my desk, feeling like someone had poured lava into my hair. I cleared my throat again, louder than before. I looked at Steven again. I don't know if I looked as scared as I felt.

"I've got something in my throat," I said. Ms. Henderson took me outside. Math class was in a metal double-wide trailer at the hill above the main school building. Each clanking step on the walkway outside triggered a new tic. "Huh huh huh!"

"Are you okay?" Ms. Henderson asked.

I didn't know. Was I okay? I only knew that I couldn't ever take another math test. And I had geography the next hour.

"Huh HUH!" I covered my mouth. My stomach filled with rocks. How could this be happening? *Why* would this be happening? And what was it? Ms. Henderson let me call my mom, who came and took me home.

I cried all afternoon. "Mom, what's wrong with me?"

"I don't know, Josh," she said. "But we'll find out. You'll be okay."

For the first time I could remember, nothing she said made me feel better. The urges to croak, stomp my feet, and clear my throat didn't subside. They kept going at dinner, and as I lay in my bed that night. I was exhausted by the effort of the twitching and noises, but couldn't sleep because of the twitching and noises.

That night my mom called Ms. Henderson and asked if I was being disruptive to the class. She had flashes of that Tourette's book in her head and needed to know if I was telling the truth about what had happened. Had I really just been clearing my throat? Had I just been making noises? Was there anything I wasn't telling her? Horror of horrors, had her husband been right and I was destined for the circus?

Ms. Henderson told her that I was fine, that I wasn't a disturbance in class, and that I didn't need any accommodations. "If you start treating him like he's different," she said, "he'll start to think he's different. If he starts to think he's different, he's going to start acting like he's different. That's not what he needs."

But I was making so many involuntary noises. There was the hooting baby owl sound. And the slobbering dog just finishing a round of wind sprints. Sometimes I whistled like wind in a ghost town. Other times I had a perpetual frog in my throat that sat there even after constant throat-clearing. But thankfully, the tics were usually at their most diverse when I was alone.

I stumbled through the rest of the year, hoping that everyone would catch a bad case of amnesia between June and August so that nobody would remember me on the first day of high school.

Over the summer I'd only gotten noisier. I was hooting and yowling and yapping and generating weird looks every time I was in public. While school was out, this was manageable. My friends knew I had tics. Everyone at church knew, but things were mild enough that most people chalked it up to extreme fidgets. At least, that's what I told myself, and my mom was willing to agree with any line of thought that made things easier for me. Even trips to the quiet library were doable—it wasn't like anything would have kept me away, but the librarians knew me. I could find a book, get absorbed, and the tics would stop. Or if that didn't work I could grab a book and run outside.

In the fall, I tried out for the freshman basketball team. I was tall enough to make the team without any relevant skills, and I wanted the status. I didn't know that being on the freshman team was about as prestigious as being the fat kid who swam with his T-shirt on, at least in our school's pantheon of sports. But I'd get to dress up. On Game Day, all Elko High School athletes dressed up. If I was among the handful of students wearing a tie on a Friday, I fantasized, girls would notice me and think *Oh, he's on the team. I should probably ask him out on a date.* Silk shirts were as popular as Hammer pants, so I asked for one when I made the team. A week later I had a blue silk shirt that, after an hour of wear, looked like a poorly erased chalkboard. I wore it with tight slacks that wouldn't reveal anything, should I fall asleep in class.

I didn't receive the adoration I hoped for the first time I wore my silk shirt, although Anna L. told me I looked nice. I had decided to complement the new look by shaving the sides of my head and growing the top out into a bushy red Mohawk. With my thick, upright hair, I looked like one of those troll dolls, except that my haircut made me about eight feet tall.

Making the team meant going to practice every day. As soon as my breathing quickened on the gym floor, my tics kicked in. The harder I played, the worse they got. And the harder I played, the more I got to play. The more I played, the more I was seen on the court before hostile crowds. The more I played in front of crowds that already hated our team, the more

I had tics in front of people who were already looking for reasons to mock me.

But there was a nice surprise that would've been completely unsurprising to anyone else—the harder I practiced, the better I got. Who knew that by repeating a task, you could improve? Our team wasn't bad either, and I realized that I liked to win more than I hated having my tics on full display.

Nobody hated our team more than our archenemies from Hawthorne,* Nevada. Our teams hated each other; our fans hated each other. Even our cheerleaders glared across the court during games. With its casinos and buffets and factories and scummy basketball teams, Hawthorne smelled like a huge dirty butt, waving in the wind.

Near the end of the first quarter against Hawthorne I caught the ball in the post and jumped for an easy lay-up.

"Don't twitch!" a voice yelled from the crowd.

I missed the shot. Had I heard what I thought I had? I looked at the home crowd on the other side of the gym. A sea of yellow jerseys and pom-poms. Who had yelled? Or were they all yelling it and I only heard that one voice? My feet were suddenly heavy and I felt sick. I gritted my teeth and played harder than ever. It worked. I shut my man down on defense. I made a few baskets. I forgot about the voice in the heat of joyous competition. Then I caught the ball down low again. I went up for a shot and heard more than one person yelling something about "twitch." I got fouled. As I took my place on the free-throw line, the crowd began to chant.

"Twitch! Twitch! Twitch!"

I hadn't imagined it. I made one out of two shots. Halftime followed shortly after.

In the locker room I was dizzy with nerves and sat down unsteadily. "Are you all right?" asked a teammate.

---

* Not the school's real name

"Yeah," I said. *I don't know*, I thought.

We matched each other point for point in the second half. The more the crowd yelled at me, the angrier I got. *Couldn't they see that something was wrong with me? How dare they!* But at the same time I was thinking, *You have to stop doing this. Of course they're laughing at you! You'd be laughing too! Just make yourself stop!*

I could hear my dad bellowing. "Kill him! He got fouled! Pass it! Good grief, are you *kidding me*?" He wasn't exactly a master at controlling himself during my games. During one legendary game against Battle Mountain, the referee actually walked into the crowd and offered my dad the whistle to shut him up. He didn't take it, but he didn't quiet down either.

Down the stretch I kept getting fouled and had to shoot several sets of free throws. The crowd chanted every time. After making my final shot, I pointed at the crowd and laughed. The Hawthorne crowd howled and stomped, but we had won. That was all that mattered. When I walked out of the locker room after the game, a group of rival students saw me and immediately began twitching, jerking their elbows, heads, and contorting their faces.

It was as visceral as being kicked in the crotch. I put my head down and hurried by. I could hear the sounds of their laughter all the way home.

"Well, at least you won," Dad said afterward. I hadn't said anything yet. "Well, you did," he repeated, while I looked out the window of our enormous red van.

"Honey, what is it?" said my mom.

"I think I want to see a doctor," I said. "I want to know what's going on with me."

They looked at each other. "We'll get you an appointment with a specialist as soon as we can," said my dad. "You know, that crowd was probably laughing at me as much as at you."

I laughed.

"No 'probably' about it," said my mom. "But you deserved it."

I turned on the light in the backseat. I'd brought a slim book that I'd grabbed at the high school library, *The War Prayer* by Mark Twain. In the book, the citizens of a small town gather in a church to pray for the young men of their town, who will soon leave for war. The service proceeds with a pastor singing the virtues of honor, and the congregation prays for victory.

A stranger walks into the building and announces that he is God's messenger. His job is to say out loud all of the things that the church members are thinking. He proceeds with the grisliest recounting of the horrors of war, pleading with God to shred their enemies' bodies with their bullets and blades.

When he's finished, the townspeople ignore him. *It was believed afterward that the man was a lunatic, because there was no sense in what he said.*

Several weeks later we traveled to Reno for another basketball game. My game had further improved and I anticipated a good fight between our teams. It was only in the fury of competition that my tics let me go. If I had time to think, I had time to twitch. But if I was shoving against someone, gritting my teeth, wanting to win just to make them lose, I had some control.

Things were going fine in the first quarter when I began fighting for a rebound with their center, a massive kid who had surely been held back eight times. He elbowed me in the back and yelled, "You can't box me out, you pussy!" I fell to my knees, then jumped up and turned to shove him. He leaned down into my face—yes, he was really tall—and blinked his eyes spastically. Apparently I was still having tics, even when I thought I had them under control. I was horrified. He laughed as we ran up the floor. I tried to avoid him but he was guarding me. Every time he bumped into me he laughed. I avoided his gaze until halftime when I looked back after he pushed me again. But I had nothing. We were getting killed.

"What's with you?" asked Coach McCabe.

"I don't feel good," I said, slumping onto a bench. "I think I need to sit out the rest of the game."

I didn't sit out, but I played even worse in the second half. When the game ended and we the vanquished lined up to shake the opponents' hands, I looked at the ground. I didn't see who slapped me on the back of the head, but I knew.

My mom told me that I'd been the bigger man, and that turning the other cheek is always better. But turning the other cheek was all I knew how to do.

I prayed a lot in the two weeks between the game in Reno and the visit to the neurology clinic at the University of Utah. I needed answers.

I thought I might have some weird form of cancer. I thought I might have some brand-new disorder that would be named after me once I died. My tombstone would say, *Here lies Josh. He just wanted to quit blinking and yelping.*

When we pulled into the parking lot at the neurology clinic I started to sweat. I was torn between wanting an answer and wanting to control what the answer would be. I only wanted there to be something officially wrong with me if it also came with a quick solution. The doctor would reach into his pocket and produce the bottle of pills that he kept on hand for those rare boys who couldn't quit barking in math class. I'd pop a couple and be cured by the time we got home. My condition was annoying, but was I making too much of it? It distressed me, but what if I got worse the second I knew what was happening to me?

My parents were out of the car for about thirty seconds before they realized I hadn't moved. My mom leaned in and squeezed my hand. "Come on."

I sat in the waiting room while my knees knocked and my hands shook like I was being marched to the gallows. My memories of the doctor are unremarkable: He had red hair and a white coat. He spent fifteen minutes having me stand with my heels together, touch my nose with my index fingers, and then watching me intently and scratching notes on a pad while I tried not to twitch too much. I was suddenly worried that if I showed him the worst of my symptoms he would misdiagnose me and give me the treatment meant for people with syphilis or rabies.

"This is Tourette Syndrome," he said, putting down his pen.

And there it was, just like that. I had a thing and the thing had a name.

"I read a book about Tourette's," Mom said. The book said this, and the book said that, and "Oh, my goodness, it's a relief to know what's actually going on, because Josh has been so nervous. Haven't you, Josh?"

"So what now?" I asked. Whatever the diagnosis, this was the only question I really cared about.

"Well," said the doctor, "I wouldn't recommend any medication, unless you feel like the situation is unmanageable. But it doesn't sound like you've had too bad of a time of it until now."

"But there are medications that would help with this?" asked my dad.

"Some patients show improvement with certain drugs that are typically used to treat blood pressure issues, and there have been studies which suggest that some people with Tourette's respond well to antipsychotics."

Now this was what I had worried about. Was I psychotic?

"But you wouldn't recommend any of those right now, you said, right?" asked my mom.

"There are side effects to many of these medications that may not be worth the cost if the symptoms are currently tolerable for Josh."

My parents looked at me. Were the symptoms tolerable? Yes, meaning I wasn't in physical pain, I went to school, I played on the basketball team and had good friends. Girls weren't paying any attention to me and my haircut was bad, but for the results-oriented person examining my life on paper, it probably looked like I had nothing to whine about. And that was a question I asked myself constantly: Was I whining? Would a tough person make an issue out of any of this? Would my dad have been here at the doctor in my place if it had been him? No way. Would my mom have been here? Probably not until she had put in another year of prayer.

"I'm doing okay," I said.

"Josh, you've actually been having a rough time," said my mom.

"I'm fine," I said.

Silence.

"I don't want any pills," I said. I didn't know whether that was true. But I said it, the doctor had other appointments, and we left without pills, prescriptions, or much in the way of progress. But we had a name. The question "What is wrong with me?" had an answer. The answer was Tourette Syndrome. My dad's knee-jerk declaration from nine years earlier had been correct.

"I knew it," he told my mom as we drove home.

She said nothing.

"Josh, I knew it. I told her!" He held up his hand. I gave him five. Then he offered his hand to her.

"Are you done?" she said.

"I knew it way back then," he told my siblings when we got home. They had almost zero reaction, since they had never heard about any of that. They knew I'd gone to the hospital and they just wanted to know if I was okay.

"So you're okay, though?" said Megan after I recapped the meeting for her.

"Yeah."

"Good." And that was the end of it.

Back at school I vowed not to tell anyone what had happened.

"I just found out I have Tourette Syndrome," I told Sarah in science class while we conducted an experiment with tuning forks.

"Yeah, I've got Tourette's," I told Mr. Williams, my electronics teacher. "It can be pretty bad."

"Yeah," I told my friends at lunch, "there's a name for what's been going on with me."

It was even a day where I wasn't having any noticeable tics. But I managed to tell everyone I could. Nobody had much to say besides, "Oh, man, that sucks," because they knew even less about it than I did, if that were possible.

During the last hour of school, the tics returned and hit with such frequency that catching my breath was a challenge.

"Mom, I'm going stay home from school for a while," I said that night. I was too embarrassed to deal with it.

"No, you're going," she said.

"It's my decision," I said.

"No, actually, it's not," she said. "It's mine, but you're not even deciding. You're letting this thing decide for you. Don't."

This was the first time I saw Tourette's as a separate being; a parasite that I was in a relationship with. I named her Misty, short for "Miss T."

Here's the crash course in how my Tourette's feels. I'm not going to explain what causes it, because doctors are still speculating about it. There are theories about dopamine imbalances and nutritional sensitivities and the hunt is on for the guilty genes, but that information hasn't ever been useful to me. What I can talk about is what it feels like to have tics, and to *need* to have tics.

Think of what it feels like when you need to sneeze. You become aware of it slowly; first there's an itch. Maybe you wiggle your nose or squint to scratch it, but the itch builds until you let it out. Of course, you could hold the sneeze in, but what happens if you stifle it? There's no relief or resolution. It feels *wrong*. You sneeze so the feeling is expelled.

When I have a tic, whether it's a noise or a movement, it's similar to the urge to sneeze. There's a pressure that builds up in my eyes if I want to blink, in my forehead if I want to wrinkle it, in my shoulders if I want to jerk them up toward my ears, in my tongue if I need to feel the edge of it slide against a molar, in my throat if I need to hum or yell or whistle. The urge can also be everywhere at once, which results in a tic where I flex every part of my body, hard and fast. Wherever it is, sooner or later, I have to let it out. But the relief doesn't last long. The pressure might fade, rebuild, and jump out again in a few seconds, a few minutes, or longer.

I can hold a tic in if I really try, but there's a price to pay for doing that. It seems that for me, I must release a specific intensity of tics each day. I can mete it out in lots of small tics, or I can hold it in and have it rage out in a blast when I get home from work, like a clogged steam valve on a radiator. I hold it in on airplanes, in meetings, in church, in classrooms, and whenever possible, on the reference desk.

For the rest of the book, you can assume that I'm always having tics. I thought about writing the noises into the dialogue, but that quickly became so obnoxious that your experience reading this book would have been just as annoying as it is to actually have the tics. So here's what I'll do: In the coming chapters, when I experience new, significant tics, I'll say so. Once I've had a new type of tic, you can assume that it stays in the rotation. Each new tic is stacked on top of what came before it.

So then, on with it.

Misty spoke her own language, but used my mouth to do it. She often started and finished my sentences, although she didn't interrupt me while I was talking. She made me say things like:

"Woo!"

"Hep!"

"Hup!"

"Dit dit deet." Whenever she spoke in multiple syllables, each sound descended in pitch.

"Ssss!"

"Nee nah."

"Hmm HMM."

"Zur."

But they're just noises, I told myself. I could handle her, now that I knew who she was.

My mom's father built a barn all by himself when he was thirteen. He lived in a tent with his family during the Depression. When it was time to feed his family of nine during the lean winter, he poached deer, despite being Moab's chief of police. This was a man who didn't make excuses, and a lot of that had trickled down to my mom. She didn't want some label interfering with my becoming a productive citizen.

Neither did my dad. For over a decade he'd risen between three and four in the morning to drive the ninety miles to the gold mine for ten-hour shifts that started at six o'clock. "Work is what a man does," he said. "Men who don't work hard aren't normal." If I was going to be normal, I'd have to work.

My first job was at a trap-and-skeet club, where I sat underground in a bunker, loading a machine with clay pigeons. The throwing arm of the machine was a thick dull blade that revolved from its base in a noisy parabola. Its arc came within inches of my chest, but it felt like it sliced just out of range of my throat. But I knew that it was completely safe, because my boss said, "It's completely safe." The shooters would arrive and buy each other drink after drink until they were sufficiently inebriated to load and operate their shotguns as I sat in the bunker beneath them with my eyes on the blade.

Soon, my hand left my lap and began tapping the blade

with the knuckle of my index finger. *Boom!* The blade flung itself in a circle just after I pulled my hand away. My heart twisted
like an uncoiling snake. My hand went back to the blade. I put
it back on my leg. The pigeon flew through the opening. I replaced it with my right hand and Misty put my left hand in
front of the blade. I didn't tap it this time; I actually put it in the
blade's path. The blade was dull—I don't think it would have
sliced my fingers off. But it certainly would have broken them.
I watched all of this in horror, from a great distance, even
though I was participating. Nobody outside knew that anything was wrong inside the bunker. But I couldn't keep my
hand still. Even when I sat on it, there was an undeniable urge
to put my hand in harm's way. It wanted to be on the blade. It
wanted to be in danger. It was as difficult to ignore as it had
been to stay quiet in Ms. Henderson's math class. But now I was
in danger. Or was I? It wasn't like I absolutely couldn't keep my
hand under me. It was more that I wanted to put it on the blade
and keep it underneath me. I didn't feel *right* until I tapped the
blade with my finger. The pressure would build. The "sneeze"
tormented me until I let it go. But the satisfaction was momentary. The urge to do it again would build immediately. Sooner
or later, I'd hurt myself.

The job didn't get easier as the weeks wore on. I desperately
wanted to quit, but no matter how I looked at it, my parents
would think I was making excuses. "So your hand won't sit still,
huh? My dad lived in a tent!" "So you're scared, huh? Try being
scared of not knowing when you'll get paid again!"

Then a solution presented itself so perfectly that I half believed it was divine inspiration. When I told my parents I
wanted to quit, my dad immediately said, "Why?"

My mom said, "But you've only been there for a couple of
months, what's wrong?"

I took a deep breath. "This is going to sound dumb, but—"
My dad nodded.

"—but I feel bad missing church on Sunday. I know it's only a couple of times every month but I feel like I'm getting out of the habit."

My mom was nodding as proudly as if I'd just given my allowance to a homeless man. My dad wasn't as pleased. "I've been working for years and I haven't always been able to get to church and I've been fine for it."

"Frank, you've told me that you miss it when you're away," said my mom.

"But I don't ignore my responsibilities, miss it or not."

"It just doesn't feel . . . right," I said. I sighed. There's a great case to be made for using religion to win arguments, as long as you only debate with other believers. My dad faced a difficult proposition: He could force me to keep my job, but that would look like he was making light of my spiritual commitment.

"Josh, we'll support whatever you decide to do," said my mom, patting my dad's knee.

I took a job as a cook at Pizza Hut, which didn't interfere with Sundays. It turned out to be more dangerous than the trap-and-skeet club.

I couldn't keep my hands under control around anything warmer than my video game console at three in the morning on a Sunday. Bare lightbulbs, seat-belt buckles that had gotten too much sun, and oven burners—all bad news. I'd get the urge to tap them with my elbow. And if one elbow tapped, the other one had to as well. Sometimes my forehead needed to touch things.

The first time I washed dishes at Pizza Hut I burned my hand on an iron pizza pan. At any moment during the evening shifts there were at least thirty of them waiting to be washed. They'd arrive about three minutes after the pizzas had left the oven, so the pans were still hot when they got to me. I'd been alone for about five minutes when I began tapping one of the pans with the knuckle of my right index finger. Soon all my fingers wanted in on the action. Not only was I playing finger-tag with the pans, the pans weren't getting washed. Although I was wearing an oven mitt, I could still feel plenty of heat and had to pull my fingers away.

Misty hadn't yet scarred me, so maybe I was just being a weenie. But if I ended up covered in third-degree burns, who could deny me accommodation or sympathy? My dad would understand a burn, and my fingers kept dancing back to the hot pans.

My parents argued over whether I should be allowed to quit. "If it's too hard for him, he shouldn't have to do it," Mom said.

"How does he know it's too hard if he doesn't try to stick it out for a while?" Dad asked.

My mom prevailed. I was off the hook.

CHAPTER 4

305.31—Lust Religious Aspects Christianity
231.74—Revelation
123—Free Will and Determinism

The public restrooms at my library are vile. Every minute some-one's in there relieving himself or bathing in the sink. The air doesn't circulate and the stench is palpable. But they have noth-ing on the teen section. To walk through the young adult area is to traverse a cloud of hormones and poor hygiene and lust and anger that's as real as a thicket of skunky roadkill.

Whenever the teenagers are quiet, I assume it's because they're impregnating each other on the library furniture. Teen-agers get so wrapped up in each other that they don't even think to hide. One night while I was closing I saw a young couple sitting on a couch. Well, he was sitting on a couch. She was sit-ting on his lap and their faces were locked together tightly enough that, had I not been able to hear their rough breathing, I might have wondered if they were alive. I tried to make my footsteps heavier, but if they heard me, they gave no sign.

I cleared my throat. I was about to say, "Look, you can't sit on top of him and do it in the library," but we were closing, so

I just said, "You've got about one minute before we close." Security had to remind them five minutes later. They wandered away, presumably down to Level 2. Level 2 is the fiction department; it also houses the Canteena, which is the area reserved for teenagers and rutting. It has a television, colored benches, and computers for surfing the Internet. It was apparently designed to distract them from reading the young adult books that also happen to be there.

Two things kept getting in the way of my carnal desires: God and Tourette's.

For Mormon boys, the sixteenth birthday is a milestone. For me it meant the great quest to rub mine against hers. Now I could date. "Getting some" probably isn't what you're thinking. To a young Mormon boy, "getting some" meant a peck on the cheek, a hand to hold, someone to breathe hot air on your neck in a car late at night . . . I wasn't choosy about the specific acts of debauchery.

The primary goal for a Mormon is to marry a worthy spouse in the temple. Marriage is part of the Plan of Salvation. I'd been taught that, before coming to earth, we were all in the Preexistence, spirits waiting for our turn to live on the third planet as corporeal beings. We knew we'd be tested to prove ourselves worthy of returning to the highest kingdom of Heaven. There are three tiers in Mormon Heaven—telestial, terrestrial, and celestial.* The key requirement to vaulting past the terrestrial and telestial heavens and attaining celestial exaltation was finding that spouse.

---

* I'd been taught that even the lowest level of Heaven is so great that, if we could see it, we'd kill ourselves to get there. But it's only in the celestial kingdom that you can have your spouse, your family, and be in God's presence. Ultimately, anything but the celestial kingdom sucks and you'd spend eternity racked with regret in the lower kingdoms, knowing you could have done better, but the chance has passed.

The grand search for a partner starts for most at age sixteen, when we're first allowed to date. By then we've supposedly learned enough about right and wrong that we won't get each other pregnant the first chance we get. Besides, it had been drilled into us endlessly that premarital sex is a terrible sin; only murder is worse. You can repent of most sins by making restitution, but you can't bring a dead body back to life, and you can't restore your virginity. We are made in God's image and God is no fornicator. The importance of remaining pure and unspotted in the eyes of God was underscored by our Sunday school teachers' constant reminders: "Nothing good happens under a blanket" and "Sleep with your hands above the covers."

I went to church every Sunday, said my prayers, and went to seminary in the mornings. I was doing my part in the Plan.

When I turned sixteen, Kellie, a pretty girl in my ward, agreed to go on a date with me. Since Elko, Nevada, wasn't exactly bursting with nightlife opportunities for kids—casinos and brothels being out of the question—I took her to see *Mrs. Doubtfire*. I was excited, but also terrified by what might happen. My fantasies and church teachings had taught me to think that an orgy was always right around the corner, and that I might very well be hell-bound by morning. I also wanted to be irresistible and smooth, and my increasingly random tics made it harder to predict how my body would behave.

"Remember who you are," said my mom. "Be a gentleman."

I picked Kellie up in my tiny Honda Civic hatchback—I was already six feet seven and I suspected that my parents bought this car hoping it would serve as a chastity belt with good gas mileage. I'd tucked a coil of fuel tubing—a circle of rubbery hose—inside the pocket of my dad's old leather jacket, which he'd agreed to let me wear even though it was June. My latest tic was to bite my lips, tongue, and the inside of my cheeks repeatedly. So my plan was to secretly slip the rubber tubing into my mouth and bite down on it if the tic showed up. I was hoping that I wouldn't need it, but if necessary, I could probably chomp away in the darkened theater without Kellie noticing, unless we got down to making out as soon as the previews started.

The biting tics lay dormant. Instead, I yipped and yapped and hooted. Luckily, most Robin Williams movies are punctuated by deafening trumpet blasts and madcap soundtracks, so if Kellie noticed (I'm sure she did), she didn't say anything. But I needed her to say something about something.

"This is really funny," I said, nodding at the movie. It wasn't.

"I *know*!" she whispered. She hadn't laughed once. But that's Robin Williams for you. The zanier he got, the less we smiled. We had that much in common, at least.

My fantasized make-out session never materialized. While our shoulders occasionally touched during the movie, that was it. I was inexplicably operating at half-capacity wittiness. If Kellie knew I was struggling, she gave no sign, but I knew the date was a dud. As I drove out of her driveway, an involuntary scream burst out of me, much louder than anything I'd done in the theater.

My mom was waiting up for me. "Did you have fun?"

"Yes," I lied. My honor was still intact, but I was too exhausted and frightened about the future to care.

"Did you put the moves on her?" Dad asked. "The moves are in your blood."

"Frank!" Mom said.

"Because if you need to learn the ropes, I can teach you. I am wise in this way. Ask your mother."

"No," I said.

As I lay in bed, tossing and turning with that particular agony known only to lusty young boys after an evening that goes nowhere, I thought about the Plan. Believing in the Plan

meant that I had Tourette's *by design*. I didn't want to saddle
anyone else with it in a partnership, but I was *supposed* to find
someone to marry. This meant that someone else's Plan was to
marry a guy with worsening Tourette's and bear his burdens.

My date with Kellie was a dud and a fluke. When I tried to
talk to girls—and I failed to try most of the time—I usually
wound up talking about myself. "Hi, I'm Josh, I've got this
weird thing so you might see this—" The girls would look at me
expectantly. These were inevitably the times when my tics
wouldn't emerge, so my opening line was to tell someone that I
had a disorder that resulted in no symptoms. Blah. Maybe my
dad did need to teach me the ropes.

It was 1994 and Nirvana had released the album *Nevermind*.
Thrift stores in Elko filled with young men trading in their MC
Hammer pants and vying for used, ragged sweaters and thread-
bare pants. I didn't know who Kurt Cobain was when I borrowed a basketball teammate's CD player during a trip and put
those headphones on. By the time we got back to Elko I knew
the words to every song. Or, I knew what I thought the words
were. It was silly to think that the howling and unintelligible
and nonsensical lyrics and the screaming feedback of the guitars had been written for me, but that's how it felt. The music
sounded like I felt. It wasn't that I was angry, or disenfran-
chised, or that I hated my life, or that I really had anything to
complain about. But I felt . . . more aggressive.

I thought I'd been interested in girls before, but by the time
the basketball season ended, I was gripped by a mania that
nearly tore me in half. One day at school I had my road to Da-
mascus moment: Every other girl was wearing a Nirvana shirt.

That night at dinner I said, "My tics were really bad today."
This always killed the conversation. Not that it stopped me

from saying it. I could neutralize any and all small talk that wasn't related to or involving me. "I want to try something with music."

"What do you mean? You mean besides piano?" Dad asked. I'd started piano lessons when I was five, and I was still taking them. Piano had given me good posture, but I'd never heard a girl say, "Why can't I just find a boy with suitable scapular alignment?"

"I think I want to learn how to play the guitar. I think it looks fun and I think it would help me."

"Electric or acoustic?" said my dad.

I pictured the girls in the Nirvana shirts. "Electric."

"Fine," Dad said. "I'll take you over to Salt Lake and we'll go to Wagstaff. Have you ever been there? Tons of guitars."

"Really?"

"If you think it will help, then yes, really," said my dad.

My mom couldn't argue with that, but she was still trying to figure out what my angle was.

"Girls love guitars," said my dad. "*You* love guitars," he said, pointing at my mom.

"Don't tell me what I love, you oaf."

We left for Salt Lake City the next weekend, as promised. We rose early and had breakfast at JR's, a restaurant inside one of the casinos. Even at seven in the morning, the cacophony of people losing money served as background music. "When we moved here, your mom and I used to come down here and play the slots," Dad said while we waited for our food.

The thought of my mom playing the slot machines was as alien as the thought of her pole dancing. This was fascinating, and not just because Mormons don't gamble. With the aim of being good examples for us kids, my parents kept their guard up fairly well, she better than he. But occasionally I'd see glimpses of the kids they had been, exhibits of the past, usually offered as evidence by one parent as a mild, good-natured indictment against the other. What else had they done that I didn't know about? What else might they *still* be doing that I didn't know about?

I looked into the casino. One row of slots was taken by a row of elderly women whose blue hair looked psychedelic under the garish lights. One of them wore a tight black glove on her slot-pulling hand to keep it rust-free. They sold these gloves at many shops in Elko, including the convenience stores. They were usually on the counter with the impulse buys. Like the scant red panties bundled into the shape of a rose.

"Did you really play the slots?" I asked.

"Just a little bit," he said. "Just for fun. We wouldn't do it now. Your mom definitely wouldn't. Hey, look at her!" He had noticed the lady with the glove.

"Was it because you don't have enough money to gamble now or because you're trying to be good?"

Dad laughed. "We definitely had less money back then, but it's both. It's a dumb habit and it's even worse when people get addicted. Do you think she's addicted?" Then he nodded and winked at the lady with the glove as she walked by. "Oh yeah, she's got to have it." We finished breakfast, got in the truck, and left Elko.

Half an hour into the drive I pulled a paperback out of my jacket pocket and started reading. My dad said, "What's your book about? Looks pretty spicy."

I closed it and wondered what to say. I'd started reading fantasy a couple of years earlier. I held a copy of Piers Anthony's *And Eternity*, from the Incarnations of Immortality series. Each book told the story of a mortal who replaces one of the Incarnations: Fate, War, Time, Death, Nature, Evil . . . and Good. *And Eternity* was about how the other Incarnations decide that God has been negligent and must be replaced. But that hadn't caught my dad's attention. The cover of *And Eternity* shows two women standing on clouds in a ray of light, arms outstretched in a pose of worship. Sprawled in front of them is a young, black-haired woman toying with a necklace. She is wearing thigh-high black nylons, a black tank top, and is lying turned to the side, apparently looking at my dad.

"Well, this series is about these incarnations—they're actually called 'offices,' like the Devil would have his own office, but his incarnation is called Evil, and—"

"Who's she?" Dad interrupted, pointing at the girl in the thigh-highs. I couldn't tell him that it was looking like she'd be the one to replace God, so I said, "Never mind, it's dumb. I know."

He laughed. "Just because it's dumb doesn't mean you can't like it." He gestured at the landscape. "Isn't the real world interesting enough for you?" We were driving through an interminable expanse of sagebrush and flatness. At its most vibrant, sagebrush looks like a bouquet of flowers that has been dropped in a mud puddle. "Fascinating," I said.

Once we got to Wagstaff Music, I wandered the aisles, not knowing the differences between the guitars, and checking out the price tags. Occasionally I'd put a finger out and touch a glossy finish, or pluck a string. I furrowed my brow, trying to look like a discriminating shopper. I even picked up one guitar and held it out with the neck pointing away from me. I squinted one eye and looked down the neck as if I was gauging something.

My dad elbowed me in the side and hissed. "*Sssss!*" He pointed across the room with his lips, where a kid was playing a guitar with his eyes closed. He swayed and nodded his head as his facial expressions changed. He'd be as blank as a zombie, then as concerned as a parent whose toddler is wandering toward the road. He was playing something heavily distorted and heavily awesome. My dad closed his own eyes and swayed in a passable, but less awesome imitation of the guitarist.

The kid was wearing a Nirvana shirt.

His guitar was black with a white pick guard and a light brown fret board. *What if he buys that guitar? That's my guitar.*

"May I help you gentlemen?" a voice asked.

I shook the sales clerk's hand and pointed to where the kid was . . . putting down the black guitar! "How much is that one?"

"The Peavey Predator, huh?"

All told, the guitar and amplifier, a beginner's guide, plus a strap, four picks, and a cord, cost my dad $250. I hugged him in the parking lot. We drove to my aunt Kathy's house and stayed the night. I opened my instruction book on the bedspread and plugged the guitar into the amp. I raked the pick along the strings and experimented with the settings on the amplifier for most of the night. When my dad banged on the ceiling above me I unplugged and kept noodling around.

I soon learned that when I played the fierce Peavey Predator, I didn't have tics. I could practice for eight hours in one day and banish Misty. I quickly started a band with some friends, the horribly named Broken Rainbow. We played at one battle of the bands (we didn't win), in our garages (we won, the neighbors lost), and senior prom the next year. To my mom's extreme dismay, soon I was drawn to heavier, more aggressive music. Nirvana was extreme in the beginning, but its effect wore off. I needed more. The most extreme music I ever got into was the band Slayer. I had Slayer T-shirts, all the albums, and I talked about the band with a focus bordering on autism. I talked about the band so much that I was given the nickname "Slaytan," a mash-up of Slayer and Satan. I thought I could get away with having it stitched onto my basketball sweatshirt. I somehow forgot that my mom did my laundry.

"Are you kidding me?" she said, holding the shirt up to my face. I couldn't believe it, but that was when I noticed that it was spelled wrong. S-L-A-Y-T-O-N. That was my escape hatch. "It's the name of a band," I said. She folded her arms across her chest and squinted at me. "You don't say?"

"Mom! You don't spell Satan with an *o*!"

"You don't say. . . ."

We didn't talk about it again.

As much as I loved my guitar, the girls weren't coming around. "Like bees to a hive," my dad had said. But no.

Then Jennie came to seminary one morning. Nothing like meeting the woman of your dreams in church to squelch your teenage dreams of debauchery. She was a year younger than I was, about five-ten, and in my mind, absolutely ravishing. I watched her as the teacher droned on, something unimportant about the Plan of Salvation and my very own destiny. I knew what my destiny was. I knew where it was too. It was seated three chairs down and was wearing a skirt. But how was I going to meet Jennie? No, scratch that. I met her the same day everyone else did—the teacher introduced her and we all said hi and introduced ourselves. Alas, I didn't say "hi" in a way that caused her to fall at my feet. But then! Salvation.

That first year with the band, Steve—our drummer—and I improved at our instruments. My other two friends, the bass player and an additional guitarist, were great at jumping around, but they were . . . uninspired musicians. Steve and I had talked about adding another guitarist, but anyone who played was already in a rival band.

Jennie's brother was Steve's age, and even though he was three years younger, he was already better at the guitar than I would ever be. He was incredible, a very special musician. Steve introduced us and soon I was jumping around in Jennie's garage every afternoon. From there it was a short trip upstairs to her room to woo and flirt. A month later I took her to the high school Christmas dance and kissed her for the first time. We were so dizzy and stupid and drunk on each other after that night that I probably wouldn't have ever graduated from high school if it hadn't been so easy.

Misty was jealous. Every time I was around Jennie, my tics got worse. I gave her my standard script, but I was nervous:

Yeah, it's called Tourette Syndrome. If you've ever seen that movie What About Bob? *you've probably heard of it. It makes me move and make noises. I've got too much dopamine in my brain. It sort of overflows and signals get sent to my body that tell it to do things that I'm not consciously wanting it to do. Sorry if it annoys you. It annoys me too.*

One night while we watched TV, I yelped and clacked my teeth together over my tongue. "Ouch!"

"What happened?" Jennie asked.

"Bit my tongue." I winced and moved my jaw around and hoped that she would want to kiss it better. Instead, she smiled, took off one of her shoes and said, "Here, you should bite down on this."

My first reaction was anger. *How dare she laugh at this!* But then I laughed. Jennie had no inclination to coddle me about this. I think she saw that it was more of a hassle for me than a burden. She waved the shoe in my face. "I just like the idea of you walking around with a shoe hanging out of your mouth. I think it would be . . . most dashing."

"Most dashing, huh?"

"Most dashing."

My mom thought we were getting too serious. The church encourages group dating. Pairing off is seen as bad news, with good reason. Leave four kids alone who are trying to be good and it's unlikely that an orgy will break out. Leave them unsupervised and in pairs and who knows? Our parents were oblivious and trusting. "Are you sure you guys can be good?" my mom asked when I told her that I was sleeping over at Jennie's house, again.

"Oh yeah. I'm sure." Her parents actually let me sleep in Jennie's room! We couldn't believe what we were getting away with! After that first kiss we slowly grew bolder, needier. It took a while, though. We were tentative and felt guilty sometimes, but we couldn't resist going further forever. As long as we told her parents we were being good, we could roll around and dry hump the sun up every weekend. We never had sex, and we knew that we wouldn't unless we were married. We drove each other crazy and took things to a point that would have caused most people to say "And you didn't? *How?*"

How? Because the church was there in the background. No matter how much fun we had, there was always an unspoken guilt. And it would have meant that I couldn't serve a mission on schedule when I turned nineteen.

We were walking around Spring Creek's disgusting, leech-filled, moss-choked marina in the spring of 1996 when I said, "When do you think we should get married?" We were about four months into our relationship. We were "in love" with that crazed certainty that only headstrong teenagers seem to be capable of.

Jennie cocked an eyebrow. "You want to marry me, huh? Why?"

"You know why," I said, kissing her in a way that, in my head, was very smooth. "Because I love you." We threw "I love you" around like someone would murder us if we stopped.

"Then we'll get married when you get back."

"Back?"

"From your mission." Shrieking children jumped off the dock, then emerged from the water shrieking even louder as they saw the leeches clinging to their clammy skin.

I had avoided this conversation. I wanted to keep avoiding it. "So I have to go, huh?"

"You do if you want me. That's how it works." I could talk Jennie into just about anything, but not this. And I didn't want her to backtrack on her beliefs. And her parents wouldn't want her to marry me if I didn't serve a mission. My parents wouldn't either. When a young man of mission age didn't go, there was always a reason. Either he didn't believe or he had sinned and his mission was delayed as he sorted out the repentance process. The process essentially entailed confessing to your bishop and then waiting for a year while remaining in good standing. I wouldn't say that a church ward has more gossipers in it than other groups of similar size, but there were plenty. Worthy young men served missions. *Unworthy* young men stayed home and set the gossip's tongues ablaze.

"Okay. If that's how it works," I said. Jennie and I hadn't talked about the church much. Doing so would have called attention to our delicious nighttime activities, which had no premarital justification. I couldn't say, "Bishop, look, I know the church says we can't treat each other like jungle gyms just yet, but biology and evolution are telling my cells that we should breed. Or at least go through the motions as often as possible." But now I'd brought up the question and couldn't take it back.

"You *are* planning on going, aren't you?" she said.

"Of course!" *I don't know.*

"Good."

I graduated from high school in June of 1996 and spent that summer working as a delivery driver. If I served a mission, I wouldn't leave until early in 1997, so I had to figure out what to do with myself by summer's end. My friend Erik was going to a college in Twin Falls, Idaho, for a semester before his own mission. Jennie still had a year of high school left. I didn't want to hang out at home and work at the mine.

"Mom, I think I want to go to college at CSI with Erik for a semester."

She was delighted. "Great! I think that's really smart to get one semester behind you before you go."

Right. Before I go.

I was the same age as my dad was when he confronted the same question about conversion. He could get baptized and marry my mom or not.

To avoid my own confrontation, I played along as if I had unshakable faith, but that semester was nothing more than a desperate grab at distraction.

Here's the least you need to know about young Mormon men going on missions:

Jesus told his apostles to scatter to the winds and spread the word. Mormon doctrine instructs us to follow what Jesus taught. Whether Mormons are Christians is hotly contested in some circles, but I'll tell you this—at that point I had watched my family worship Jesus Christ, and *only* Jesus Christ, for eighteen years. Regardless, Jesus said that other people needed to hear his message, so that was why we served missions.

When Joseph Smith got the party started over in America a couple of millennia later, it couldn't have gone anywhere without missionaries. There was no Twitter and you couldn't put a stupid Facebook ad for the church in front of everyone. Those early elders took their Books of Mormon, chose a direction, started walking, and preached. It's the same idea now. When it's time, you submit your paperwork and then wait for your mission "call" to arrive in the mail. You don't know where you'll spend the next two years—missions for elders last twenty-four months, versus eighteen months for sisters—until you open that envelope. The Philippines? Guam? Toledo? Los Angeles? Okinawa? You don't know. Once you learn where you're going, you get started at a missionary center and then you're out in the field, trying to baptize everyone.

It is assumed that you'll go when you're nineteen if you're a male. Sisters don't go for a couple more years, and many marry during that extra time. Mission expectations are different for women. Nobody is forced to go, male or female, but if a woman was to say, "I'd rather stay home and go to school or get married or work," nobody would question that.

During that semester I took some introductory classes that were as boring as they sounded. The one exception was a psychology class. As I read the syllabus I noticed a Tourette's discussion during the abnormal psychology unit. The lesson was a disappointment, however, and merely restated what I'd already heard: There is no cure for TS but doctors are working on it.

My relationship with Misty was getting painful. She wasn't violent, but the repetitive strain was taking a toll on my joints. I saw how much pain I could eventually be in if the current level of tics maintained over the next few years or even decades.

I drove home to see Jennie on the weekends, but we spent much of the time fighting about things that didn't matter. I was always in the mood to argue. One night she asked, "What's the worst part about having Tourette's?"

I bit back whatever I was going to say. "You know . . . I'm not sure."

"Think about it. I'm not sure what's going on with you, but I don't like you much lately." I wasn't ready for the "I'm not sure I want to go on a mission but can we be together anyway?" discussion. Or maybe I wasn't sure that Jennie was capable of it. I didn't know how to tell her that Misty was trying to rip me away from her, which is how it felt. When I started dating Jennie, everything felt new. Every day felt like the morning after a rainstorm when everything glistens and smells fresh. We were unblemished and faultless. We knew just enough about each other to want to know more. Now we had been together for over a year and we knew enough about each other to want to keep certain things to ourselves.

"Jennie, I'm not sure I'm able to be happy," I finally said.

"Well, that's pretty melodramatic," Jennie said as she hugged me. "Of course you can be happy. That's why I love you. When you're happy, you're happier than anyone I've ever met."

I tried again. "Okay, I think the worst thing is that I'm always waiting for something. And I'm not talking about waiting for time to pass. Not like waiting to go to college or waiting for a basketball game to start. Or waiting to see you or to go do something fun or go on vacation or anything. I mean. . . ."

Why was this so hard to explain?

"I feel like there's someone else here. Like I'm not able to make all of my own decisions, because there's this thing in my head that decides what I'm capable of. I hate it that I can't make you understand exactly how it feels. I know I've been a jerk, but when it's bad, I feel mean. I don't know how to say it any better than that. I'm not very good at waiting for things, and now I'm always waiting for the next tic. I never know what's going to happen, even though it's not that bad. It's exhausting. I don't know if I know how to be happy or nice when I'm this tired and anxious all the time. What if I can't do the mission? What if you can't ever rely on me for anything?"

"You'll go and I'll wait for you. You'll do what you can, and that will be enough."

"But—"

"It will be enough for me."

"Do you really believe it all, Jennie? The church?"

She looked at me for a long time before nodding. "It feels right to me. It feels real."

I drove back to Twin Falls the next evening. Erik wasn't home. I let myself into our place and sat in the dark. I listened to the clock ticking and the cows lowing outside in the nearby pasture. I was annoyed to realize that I had tears in my eyes. Too many tics. Too many unmade decisions. Too much uncertainty and worry that things might not get better. And worry that things weren't all that bad to begin with and that they simply *felt* harder than they should. That somehow by feeling so burdened, I was proving that I was weak and weak-willed. The house was suffocating. I ran outside, into the driveway.

It started to rain when I got into my car. The paved roads turned to dirt as I left the city and drove to nowhere. How many years were in the average life? If I were lucky enough to have a long life, how many tics would be in those years? On that road, in the dark, it seemed that there was so little to believe in. So little cause for hope. The road ended and I stopped the car. The rain beat at the windows from every angle. Looming over the doubt and dread was the awful suspicion that I was just being a stupid drama queen and that I should really just suck it up and get to work. *That's what Dad would say.* Was I just a kid, experiencing a kid's immaturity and worry about the future? Was this just teenage melodrama? Even if that were true, wondering about it, acknowledging it in some way . . . wouldn't have made it *feel* true. What felt true was that I was wracked with panic and tears. What was true was that I was sitting in a car that was much too small for me, out in the middle of rural Idaho, at the end of a rutted road, far from the reach of the town's lights.

I cried embarrassingly hard. There was a set of Scriptures under my seat. They usually got put there on my way to church and then forgotten for the rest of the week. I opened the books at random, settling on Section 6 of the Doctrine and Covenants, a series of "revelations" to the prophet Joseph Smith and others. Section 6 was a revelation given to Oliver Cowdery, the scribe who had assisted Smith in the translation of the Book of Mormon. Verse 22 is allegedly Christ speaking to a doubting Oliver:

If you desire a further witness, cast your mind upon the
night that you cried unto me in your heart, that you
might know concerning the truth of these things.

I'd said hundreds, if not thousands, of prayers, simply going through the motions. I knew the words. I knew the actions
and the reverent posture. I knew how it was supposed to work
and how it was supposed to feel. But I didn't know what it
meant to really cry out in my heart. To beg for an answer. To
need an answer for my own sake. Relying on my mom's faith, or
whatever Jennie wanted me to do, wasn't enough tonight. I
started talking. "I need to know. I don't know what to do. I
have no idea what's going to happen to me and I have no idea
how strong I'm supposed to be before I deserve help from you.
I don't even know if you're there. I hope you are, but I don't
want to believe things because they make me feel better. I want
to believe them because they're true. Is it possible to know that?
Is it?"

The wind stopped. The rain stopped. Despite the goose
bumps that stood up on my arms, I was warm and calm inside,
as still and peaceful as the weather outside. If you've ever lost
control of your body to sobbing, you know it's hard to calm
down until you're cried out. I'd been in the thick of that, nowhere close to drying up. And yet it had happened. One moment you might have thought I was weeping at my mom's
coffin. The next . . . everything was fine. Clarity and calm
flooded through me. Part of me watched this happening from a
distance and said, *Now hold on . . . is this really an answer?*

But it was a small part of me. The rest of me marveled at
how *different* I suddenly felt. I wish I could describe it better. I
would tell that to a bishop later and he would laugh as he said,
"Why should you be able to use mortal words to accurately
describe something divine? Doesn't the very use of words
cheapen the experience? How could it not?"

Feeling was enough for my parents, for my leaders, for the girl I planned on marrying. And now it felt like it would be enough for me. I couldn't explain away what had just happened, because I'd never felt that way before. I didn't say *That was an answer*, but it was close enough for me to decide. After the next week of school Erik and I drove home to Elko again. That night at dinner I said, "I think I want to put in my mission papers."

"Good!" said my mom.

"You sure you're ready to leave your girl here for the wolves?" said my dad. The dinner passed in predictable chatter. "I wonder where you'll get sent?" "Where do you want to go?" "What language would you want to learn?" "Are you scared?" It wasn't much of a scene because I don't think anyone but me ever doubted it.

I told Jennie I was going. "I'm scared," I said. "How do you feel?" had been her second comment, right after "Oh, *Josh*!" I let her be proud of me. It felt good. It felt right. It gave me purpose; her happiness seemed like an end worth pursuing.

I spent the next month doing paperwork, getting a physical, applying for a passport, checking boxes, getting fitted for white dress shirts, and wondering where I'd go.

My call arrived in the first week of December. I held the envelope while my mom called my dad at work. "Yes, he'll wait until you're all here."

Another cliché: That was the longest day of my life. Inside that envelope was a summons to do something utterly foreign to me. It was a membership card to the ranks of the missionaries, plane tickets that needed to be booked, a physical symbol of the conviction I said I had, a sign to Jennie that I wanted to marry her, and the end product of a revelation I had received during a rainstorm, that now looked far less portentous and insignificant inside of an eight-and-a-half-by-four-inch square of paper.

By seven P.M. everyone was there in my living room, watching and smiling. My heart leapt about. "Everyone," I said, "I'm not sure how I feel about all this. So if it's okay, after I read it, I don't want a bunch of cheering and hugging. I just want to go outside and think."

My mom visibly deflated. Jennie's mom nodded. My dad laughed. "Do whatever you want. It's your night." Jennie rubbed my shoulder as I opened the envelope and read aloud:

> Josh Hanagarne, you have been called to serve in the Washington DC North Mission, where you will teach the gospel of Jesus Christ in the Spanish language.

I would leave on January 7. One month away.

Everyone gave me the distance I'd asked for. "Fix the government while you're there!" said my dad. I stood and exited through the front door. I walked out into the center of our yard, the snow crunching beneath my feet. It was an impossibly clear night and the air was pure and sharp. The door opened and closed somewhere behind me and Jennie was at my side. "You think you can see stars like this in DC?" she asked, kissing my cheek.

I smiled but didn't say anything.

"How do you feel, Josh?"

I half succeeded in smiling but couldn't put it into words, so I just said, "I don't know. I really don't. I'm going to miss you all. I'm going to miss you."

"We'll be here when you get back."

CHAPTER 5

289.3—Mormons Missions
193—Knowledge, Theory of

"This is the nonfiction floor, right?"

"Yes, sir, it is." He looks beyond annoyed at my answer.

"Okay . . . Josh," he says, leaning in to sneer at my name tag. "Then why is the religion on this floor?" And now it's clear. There's a shrill atheist standing before me. But his question is valid. It's a question for Mr. Dewey himself, I suppose. As cataloging issues go, this was thorny.

If you classified religion as pure fiction, you'd annoy the devout. And the fiction department that already groans under the weight of so many James Patterson novels would be stressed to its limits. But if you classified religion as nonfiction, you lent it credibility by placing it on the same floor with the sciences and books about cupcake decorating.

People who raise this issue never ask about the Sylvia Browne books or the occult mysteries section, also on my floor. They're never annoyed that the healing power of crystals is advocated at great length one mere aisle away, or that the massive books of reptile-paranoia guru David Icke take up a square foot here and there. They accept that people who want to summon fairies would visit my department, but that anyone who prays to a God or Gods is an imbecile who mustn't be tolerated.

Even as a mildly religious person I am fascinated by this question. My fascination rarely makes atheists less irritated, but I find this the ultimate distillation of theory vs. experience. Anecdote versus empiricism. This floor also houses the psychology and psychiatry section, the self-improvement books, books on reflexology and alternative medicine, and the endless, trendy volumes of stock speculation. I find these books every bit as dodgy, in terms of verifiability, as the religion books.

"Well, who can I talk to about getting this resolved?" he asked. What ambition he had! The debate of believer versus nonbeliever has been raging for—oh, I don't know, since we can't even agree on how old the earth is, but it's been at least a few thousand years, even for creationists. But this man was going to resolve it. Once and for all. I sent him to admin on Level 5.

Maybe our library director could handle this softball.

Every Wednesday, hundreds of missionaries enter the Missionary Training Center (the MTC) in Provo, Utah. Most of them are young men between the ages of nineteen and twenty-one, but there are plenty of senior citizens serving various types of service missions, and there are the sister missionaries.

As my parents drove me to the MTC, we didn't talk much. My mom stared out the passenger window and sniffled occasionally. My dad wasn't doing much better. He kept glancing at me in the rearview mirror. I'd try to smile but only manage a hideous twist of the mouth that betrayed my nerves and excitement. Nowadays, parents drop their missionaries curbside where they are whisked away by other MTC trainees. They say their good-byes in the car and away they go. But when I went through, parents and kids went in together and checked in at the front desk. The MTC resembled any college building—long hallways, high ceilings, classrooms, dorms, auditoriums. But here pictures of church leaders past and present lined the walls. They watched us walk to a conference room with a couple hundred other newbies.

The president of the MTC—this was a calling as well—spoke about the great work we had embarked on. He commended our red-eyed parents for their sacrifices, but assured them that we'd be protected and watched over. I wondered if he was thinking, *Okay, everyone, toughen up. Good grief.*

To us, he said, "Remember that because you have made this choice, the time in the mission is not yours. You have dedicated it to the Lord. Serve with honor and you will be rewarded. And the families you find will be blessed." Then we were all standing up and hugging. My mom wrung her skirt in her hands and stared at the ground as my dad embraced me. "Seven hundred and thirty days," he said in a shaky voice. "See you then. I'm so proud of you." I turned to my mom.

"I love you, Josh." That was all she could say. Of course this made me cry too, but not as much as I'd expected. All around us were the sounds of backs being slapped and noses being blown and apron strings being snipped. Then it was time. The parents left the room. We were now missionaries. Righteous, anxious kids in new suits and skirts being herded into processing.

I received a packet with my dorm room number, the name of my companion (Elder Sansom), a room key, information about the cafeteria and class schedules, my district (the dozen or so missionaries I would attend classes with), and a list of study materials to buy at the missionary store. The first priority was to buy the six missionary discussions that were the core of the structured teaching material. After finishing my shopping, I walked to the male dorms. En route I passed some laughing sister missionaries who were impossibly attractive now that they were completely off-limits in any way I cared about. There would be six sister missionaries in my district that I'd see daily for the next eight weeks, but it's not like we could sit around and flirt and kiss and do anything fun. We weren't there for fun. It wasn't our time.

My room was the size of two large elevators. Two sets of bunk beds bookended the narrow space. I set down my luggage, sat on the bottom bunk, and said a prayer. *Thank you for getting me here. I hope I can accomplish what I'm supposed to.* Did anyone hear me? Was I was just a nineteen-year-old boy sitting in an empty room, trying to feel something that wasn't there? Either way, it was still and peaceful—besides the tics, of course.

As the building filled, the most common question was "So where are you going?" The Philippines, Japan, rural Nevada, Vietnam, Canada, Washington, DC. The breadth of missions was staggering. This was a big production. This was serious business. And how incredible that we were all there of our own free will, and unpaid. Elder Sansom, my companion, was a stocky blond man headed to Costa Rica

By nighttime every room was full. Some elders had a contest to see who could climb all the way to the ceiling by supporting their feet on one side of the hall and their hands on the other. Footraces down the corridors. Constant pranks. Everyone swapping pictures of girlfriends and bragging about where they were from and how they had played in a band and who wanted to arm wrestle?

There were those who remained wholly incapable of levity. They sat in their rooms and scowled at the noise, reading their scriptures and shaking their heads at the tragic loss of solemnity.

Everyone I talked to cared about being there. But come on, a nineteen-year-old boy is a nineteen-year-old boy. Put them all together and don't be surprised if there are some shenanigans, a stench that was referred to as "the wall of flame," and lots of noise.

Classes started the next day. Because I was learning another language, I'd be at the MTC for eight weeks, versus the three weeks for English-speaking missionaries. I had to learn how to teach the six discussions, but I also had to learn Spanish, which added new frustrations and satisfactions.

The routine: wake up at six A.M. and shower. Get to breakfast by seven. Classes started at eight. There were three classes each day, in two- to three-hour blocks. Teachers were former missionaries. Each class opened with a prayer; then we'd drill the language. Everyone in my district was going to a Spanish-speaking mission, but I was one of only four who would go to Washington, DC. The language training was predictable.

Teacher: *"La cama!"*

Us: *"La cama!"*

Teacher: "The bed!"

Us: *"La cama!"*

Teacher: *"El evangelio!"*

Us: *"El evangelio!"*

Teacher: "The gospel!"

Us: *"El evangelio!"*

We had a message to share, but didn't know the words yet. So we drilled basic conversation. The plate, bed, wall, Bible, table, Savior, how to say your name, an introductory "Hi, we're missionaries" script, and gospel principles. When we learned to say words like "beautiful" or "I love you," I found myself staring at the sisters. I missed girls.

When we weren't learning languages, we practiced teaching

the six discussions. The discussions began with an introduction to church fundamentals—Joseph Smith's vision, the Book of Mormon, and the centrality of Christ to the religion—and the sixth lesson ended with the newly baptized member's integration into a ward.

Sometimes our teachers taught us and we'd play the investigator, which was the word for a prospective convert who showed interest. Sometimes we'd reverse roles. Sometimes we'd commit horrific vocabulary errors, like accidentally requesting a whore instead of a napkin. Swearing in Spanish didn't feel vulgar at all. We used the word *chingar* constantly and thought nothing of it until a Mexican elder heard us, walked in, and said, "All of you shut the fuck up." We were outraged!

"Elder!" I said. "You can't— We're in the MTC!"

"That's what it sounds like to me when you use the word *chingar.*"

We stopped.

We were always with our companions, but I was lucky; Elder Sansom and I got along well. I hated never being alone, but I knew myself well enough to accept the reasoning behind it. It was very easy to catch an elder staring out the window at the sisters' dorms and know that he was imagining all those young women. And probably not imagining them studying their scriptures and practicing their languages. I could've talked myself into many adventures, had I been alone, courageous, and suave. But because we were always with the district—or at least with our companions—we kept one another in check. No girls, no swearing, very little English, and no mercy for the losers who refused to have fun.

I worked hard, but there were always distractions. The worst thing Jennie ever did was send me a calendar with her picture on every page. One night I flipped on my reading light in the dark and opened to the page detailing her family's trip to Lake Powell. There she was in a nightshirt and a sombrero, long tan legs bent at a saucy angle and lips blowing me a kiss. Damnation, that made it hard to sleep.

I think I missed my pleasure reading as much as I missed her. I read constantly, although all I could read was the King James Bible, the Book of Mormon, the Doctrine and Covenants (a book of revelations recorded by Joseph Smith), the Pearl of Great Price (more canonical writing translated by Smith), the missionary discussions, and various teaching guides.

I needed it. Despite my years in seminary and Sunday school and family home evenings, I'd never read the Book of Mormon all the way through, and it was the cornerstone of our teaching. Everything in the church hinges on the Book of Mormon being the word of God. It's what we have that no other church does. It was translated by a prophet that no other church had. It clarified the confusion caused by the various interpretations of the Bible. It was the missing piece. And it was boring.

So I missed my books. I missed my authors. I almost asked Jennie to flout the rules and send me a copy of *Catch-22*. I didn't ask, but I walked right up to the edge and got on my knees, ready to beg.

But, no, I was here because I knew the truth and I would help others know it as well. Unless I spent too many nights looking at spicy pictures of the Lake Powell trip.

There was the occasional scandalous departure from the MTC. There were always rumors about "the sister missionary that the dorm leader got pregnant" and similar tales. We'd all heard stories about missionaries who entered the MTC unworthily and then got slapped silly with guilt as the weeks passed. While applying for a mission, you went through interviews with your bishop and stake president (a stake comprises several wards. The bishop in each ward reports to a stake president). At each of these you were asked if you had any unresolved transgressions. You could lie to these men and say no, but you couldn't lie to God. One elder confessed to us with a hilariously inappropriate tale of the lurid acts he'd committed with his girl-friend days before coming to the MTC.

"And the thing was," he said, "she was just so . . . virginal . . . that . . ."

"Okay, enough," said Sister C.

"I just need you to understand that what we did was—"

"We understand."

He left that night.

My only day of real doubt arrived in the form of a letter from my mom. Amid the normal reports and pleasantries was the sentence: *I thought you would want to know that Alan D. died unexpectedly. Complications with surgery.* I set the letter down and stared at the wall. "Are you all right?" asked Elder Sansom.

"No."

Alan was a twelve-year-old boy who was born with spina bifida. He was a fixture at church. He couldn't walk, stand, or speak clearly, but those of us who'd spent enough time with him understood him. If he liked you, he'd take your hand and press it to his face. I thought of the last time my hand was on his face and I broke. This was someone I loved. A happy kid, even though he'd been dealt a terrible hand. A child born to a wheelchair and a life of surgeries and pain, and now he was dead. He'd never done anything wrong. He didn't deserve his fate. He deserved to be rewarded for being so brave. He was tougher than anyone should have to be. Now he had come and gone and I wondered how his poor family was feeling. If I was upset, their grief and anger must have been profound and bottomless. Were they asking the same questions I was?

Why? How could You?

Or did they picture their son in a better place? In a better body?

What was I doing here? Each question—all the same question, really—was a door with a different answer behind it.

Is there a God? (Yes, and he killed Alan.)

Is there a God? (No, obviously. Alan is dead and you're wasting your time. Go home and bang your girlfriend.)

Is there a God? (Yes, and He has a plan. Alan's death is part of that plan. You might not understand it, but what do you expect? You're not some divine, omniscient being. Quit being an arrogant dick and thinking you *should* understand.)

Is there a God? (Maybe. You know how to find out.)

The prayer was short. *I don't know what to do. If You are there, please help me understand what I'm supposed to do. Or I don't know if I can stay here. Please give me an answer.*

That night I had a cinematic dream. It began with two white feet walking along a path. Gradually I saw more and more of the person attached to those feet; it was Alan. When I saw his face—his clear, relaxed face—he began to sing. A clear and lovely melody, the hymn "I Stand All Amazed." He turned and I saw that there was someone on the other side of him. Someone holding his hand. Each time I moved to see who it was, Alan moved and blocked my view. In the dream I knew that Alan was walking with Jesus Christ. Walking, and singing, and smiling, and not holding the slightest grudge about the challenges he'd endured on earth.

I'd woken up from dreams screaming. I'd woken up from dreams with tears in my eyes. But I'd never woke feeling like this. It felt like clarity. Warmth. Certainty. Confidence. Above all, it felt like an answer. That night I believed that I wasn't alone. I rolled out of bed, knelt, and said, "I will stay."

March arrived. It was time.

On our last night, I knelt with my district, a bunch of kids in ill-fitting suits and modest dresses, about to be scattered over the earth, charged with a great responsibility. One of the sisters led us in prayer.

"Please help us to find the people who are ready to listen. And thank you for bringing us together here." Her voice broke and then we were all bawling like infants. I don't think I've ever packed more hugs into a five-minute period than I did that night. I was scared, I was happy, I felt like I was doing the right thing, and best of all, I'd get to see Jennie the next day at the airport for a few precious minutes. It's ridiculous, but for those of us who had girlfriends coming to see us off, "Are you going to kiss her good-bye?" was a topic of intense debate. For the people with sticks up their butts, the subject was closed:

"You accepted the calling to be a missionary. You promised to sacrifice these two years without distractions or temptations. If you weren't allowed to kiss your girlfriend the night after you entered the MTC, why would that be different now?"

I got off the bus, saw Jennie beaming from the curb at the airport, and smashed my lips against hers so desperately that it took my Clydesdale of a father to drag me off. I'd planned on kissing her good-bye no matter what, but I got to kiss her hello as well.

"You look different," said my mom.

"You're uglier than ever," said my dad.

"We're so proud of you," said Jennie's mom.

Jennie's dad nodded. "Your dad's right, but so is Jennie's mom."

I hugged my siblings. My teary, sobbing siblings. That's when I knew what it means to be a big brother. Three sets of arms wrapped around me, attached to people I hadn't always been kind to, but whom I would die or kill for without hesitation. I pried them off so I could kiss Jennie again as the missionaries from my district—those going to DC—either smiled or shook their heads in lame disapproval.

In the MTC we were groomed to feel as if asking someone to change their entire life—and their faith—would be simple. That if we could just find the courage to open our mouths, over and over, the words would be there. "The people who are prepared to listen will hear what you have to say, even if you don't say it well," our teachers reassured us. It would be so easy. I had visions of clambering up the Washington Monument, whipping out a bullhorn and shouting, "All right, people, listen up. Shit just got real!" The mall would fill with people begging me to baptize them in the reflecting pool.

As the plane descended into DC, however, some of my self-assurance vanished. This city was full of people I'd never met. Somehow I'd have to go meet them all and share something with them.

I'd split most of my life between the small towns of Moab, Utah, and Spring Creek, Nevada. I hadn't ever seen a city larger than Salt Lake. I don't even remember ever going to school with a black student. But my early impressions of DC had nothing to do with the size of the buildings, the color of people's skin, or the bustling streets. It felt mean. It was crowded. Nobody seemed to like each other. All of the faces were mixtures of anger and weariness. I was almost terrified. Had there ever been people less interested in me? How was I going to do this?

Enter my trainer, a missionary I'll call Elder Santiago. If he had doubts about my abilities, he didn't show it. On our first day on the street, he walked right over to a black man waiting for a bus and said, "Sir, have you received your free copy of the Book of Mormon yet? It's another testament of Jesus Christ." I watched this display of confidence and verve from a distance before remembering that I should've been standing beside him. I got there just in time to hear the guy say, "I don't want to hear it. Leave me alone." The next man said, "I won't waste your time, but don't waste mine. We got nothing to talk about."

At the MTC we'd been assured that if we just told people

what we knew, the Spirit would help them feel the truth of it. "I know this is true," I said to an amiable man on the subway. He laughed and said, "What do you mean, you *know*? How do you define the word 'know'?" I tried to explain what it felt like to receive an answer. "Young man, I can tell you mean well, but listen—feeling is *not* knowing. We can't have a productive conversation about this if *I* think but *you* feel."

Others weren't so kind. I'd never had someone tell me to "fuck off" before. Now I'd heard it three times in two hours. And my verbal, choking, and yipping tics would flare up with each rejection. This terrified me; it was obvious that rejection would be the most reliable part of our routine.

People looked down at their purses or briefcases when we approached them on the sidewalk. They started conversations on phantom phones. Some smiled and nodded patiently while sneaking glances at their watches. The people most willing to talk with us were priests and preachers, and they just wanted to argue. The success I'd dreamed of didn't arrive that first day, but it wasn't a bad day. I was doing what I'd come to do. I hadn't crumpled into a cowering ball of uncertainty. Nobody mugged me. I wasn't a brilliant orator but I was opening my mouth and trying.

If we had any success that first week, I couldn't see it. We hadn't taught one lesson, let alone committed anyone to baptism. But I told myself that we were planting seeds. Maybe later someone would remember those two boys who'd knocked on their door, remember that they had slammed the door in our faces, and wonder if they'd been wrong. Or something.

One day we were almost home for the night when a voice behind me uttered the sweetest words: "Excuse me, Elders, could you please come and talk to my mom about Jesus?" I turned to see a man gesturing to me. His hand was missing several fingers; the remaining ones ended above the largest knuckle. The stumps oozed what looked like syrup. He was maybe thirty years old, wearing a gray sweat suit. He pointed behind him to a woman a block back. She appeared to be crying.

"Of course," I said.

"Elder Hanagarne," said Elder Santiago.

"We'll be right back down," I told the man. "I'm going to go set up a couple of things." Because I'd been called to teach in Spanish, all interested English-speaking investigators were turned over to the English-speaking elders as soon as possible. Four of them lived on the floor below ours. They didn't answer my knocking. I dragged Elder Santiago to our room and he watched me silently as I took a Book of Mormon out of my drawer, forty dollars of my own money, and a loaf of bread from the refrigerator. The man was waiting downstairs. His mother was nowhere in sight. "Oh, you brought me a Bible!"

"Sort of." I put it in his hand, along with the money and the bread. This was more like it! Someone needed help and I could provide it.

The man said that he could meet with the English elders the next day at eleven. He gave me an address and a phone number, which I wrote in my planner. Then he grabbed the money and the bread and jumped into a car that was suddenly at the curb. I watched the car drive away and smiled at Elder Santiago.

We didn't get in touch with the English-speaking elders until later that night. I was so proud. "He says you can call anytime tomorrow between—"

They all laughed. "Is this the guy with no fingers? Don't talk to him again, man. He's not interested; trust us. He wants money. Get used to beggars and scammers." They'd all dealt with this man more than once. The first person who'd been interested in the message had pretended.

I flopped into my bed. There were too many sirens in the city. Even with the blinds pulled the room was too bright. I stood and looked out the window. When I noticed that I couldn't see the stars, I thought of the many nights I'd spent sleeping on the trampoline back home with my siblings, endless galaxies spiraling away into nothingness over our heads.

I missed my family.

It had been a hard day of toil and rejection. We'd probably talked with three or four hundred people—an average day—without success. I was getting used to having doors slammed in my face. Of having girls wink at me and not being able to offer anything but salvation in return. Of being stood up for five appointments in one day and wondering how to fill the time.

Elder Wrigley, a district leader, came to check on our group. He was a giant, an inch taller than me. He sent his own companion with Santiago and worked with me that day. At the first door he knocked on, he said, "Have you ever wondered why Hispanic people are more likely to let us in?" I didn't have time to answer. The door was opened by a small woman from El Salvador. She spoke no English. But she insisted that we come in. *Pasale, pasale.* And suddenly I was teaching my first full discussion. She listened while Elder Wrigley and I spoke and gave us some water to drink. She declined to be visited again, which confused me since she had ushered us in with such gusto.

Outside, Wrigley said, "A lot of these people think we're from immigration. They've just arrived from Nicaragua or El Salvador or wherever and suddenly there are two white people wearing ties at their door, looking serious."

"So that's why she didn't ask us to come back?"

"Yeah. I'm sure she would have kicked us out sooner if she could have figured out how to do it nicely. Their culture's a lot more polite than ours."

This was true. The Hispanic community certainly had its share of people who couldn't stand us, but most were willing to talk, even if just to heckle us. In my experience, black people would usually hear us out and invite us in. We knocked on a door once and a small black guy with a huge smile opened the door. He invited us inside and asked, "Can I look at those books?" He ignored us while we tried to teach the first discussion. He flipped through the Book of Mormon and stopped on each of the inset pictures. "So what's happening here?" The picture showed a fat man in a purple robe—a bad king named King Noah—condemning one of God's prophets to be burned at the stake. I related this story and he slammed the book down and yelled, "Mother*fucker*." He sat back and shook his head, staring at something over my shoulder. "You telling me this fat fuck burned up a man of *God*? God*damn*." These sorts of interactions weren't all that productive, but they were lively. And way better than slammed doors and rolled eyes.

By the six-month mark I had helped baptize two people. The average for our mission was seven baptisms over two years. This was pretty standard for stateside missions. Compared with places like Santiago, Chile, where a missionary might teach *and* baptize ten people in a day, our success felt paltry.

Our success stories were two teenage boys who let us in when we knocked on their door. Elder Santiago and I were there to follow up with their mother, a contact made on the street. She had urged us to visit and then didn't show. The boys were obviously bored by everything we said about the church, so we started talking about sports. We went to the park and played two on two for a while. When the game ended, Elder Santiago said, "Have you guys considered getting baptized?"

They shrugged and said, "Sure, we'll do it." We taught them the rest of the lessons, baptized them, and managed to be surprised when they never came to church and stopped taking our calls.

But we'd done it. We'd gotten two baptisms, and I hoped that this success would sustain me and drive me to work even harder.

It did, but then everything changed.

Eight months out, I was out on the street on a sunny day when I suddenly punched myself in the face. Boom!

It hurt.

I looked at my bloody hand. What the hell? People gawked at me, but they weren't nearly as surprised as I was.

Everything looked the same. The sky was still blue and the clouds were still white. I still had my Book of Mormon in my unbloodied hand and I was still sweating like a tall, skinny faucet in the August heat. My feet still ached and I still had a terrible haircut. Elder Miller—the best friend I would make in the mission—gaped at me. "Are you all right?"

Before I could answer, it happened again. Wham! "Let's go home," I said. I managed to get on my bike and pedal. I didn't hit myself while on the bike, but I did scream a couple of times. We rode for thirty minutes and I collapsed onto our couch and sat on my hands.

"What can I do?" Elder Miller asked.

"I don't know." *Wham!* My right hand had sneaked out from beneath me. I wanted to call my mom. But I couldn't. We were allowed to call our families on Mother's Day, long past, and on Christmas, which felt like it was a century into the future. For the rest of the afternoon I yelled, hit, and scratched myself raw.

It was too much. The next day I called the mission president and asked if I could call my parents. When my mom answered the phone, I blurted out what had happened to me and waited for her reaction.

"I've never heard of Tourette's doing this," she said.

"What should I do?"

"See a doctor. Do what he says. Let us know how it goes. We love you, honey, hang in there."

Elder Wrigley drove me to a neurologist in Bethesda. President Graff came as well. The doctor outlined the profiles for various pills and asked which I felt most comfortable trying.

I agreed to take the drug Klonopin. After a week I'd report back to President Graff. There wasn't much to report:

"It's making me really sleepy, but it's not helping with anything."

"Can you continue to work?"

"Yes. We're going out tonight."

"Please let me know if I can help. Go out if you can. Someone might need to meet you today."

The tics weren't as bad after that first horrible, violent day. They hurt and they made it hard to go outside, but I was doing all right. After about a month, the worst of the injurious tics—hitting and scratching myself—stabilized and I was merely walking around screaming, "Huh huh huh!" at the top of my lungs, like a quarterback calling for the huddle.

I continued to work and it paid off. Elder Miller and I met the person that missionaries dream of—the one who'd been prepared for us. We knocked on Sonia's door and the first thing she said was, "I knew someone would come. I've been praying for someone to come talk to me about God." She accepted everything. Instantly. The most fascinating thing was that she'd met with missionaries before, in her home in Bolivia. She'd even taken a couple of the discussions. But as she put it, "It was never *you two*."

"What do you mean?" I asked.

"You know how there are so many self-improvement books in the bookstore? They all say the same thing. So why do people keep reading them? They basically all say 'You can do it!'"

I laughed.

"Well, Elders, you do not know this, but you are the same as all the other elders, and you are different. You are *not* them, even if you tell me all the same things. I *feel* things when it is the two of you that I do not feel with others, even if the words do not change so much."

I was unprepared for this eagerness and openness after the

months of fruitless toil. We baptized Sonia a month later. It
was a small ceremony at our ward building. She wore a blue
dress with a white collar to the church and changed into a
one-piece white jumpsuit for the ceremony. The bishop gave a
brief talk in the chapel, then the handful of us in attendance
guided Sonia into a room with a baptismal font. Elder Miller
stood next to Sonia and intoned, "Sonia, having authority
given me of Jesus Christ, I baptize you in the name of the
Father, and of the Son, and of the Holy Ghost. Amen." He
guided her under the water, supporting the small of her back,
then pulled her up. I was one of the two required witnesses
who made sure it was done properly, "just like Jesus," according to the Book of Mormon. Sonia's husband wept. He hadn't
attended the discussions, although he supported Sonia's decision. "This felt very important," he told me. "I think I'm ready
to start learning."

When Sonia emerged from the dressing room later, she
hugged us with tears in her eyes. "Thank you thank you thank
you. I feel . . . new."

Feeling is not knowing. I'd been hearing this unwelcome
echo since the day I'd hit myself.

When we got home, Elder Miller said, "Elder, that was a
good baptism. That's why we're here." After dinner we studied
until he fell asleep. I looked at the clock and listened to my
body groan as it tensed and shook, twitched and rigidified.
Twitch. Twitch. Twitch. Slap slap slap. Suddenly all the food in
my stomach was rebelling. This was a recent development. I was
now contorting so badly, so frequently, that food wasn't settling
in my stomach very often. The more this happened, the more
my body thought that was how it should deal with food: by
rejecting it.

I walked into the backyard, looking for stars. There were
none, although there was a perfect October Halloween moon,
the kind of moon that exists for bats and witches to fly across in

silhouette. The house next door had an eerie decoration—a rubber gorilla head on a pole. When the wind blew, which it did often, the gorilla's mouth moved and fluttered. Tonight it was saying: *Feeling is not knowing. Why didn't you tell Sonia that you haven't prayed in a month?*

How could I? How could I tell Sonia that I was furious at God? The worst part of Tourette's wasn't the bodily harm or even my inability to go outside sometimes. It wasn't that I was being driven toward increasing isolation. It was the uncertainty. It felt like driving at night, with headlights coming toward me, and every car seemed to be in my lane. I no longer had a destination. I only knew that everything coming toward me had the potential to wreck me, to derail any plan I could make.

I'd heard the saying, "If you want to make God laugh, tell him your plans." I didn't want to talk about anything with Him, let alone my plans. I didn't care that Christ, when he took the sins of the world on Himself, felt every pain that anyone would ever endure, including what was happening to me. I didn't care that there was a world full of people who needed to hear our message. I didn't care about any of it. I just wanted to sit still. I wanted to be able to think again. To focus. I wanted to stop losing weight from my already whittled frame. How could I tell Sonia that I, an ordained missionary, resented her relationship with God? That she was much closer to Him than I was capable of? That I was disgusted by the whining in my head and tormented by my own questions?

"How?" The gorilla head said nothing. The wind had died.

The next two months were worse every day. The tics were constant and brutal. The weight loss scared me. I'd lost control of my body, my faith, and had nothing that resembled a fighting spirit. My birthday was on December 1. Our district went bowling. In the bowling alley I bit the insides of my cheeks until blood was leaking out the corners of my mouth. I managed to hide it before anyone saw. That night I called Elder

Wrigley and asked him to set up a meeting with President Graff and me.

The next day my mission president and I sat across from each other at a desk in a church office in Bethesda. "The medication isn't helping, is it?" he said. He had the kindest eyes.

I shook my head. "I don't know what to do."

"Elder, do you know how much you weigh? Right now?"

"No, but I'm having a hard time eating."

"Do you feel like you can still do the work?"

"I want to. I want to be able to do it. I—" Good grief, crying again. I'd probably cried more in the last two months than in my entire life. "I think I want to go home. But what if I'm just giving up? How do I know if I've done enough?"

President Graff reached across the table and grabbed my hand. "Oh, Josh. You've done enough. You served with honor and if you choose to leave now, you need to know that you served your entire mission. You did all you could and you did all that was asked of you. The families you reached would agree with me, whether you know it or not."

I'm not sure if I let him convince me, or if I'd already made up my mind, but it was enough. I nodded. "Okay. What happens next?"

When I stepped off the airplane in Elko, Nevada, my family was waiting for me. My mom hugged my emaciated frame and cried while my dad and my siblings watched. Then they all hugged me, and believe me, you've never heard such sniffling. But it felt good. It felt right. It felt like home.

"Son," my dad said as we headed home, "we talked to President Graff. He said to make sure to tell you that you did enough. We're going to get you some help."

"From who?" I asked.

"We'll get you help," said my mom. "We'll try everything, but you have to keep trying too. You don't get to give up."

I'd awoken that morning as a missionary, Elder Hanagarne,

on the other side of the country. Tonight I was just Josh, a kid unpacking his bag in the bedroom he'd left a year earlier. I spent most of that night in my bed with a reading light and *Catch-22*, trying to find the things that used to make me laugh.

They weren't there anymore.

CHAPTER 6

364.163—Fraud
613.71—Bodybuilding
808.5—Voice—Social Aspects
646.726 Botulinum Toxin—Therapeutic Use

There are always two LICs on duty at my library. Librarians in Charge. This title makes you the first responder to events weird enough to merit a first responder.

When I'm LIC, I walk the building and ask at each desk, "I'm the LIC, do you guys need me to do anything? Anything you've been putting off?" They usually say, "Well, how nice!" as if it's the most surprising thing they've ever heard. I don't do it out of altruism, misguided or otherwise. I do it because I have this nagging memory that there's a spreadsheet of rules and procedures out there somewhere that says I'm supposed to do this.

Admin takes library process seriously. "Crucial," I've heard it described.

It's not crucial.

As I descend the spiral staircase between floors I hear: "Oh, he can help you! There's Josh! Josh can help you! Hey, Josh!" The employee—let's call him Jim—waves me over. Standing before Jim is a person in a pink sweat suit, with long gray hair and a gray goatee.

"Hi, can I help you?"

"Yes!" booms a sonorous baritone. "This . . . person"—pointing at Jim—"won't stop calling me sir and I'm a legal female!"

I am so proud of my straight face. Librarians in Charge don't surprise.

"Is this true, Jim?" Jim has pulled his feet up into the tall chair he sits in. He covers his face with his hands, then looks at me through spread fingers. "I have no idea what's happening here."

"Oh yes, you do!" A driver's license appears under my nose. The person's thumbnail points at what looks like the letter *F* under Gender. The card vanishes before I see a name or photo.

"See! See!"

"I've worked with Jim for a long time," I say. "If he'd really seen what you thought you were showing him, I don't think he would've been antagonizing you on purpose."

"Oh, so you're taking his side? You're going to lie too?"

"It's got nothing to do with sides. I'm just giving my opinion."

"Well, you don't get to say you're something you're not, and he doesn't get to say I'm something that I'm not! I use the ladies' restroom!"

"I agree. I just think it's a misunderstanding."

"You probably just think I'm off my meds."

"Look, is there anything I can do to help?" I say. "I don't want you to leave angry, but we're not getting anywhere."

"Okay, okay, look. I'm putting my hands in my pockets to show you that I'm not a threat to you. Okay?"

It's true. "Okay, you're not a threat to me," I say. "We agree."

The hands are back! Fists under my nose! "If I wasn't a lady!"

I'm in danger of laughing and never being able to retrace

the steps to equilibrium. "Can I do anything else for you? Did we get this figured out?"

Not quite, because the guy points into the lower Urban room, to a display about the benefits of voting. "That sign out there says the vote is the great equalizer. Take it down."

"No."

"Well, I've studied a lot and I'm going to tell you something. Something that you might not like. Are you ready to hear it?"

"Probably not."

"You probably think we're hard enough on the Japs, but you're wrong. We can't let everyone forget what they did. We can't." I shake his hand and he leaves.

I walk behind the reference desk where Jim stares into his computer. "Are we done?" He looks up. "Oh good, he's gone! Now what in the world was he saying about his ID? I had no idea why he started yelling."

"Go," said my mom.

I looked around. I could have gone into another building and started gambling, or taken a prostitute for a spin, or purchased a shiny new saddle. I could have—

"Go," she said. "We've got to try this."

"This is stupid. I don't think I can."

"We're here. We're going to try it. Gail said he really helped her once."

"He gave Gail a lemon potion so that—"

"It wasn't a potion."

"—so that her knee would feel better."

"It *wasn't* a potion."

"But how's her knee?"

"It's still bad, but she didn't go for her knee, so you don't know what you're talking about. Please. Just go." She shoved me in the chest.

"Hey!"

Mom turned the edges of her hands into blades and threatened me with karate chops, a tactic she often employed when we said we were too sick for school. She sliced the air between us. "Yah! Yah!"

I climbed the stairs, Mom trailing.

My first week home we'd all had a great time getting reacquainted and sharing stories and laughing and moaning about poor Josh and how we were going to do "whatever it takes" to fix things. A couple of weeks after that my siblings were finding other things to do than sit around and watch me cry. I didn't blame them. Misty was uncontrollable. The noises were louder, the punches were harder, and she never left. I could barely think. I drove to Salt Lake to visit Jennie, but after a couple of weeks with her I could tell that she was wondering whether she had other things to do than be my nurse. I couldn't blame her; there were no signs that things would improve. We spent the next few months talking about getting married once I got better. Then we stopped talking about it altogether. Then, in a burst of loneliness, panic, and impulse, I kissed another friend in Elko when she was over late one night, told Jennie about it, and she dumped me. This was heartbreaking, but then, everything was. I was a twitchy, delicate little daffodil with feelings made of porcelain.

My mom didn't know what to do about my emotional state, but she was determined to stop Misty.

Wind chimes greeted us as Mom and I entered Dr. H's office. Somewhere a tiny band of pan flutists piped away. My doubts grew at the sight of the Kachina doll on the wall, at the smell of incense, at the sound of cowboy boots clomping down some dark corridor toward us. The man who emerged from a bead curtain had definitely read Stephen King's *The Stand* and modeled his appearance after Randall Flagg, the Walkin' Dude.

Jeans. Boots. Smiley-face button. Denim jacket over a collared black shirt. A long, thin gray ponytail unfurling behind him like the remnants of an old cape. A predacious smile. He offered a hand. I shook it. His hand was very soft. The pan flutes played on.

"Well, we're here!" said my mom.

"Yes," said Dr. H. "Yes, you are." He locked eyes with me, trying to convince me that I was a toothsome cut of pork. He stepped closer. When I retreated and groped behind me for the door, he said, "Welcome to the place!" and hustled us inside. He was a chiropractor. "But so much more." He bid me look at the table with its doughnut-shaped headrest. Stuffing leaked out from the cracked upholstery. Pictures and paintings of elk and meadows and angels covered the walls. "I am a healer, Josh."

I looked at my mom.

"I heal." He invited me to lie facedown on the table. "Ever been to a chiropractor before?"

"No."

"Good, because I'm much more than a chiro. All right, just relax then. What religion are you? Wait, don't answer that yet." Dr. H placed the heels of his palms on top of my fifth lumbar vertebra. "Exhale." *Crack.* He pushed, something gave, I gasped, and yelped, a tic that sounded like "Woo!" *It's not working.*

"We're some of those Mormons," said my mom.

"Correction, you are *two* of those Mormons," he said. "I shared your faith for a while. I share it still at times. It is all in the sharing. Ever been on a vision quest?" *Crack.*

"No, I—"

"Don't answer that . . ." *Crack.*

At his behest I turned faceup.

"When I was on my first vision quest I saw who most people might refer to as the Lord. Turn your head to the left, please. Relax." He placed one hand against my ear, one on my shoulder, and cracked my neck.

"But it wasn't the Lord," said Dr. H, "because how can we really tell, do you understand? Oh my, your jaw is tight. Open your mouth please."

His ring tasted the way you'd expect a piece of metal that had been on a finger for years to taste. Having my jaw cracked was not unpleasant, however. There was release in it. Much of my pain was from overuse and rigidity. Beyond the specific pains in the tense areas, there was an overall systemic tension that I hadn't been aware of—until this valorous healer began pretzeling me. He stepped back and put his hands on his hips. "Do you want to know about perfection? Do you want to know about calm?"

I looked at my mom. The interlaced steeple she'd been making out of her white-knuckled fingers was drooping under the burden of this folly. When she saw me looking, the sagging frame sprang back to life. "Sure!"

"Do you believe there is a cure for you?" Dr. H asked, leaning into my face. If I'd had any money, I would have bet that the white fleck in his beard was a small chip of long-dried Ramen noodle. "The key to your cure is to become as calm as young Joseph Smith was when he walked into the Sacred Grove and saw God. Do you know what Tourette's is? Do you know what causes it?"

"Dopamine?" I said.

"The same thing that causes all of mankind's ills. Have you read *Brave New World* by Orwell?"

"Aldous Huxley wrote *Brave New World*."

"Ah. But do you want to know what causes your Tourette's?"

"Sure!" said my mom.

"A lack of perfection." Dr. H extended his arms to his sides as if he was about to be pulled apart by horses. "Now, I want you to imagine yourself in a perfect, perfect circle." He brought his arms forward in a slight curve. "If you can imagine that perfect,

perfect circle for seventeen seconds, you will be healed. Do you think that Joseph Smith could have seen what he did if he had not been able to stay still for a measly seventeen seconds?"

"Well," said my mom, "there was actually more to it than that. . . ."

Or less, I thought.

"Well, perhaps," said Dr. H, "but—"

"I'll try," I interrupted.

"I'm proud of you, Josh," said the good doctor.

"Thank you." I concentrated. But alas, I only made it to fourteen "perfect, perfect seconds" before Misty'd had enough and tasered me.

"I'm still proud of you, Josh," he said. "We can't all connect the first time out, can we? When was the last time you read the Book of Mormon, by the way?"

I'd come home prepared to avoid the slump I'd heard about from other returned missionaries. Suddenly you're home and there are all these other things you want to do and if you let it go you'll fall out of all the habits you've gotten into, like reading your scriptures all the time.

"I read some this morning," I said. I'd actually spent most of the morning reading *The Shining*, a welcome-home present from Jennie.

"Good, then this next part will go easier." Dr. H vanished into another room. "We can still cure you," his voice announced before his body reappeared. "And don't worry about the circle. It will always be there when you're prepared to revisit it." He was brandishing bottles of clear liquid.

He set the bottles down with great aplomb, announcing them as if they were visiting dignitaries. "Zinc!" *Thump.* "Copper!" *Thud.* "Tungsten!" He looked down at me as if expecting me to jump up and scream, "Oh yeah, now you're talking!" before we exchanged thunderous high fives. When I didn't move, he sighed and tutted and said, "Cross your arms."

I crossed my arms. He placed one of the bottles—I think we started with zinc—atop my crossed arms. He grasped my right wrist with his hands and said, "Now I'm going to pull back. I need you to resist. Can you resist?"

I inhaled. "I can resist." I was tired and wanted to resist the teeth out of his head. I resisted while he pulled my arm. I resisted in my head when the result seemed to please him. He produced a little notebook and jotted with as much exuberance as one can jot with. He performed more tests to determine which minerals my body needed. Bottle after bottle on my chest. "Resist me! The body speaks!" he said each time. Based on the resistance, he prescribed bottles of copper and zinc water, which Mom purchased.

In the parking lot later, Mom looked at the bottles clinking in my lap and said, "That was so stupid."

I laughed. We went to lunch and said, "Resist me!" for an hour.

Dr. H eventually went to prison for a year. No matter what anyone tells you, there's no magic bath that cures cancer.

He hadn't been the first stop. My neurologists—in DC and now one in Salt Lake—had already prescribed several medications, with mixed results. The problems with the pills were that 1) they didn't work and made me feel like crap; or 2) they seemed to work and then stopped because I'd outlasted the placebo effect; or 3) they actually *did* work but then they stopped, which was worse than never working to begin with.*

---

*   Over the years I tried everything that neurologists try. The Klonopin didn't help. Neither did Risperdal. Or Haldol. Or Clonazepam. Or Clonidine. Or Zyprexa. Or Tetrabenazine. A neurologist put me on a nicotine patch, which apparently had helped someone in some study. Every few months I tried something new. Every few months, a new letdown. My neurologists said they hadn't dealt with many cases as severe as mine. They seemed delighted to have this chance to experiment.

Dad wasn't surprised when I recapped our visit. "Criminy, what did you think would happen with that guy? I saw Gail the other day and she was limping around like a cripple."

"Frank!" Mom said. "She didn't go to him for her knee!"

Dad winked at me. The next day he walked through the living room, saw me lying on the couch half awake, and nudged me with his boot. "Get up. Get some shorts. Get in the truck. We're going to the gym."

I reached for a ready-made excuse. The bag was empty.

We drove to town. "Why do I have to do this?"

"You don't have to." He turned on the stereo and fired up a Dwight Yoakam tape that my mom hated. "But you need to. And so you'll do it."

"I don't want to."

"Then you shouldn't have gotten in the truck, smart guy."

"I'm smart."

"Then you'll admit that the chances of that couch you're so in love with driving itself down this road with you laying on it are pretty poor, right?"

"Lying."

"What?"

"Lying on the couch. Not 'laying.'"

He whistled. "Wow, is it nice? Being a genius? It looks nice. Thanks for the correction. I'll turn around and tell your mom that she's got nothing to worry about. All I meant was that if you'd stayed on the couch, you wouldn't be in the truck."

"Okay."

"No. Not okay. You're going to the gym with me. I think this will be good for you."

"Why?"

"Because I've been depressed before. I know some things. But listen, can I ask you a question?"

"Yeah."

"Is there anyone you look up to? I'm serious, now. No jokes."

"I don't know," I said. What good would it do to say I looked up to my dad? Or my grandpa? Or the prophet or Pee-wee Herman for that matter?

"Well," Dad said, "you've got to find someone to follow. Do you know who that is?"

"You?"

"I wish. But no. It's you. You have zero confidence."

"Yes, I do."

"Yes, you have zero confidence. No, I know that's not what you meant, but, no, you don't, and do you know how I know?"

"Because you're in touch with Navajo spirits."

He exhaled hard through his nose. "Do you ever get tired of being so funny? It's a nice little smoke screen, but I know you. Confident people do stuff. They get stuff done. They make things, even if it's just making money. You know what you're making?"

"It doesn't matter."

"You're making our couch sag. That's about it. You're making your mom sad because you're not trying. You're making your siblings miserable because you're acting like you're miserable."

"I am. I'm depressed and on a bunch of drugs. I want to take more of them every day just to feel different."

"This isn't depression and that's not their fault. But I don't want to fight. I think what we're about to do is going to give you a way to make some progress."

"There's nothing important about lifting weights."

"There's nothing insignificant about progress. Let's just give it a try."

Dad had been lifting inconsistently for most of his adult life. He'd usually go until he injured himself showing off, take a couple dozen months off, wait for New Year's to roll around, and then decide that this would be the year he got his bench up to 350. He once hurt himself in a Denver sporting goods store by bench-pressing for the Broncos cheerleaders, who were duly impressed as my mom let him lean on her for support as they exited.

The gym parking lot contained few cars. Nothing about it screamed "Salvation!" or "Remake yourself!" Except for the poster on the wall: a man in a black string tank top doing curls under the words "Remake yourself!"

My dad scanned his card. "And he needs a guest pass," he told an old guy behind the counter. "And he'll need one of those slinky tank tops from that poster he's looking at."

"Don't sell 'em," said the guy.

There were four other people there. Two peppy women in spandex hopped up and down while holding tiny dumbbells under their chins in both hands, as if they were trying to fill chalices with the sweat of their labors. "Wow, they're really laying it all on the line, aren't they?" whispered my dad. "This place gets some weird customers."

A short guy wearing a fearsome black bandanna stalked before the wall-length mirrors. He yanked up the hem of one leg of his Daisy Duke denim shorts and flexed his quadriceps in the mirror. He nodded. He had an enormous tattoo on his calf.

"We need to get you some little shorts like that," said my dad. "Man, you're skinny. Let's get started."

"Okay. How?"

He led me over to the rack of free weights. "Just find a couple of dumbbells that you can put over your head and start pressing them until you can't. Let's start there. I'd like to see your shoulders get a little bigger."

"Why?"

"I'll tell you later. I'm going to go bench. Now lift."

I tested a few dumbbells and settled on a pair of 45-pounders. I could only manage a couple of consecutive overhead presses before I got wobbly and pulled out of alignment. I felt silly. But as I began to fatigue, the other people faded. There was just me and my body. My stupid, thin, Benedict Arnold of a body. I could focus on getting the movements "right" or I could worry about everyone else. I focused on the details.

"Just rest until you can get a couple more reps, then get a couple more," said the guy next to me. "There's no trick. Only patience. And food. And sleep."

When I couldn't lift the 45s, my dad appeared and said, "Keep going down the rack. Do what you can with the 35s, then the 25s, then the 10s. They'll start feeling heavier." I ran the rack. It astonished me how something so light could weigh so heavily on my body when moments earlier it had been so easy. For forty-five minutes, I repeated the process with various exercises. Back in the truck I realized that I hadn't thought about my tics for nearly an hour.

"Was I having tics in there?" I asked my dad.

"Yeah."

I wanted him to say "No and that's what I was getting at! You're cured!" But if I was oblivious to my symptoms, wasn't that the same result? "Huh. Why did you say you wanted my shoulders to be bigger?"

"It'll change the way you walk. It's hard not to be confident if you walk like you're wearing a cape, with it blowing out behind you. Big shoulders help with the cape. Should we come again tomorrow?"

"Yes." I did want to go again, to see if I could replicate that experience of feeling like I had control of myself, or the experience of not worrying what anyone else thought about my tics.

"Great. In that case, we've got to make a stop." We pulled into a store where Dad bought a spiral-bound notebook. "You'll want this."

"Why?"

"Because that"—he tapped the notebook—"is a small victory. That's where you track your wins. Find a way to win and you start getting things done."

Not only did I go back to the gym the next day, I went back every day that week. I even went alone once. I got a look at the short-shorts guy's tattoo: It was of himself, wearing his workout outfit, *doing the leg press in a column of fire.*

Misty fussed harder than ever, but it was as if she were barred from the gym. Afterward, yes, I would pay for it with savage tics. But during those sessions of clanking weights and sliding pulleys and yes, even the stupid guy with the aviator shades admiring his thighs, I forgot about the price I'd pay. What I did in the gym made everything outside easier. What a fascinating, bizarre turnaround; I was choosing to do something so difficult and painful that my symptoms didn't seem as bad.

I grew. I no longer looked like a svelte bone with glasses. I was wearing the cape.

That was in the spring of 1998. I spent the next year at home with my family, recovering. I lifted almost every day and put most of the weight back on. But the biggest change wasn't physical. It was spiritual; I could go to the gym and lift myself into a quiet oblivion, but Misty insisted on tagging along when I went to church. Being in that quiet chapel was too much, so I stopped going. At first, I missed it. I felt guilty being home while my family worshipped. Soon I stopped feeling guilty and looked forward to the three hours of quiet each Sunday when I had the house to myself. Well, myself and Misty.

I got a letter from Erik, the friend I'd attended college with in Idaho before our missions. He was finishing his mission in Brazil and let me know that he'd be going to Rick's College— an LDS junior college that would later become Brigham Young

University–Idaho—in the fall of 1999. I resolved to go with him.

"That's great," said my dad. "I'll help you pack. Let's go do it right now."

We didn't pack that day, but a year later my dad said, "Do you really have to take these?" as he taped up another box of my books.

"It's not that many," I said.

"It's eight boxes. That's eight boxes too many when you're going to have other books to read, like your textbooks that I'm paying for."

"Yeah, I know, but . . ."

"But what?"

It was a good question. "I want to take them."

"He wants to take them," said my mom. But then, after hefting a box herself, she said, "Now why do you want to take these?"

That evening, the first one in my new apartment, I unpacked those books and filled our living room's one bookcase with Stephen King, Socrates, a bunch of *Far Side* anthologies, and a bunch of other volumes that, yes, I truly didn't need to bring with me. But it was too late.

College life at Ricks was fine, but I was surprised to find that going to church was one of the best parts. Every Sunday, everyone in my ward—a few hundred kids comprising a few apartment complexes—got dressed up and went to church to check one another out. It's an interesting experience to watch religious males try to out-righteous one another to catch the eye of the women. A bizarre bit of posturing, everyone trying to put the "stud" in Bible study. I got caught up in it, which was great for my spirituality. If our Sunday school class was going to be discussing the Book of Mormon, I'd better be ready, so I read. If we were going to do a service project, I'd be the first one there.

I'd decided to major in philosophy. I really don't know why, except I liked the idea of myself thinking deep thoughts. It was kind of like when I decided to be a chess prodigy. It was more like I thought, "You know, I'm the sort of person who should be a chess prodigy." But then I realized I had to practice and study chess matches and so I quit. I liked the idea of Josh, the philosopher. I liked it so much that I enrolled in an ancient Greek class. Misty didn't appreciate my studies. If I sat in the library, she had me shouting, then up and pacing around, trying to outdistance her with my lengthy stride. But she was a shadow that didn't fade with the sunset. And she wasn't merely attached to me at the heels. Every single cell in my body had a parasitic shade clinging to it. There were no depths or heights that I could descend or climb to in order to leave her behind. There was only the hope that she'd get distracted.

"I'm really sorry, sir," said a voice that really and truly did sound really sorry. "Someone has complained about the noise. Is there anything I can—" I was studying for a Greek test. I had managed to escape into the Middle Liddell Lexicon as I prepped for a frenzy of conjugations and translations the following morning. Suddenly, a hand on my shoulder.

I was already up and gathering my things. "No, no, you're fine," I said.

"I just meant—"

"It's not your fault. I can't help it but it's not going to stop." I hadn't even known I was doing anything. This was something new. I'd been absorbed in something and still having tics. Was nothing sacred, to bellow clichés at the sky?

"No, I had no idea it was happening," I told my mom on the phone that night.

"Really?"

"Yeah."

"Well . . . shoot."

I lifted weights exactly one time that school year. It was a night when I was trying to study for a Book of Mormon class. Every time I tried to take a note, Misty yanked my pen across the page. One page ripped, then another, and then the pen moved past the page and now there was a big pen mark on my desk. I put on a sweat suit and walked to the school's weight room.

It was full of people. A big line of guys waiting to bench press, groups of girls talking and laughing, a bunch of people on treadmills, and me. Everyone looked like they had so much energy. The current medication made me slow and weak.

"Huh!" I yelled. Misty had followed me. Nobody looked. The room was full of grunting, so hopefully we'd go unnoticed. And maybe if I slapped my face, everyone would think I was just psyching myself up for a big lift.

I went to the squat rack, which of course was not being used—squats are hard and legs aren't mirror muscles. I put 135 pounds on the bar. I put it on my shoulders, squatted down, and . . . that was that. I couldn't stand back up. I sat down, letting the bar find the safety pins that were three feet off the ground. I rolled onto my side and crawled out of the rack. I noticed a couple of people watching. When I stood back up, my head swam.

I couldn't stand to be weak, but having people see it was worse.

I didn't go back.

"Have you given any more thought to the Botox?" asked my mom during a desperate phone call. The first semester had ended and I told her that I wasn't sure I could handle the spring term. She'd heard about an experimental treatment. Botulism toxin to paralyze the vocal cords. No more screaming, in other words. This wasn't the final frontier for youth-obsessed people who simply had to know that their potentially sagging vocal folds were restored to the peak and vigor of their twenties. This was for people who treated public spaces as if they were recording booths for gag-reel noises. This was for people who, when they happened to make noises, made the wrong ones.

"No. Yes. Yes, I have, but just right now. Okay."

"Okay what?"

"Okay all right. I guess. I'll come do it."

You might think that before agreeing to something like voice-stealing injections in your windpipe, you might study up and figure out what you were in for. Nah. I was much more interested in figuring out how I could convince a girl I was pursuing to come with me for the procedure. Cyndi. She was tall. She had red hair. She said that if I ever wrote a book she'd read it. She'd never date me, but we hung out constantly. She wouldn't kiss me, but she said she liked me as much as she'd ever liked anyone. Maybe that was why Misty tolerated her: Cyndi made it look as if there were a We, when in fact it was still just me.

Cyndi agreed to go with me. I wasn't sure how the injections would go, but I'd be able to dazzle her with courage and comeliness under pressure.

On the way to Salt Lake, Cyndi and I stopped for dinner and then drove to a park. I had my guitar and a blanket in the back of the car. "Do you mind if I play for you for a while?" I asked.

"Sure," said her mouth. *What are you up to?* said her eyes. *Don't get any ideas*, said her arms, which were now folded across her chest.

"I just want to play for a while. I don't know when I'll be able to sing again." This was going to be my sentimental trump card but my voice broke and I realized that it was true. So I sang. I strummed and sang while the stars came up. Cyndi wrapped the blanket around herself. My fingers were numb but the songs were as clear as they had ever been. I finally stopped when I had played every piece I had written or learned. As the final note died away, I had a tic. I could see it in the cold air between us, this sudden burst of breath and nerves.

"That was nice," she said. "But they were all sad songs."

"Sad songs are all I know," I said.

Then we drove to my aunt Cathy's house, where we'd sleep. My mom met us there.

Otolaryngology clinic. What an ugly word. What an ugly place. Nobody in the waiting room smiled. Why would they? They were ostensibly all here to get their throats or larynxes snipped or molested or savaged. They'd all be shambling away in a couple of hours, greatly changed. Diminished.

But I didn't expect this demeanor from the staff. For all his nonsense, Dr. H's inane cheer had been more calming than these icy cyborgs. An unsmiling woman signed me in. An unsmiling orderly shuffled into the room and stooped about, replacing tissue boxes.

The doctor who would change me was bald. So very bald, with the type of gleaming skull that one only affects in order to convey an air of menace and sociopathy. His glasses had no rims. He was utterly mad and soulless.

One knows these things.

"Hello," he said, unsmiling. "I'll be back in a few minutes after you've been prepped."

The madman's assistant robot monotoned the procedure.

"You will lie on the table. You will have gel applied to your temples. The doctor will aim needles through your throat over and over until his arms are exhausted. You will be voiceless forever. Cyndi will never kiss you. Bleep bloop."

The reality didn't feel any better than my mental interpretation. I sat in the reclined chair. The man I would come to know as the Joyless Healer swabbed my head with some foul goo that smelled like the inside of a Halloween mask. I turned my head to look at my mom and Cyndi.

"Hold still," commanded the orderly with a whir of grinding gears.

"We're here," said my mom.

"Heh-heh," I said, "this reminds me of that scene in *One Flew Over the Cuckoo's Nest* where they get him ready for electroshock."

"This is quite different from that," said the revenant doctor. "This is not electroshock therapy and this is not a liquid conductant. You are getting botulism injections in your vocal cords. Now, lean your head back, don't move. Don't swallow. "After inserting the needle I will need to move it slightly to get into position. Hold still. This will be uncomfortable."

Pressure in my throat. A pinch. Momentary release as the needle punctured my windpipe. It was unpleasant but not agonizing. Just uncomfortable.

"I said don't swallow," said the doctor. "Do it again and we may have to start over. This is not a booster shot." It tasted sort of like the mist of an asthma inhaler. An antiseptic tang that I felt as much as tasted.

Finally he withdrew the needle. I unclenched the hands I didn't even realize I'd turned into fists, and began to sit up.

"That was only halfway," said the doctor. "Sit back. Don't swallow."

Vocal cords! Plural! Silly me.

When it was over, I felt my face to see if I'd been crying.

Nope. My mom, on the other hand, looked as though someone had been sticking needles into the throat of her firstborn as she watched with a dreadful mixture of horror, hope, and fascination. Cyndi looked bored.

"All through," said the Joyless Healer with what sounded like tremendous disappointment. "Your voice will probably begin returning within weeks. Please see the nurse on the way out if you'd like to schedule your next round." He departed in a whoosh of lab coat and malice.

I stood. "Well," I said. Wait! I could still talk!

"Are you okay?" said my mom.

"Let's just get out of here."

Cyndi took my arm as we walked down the hall. She didn't look at me, and nothing about her said anything to suggest that I should grab her hand or propose to her or kiss her, but it was good. We walked to the parking lot. My mom hugged me. "It's going to be all right."

I nodded. "I hope so." Then she was gone, driving west to Elko.

Cyndi and I stopped at a gas station and bought sodas for the drive. In the car I turned on the radio. "Oh, I love this song," I started to say before realizing that my voice was losing power. By the time we made it back to school it was nearly gone. A week later it was as gone as it would get. I could whisper, but not with enough force to speak over the phone.*

It took tremendous effort to whisper.

I toyed with the idea of wearing a sandwich board that said in big, blocky, crooked letters: CAN'T TALK MUCH. STILL LIKE TO TRY. WANT TO MAKE OUT?

---

* From here on, just assume that if I'm talking, I'm whispering. I could communicate, but I only had the energy for five-to-ten-second bursts of whispers. Most of the time, it just wasn't worth the effort.

The tics: While it was true that I could no longer scream, and being in public was easier, I finally had a verification of something I had long suspected—there was a daily intensity quota that must be met. I had to expend a certain amount of energy on tics each day. It could be meted out over many small tics, or a few dozen huge ones. So even though I wasn't screaming, my body was still trying; it just couldn't make the noise. If I couldn't be noisy, I could still be an abomination of motor skills gone amok.

With sweat pouring down my face I traversed a crowded café on my way to class. "Hey!" My flailing arm had just knocked soda into a kid's face. "Oh oh oh I'm so so sorry," I whispered, grabbing a handful of napkins off someone else's table. It seemed very quiet as I reached toward him. Then I realized he didn't want me mopping up his face. "I've got . . . I've got—"

"It's okay. It's okay. I get it. Just please stop."

"Really?" *Really? Please explain it to me.*

Every five or six weeks, my voice would return to the point of making me self-conscious and uneasy. So I'd head over to Salt Lake and surrender my voice to the Joyless Healer. I was still doing my silent screaming all the time, which gave me six-pack abs for the first time because every single cell in my torso contracted with great force from sunup to sundown.

But the shots helped me get through both semesters. I went home to Nevada after spring term with more confidence than I'd had in a long time. I worked as a delivery driver during the day and went to the gym at night.

As long as I was making some sort of progress in the weight room I could make progress in other areas. I couldn't put it into words yet, but I was learning that the more I could do, the more I could do. Progress in one direction made progress in other directions, if not easier, more likely. It made me want to engage with other challenges. It made me want to go back to school and get going again. I had something resembling hope. Perhaps I was benefiting from an illusion of control in a universe of chaos, but the results were so good I couldn't slow down enough to care.

Until one morning when I was getting in the shower. I wasn't one to sit around and stare at myself in the mirror all day, but I wasn't above the occasional appreciative look at myself to verify that, indeed, I was lifting weights. I enjoyed seeing a new muscle, a new vein, a new narrowness.

But nothing this new. A pink bulge the size of a peach sprouted from my abdomen, just to the right of my groin. I tentatively pushed it with my finger. It slid back into my body. I flexed my abs. The bulge reappeared.

"Mom, I think I've got a hernia," I said.

"Let me see!" I let her see.

"Yeah, no doubt about it, that's a hernia. Well, shoot, honey, I'm sorry." I saw a doctor that afternoon. A week later I had hernia repair surgery. I woke with a mottled black-and-blue abdomen. If you've ever quit an exercise routine, you can probably guess what happened to me six weeks later when I was allowed to lift again.

I didn't lift. I didn't strive to regain the strength. The element of control was gone. I let it go, but it was gone nonetheless.

And when it was time to go back to school, I couldn't face it. So I didn't.

CHAPTER 7

646.78—Marriage
591.473—Mimicry (Biology)

There's no lovelier place to watch a snowstorm from than the reference desk on Level 3 of the Salt Lake City Public Library. In the fading light, in this glass magnificence, it's a happier world out there, something from a Christmas card. Even during this phone call, I can't keep my eyes off it. Yet . . . an urgent situation of considerable shrillness is developing behind me.

Our desk is round. Librarians sit inside the hole of the doughnut. Voices behind me are now raised so loud that I turn around, hand the telephone to my colleague, and say, "Take this and take a break." He does.

Now we are alone. Our eyes meet. Above her right orbit, a thin purple eyebrow drags its right edge toward the siren call of something beneath her large straw hat. She presses her heavily lined lips together. They are so glossy that I can hear the noise of them closing.

"He is"—she gestures toward my receding colleague's back—" . . . unsuitable person." She relaxes her face. The eyebrow stays on high alert. "I wonder if you—could you be . . . suitable?"

I smile my least confused smile and ask, "How can I help you?"

"He is unsuitable person."

"Yes, but how can I help you? They don't get much more suitable than me!" I sound much peppier than I feel. How can there be that much snow in the sky? How can it fall so quietly?

"Yes, I have problem. Downstairs I am trying to listen to compact disc. The machine does not work. Fix it. You fix."

"This is Level Three. We don't have anything to do with that. Have you told them about the problem down there? Would you like me to call them?"

"I ask them once. The American girls laugh. They are not interested in helping. You fix it." After several iterations of this routine I agree to send an e-mail to the technology department.

"No. I will send. You give me their address."

I print out their e-mail address and hand it to her. "Here you go."

She looks at it and makes a sound that sounds like *pyeh!* "You can't send?"

"You said you wanted to do it."

She squints at my name tag. It's an old one, a spare. At one time it read:

The City Library
Josh
Manager

I'm not a manager anymore, so now it looks like this:

The City Library
Josh
~~Manager~~

I only use this tag when I forget my usual badge.

"Is not even you? Pyeh!"

"Yeah it's me. Manager's crossed out, not Josh."

"You send that e-mail. You send now."

I send the e-mail. It says:

Computer Services, I told someone I would send you this e-mail. I know it's not your department. I asked her to contact AV first. But she insisted that you see the e-mail. Good luck. Josh.

"Sent!" I say.

"Americans . . ." She looks around. I see how long and thick her ponytail is. It is glorious. I am ready to forgive it all. I'm ready to—

"You know what I say if American millionaire asks to marry my daughter?"

"No."

"I forbid. I forbid it ten thousand times!" She narrows her eyes as if I'm hiding a cushioned ring box behind my back, ready to surprise her daughter—whose name is almost certainly Svetlana, or maybe Pyeh!—from bended knee.

"That's a lot of forbidding."

"You think I don't know this? I was teacher. We are not stupid. Some of us are teachers. My husband. Teacher. You Americans."

I shake her hand, say it was nice to meet her, and watch her walk toward the stairs. "Stay dry out there!" I say.

She turns, glares, sets her bag down. "What is mean by 'stay dry'?"

"It means that it's snowing out there and don't get your hair wet."

"There is only one meaning of this phrase?"

"Are you really asking?"

"You are saying I am drunkard, yes?" She tips her thumb toward her mouth as if she is stumbling intoxicated through the streets of a Primorye province village, as I'm apparently implying.

"No. Don't get your hair wet. That's all."

"If . . . if I find there is more than one meaning for this phrase, I will return." She looks at me over the top of her glasses. She points at me. Her eyebrow wriggles with her disapproval.

"I will verify . . . I will. I hope that you are honest tonight." She leaves.

The snow didn't stop until late the next afternoon. It was a beautiful storm.

"Josh, I've found the perfect girl for you. Her name is Janette." Mom was home from church looking triumphant.

"No thanks." I was done with dating. Jennie had taught me that modern females didn't consider weepy, frail men the ultimate aphrodisiac. Besides, who had time for dating with my busy life? Since I hadn't returned to school, I now had a breakneck schedule of weaning myself off my medications, napping, visiting the Joyless Healer to surrender my voice, and staring at the walls. I rarely left the house. The days slogged by.

Maybe Mom was right. Maybe dating would shake me out of this no-life. On the other hand, Mom's track record with "perfect girls" for me was blemished. She'd never actually set me up with anyone, but she floated trial balloons.

"You know, I sure do like the Wallace girls. Are they dating anyone?" Or "That Kimberly sure is getting pretty." I acknowledged and ignored.

"Okay," I said an hour later. "How can I meet her?"

"She's singing in our ward next Sunday so you'll have to come."

Ugh. One upside of the previous year was that Misty didn't want me going to church. She wanted to stay home and watch movies or read. This placed my soul in jeopardy, but I never felt like I was missing much. Still, I had to go the next Sunday if I wanted to meet Janette Watts.

That morning I put on my suit and went to church with my family, where I watched Janette on the stand—the area behind the pulpit where speakers sit before rocking the mic like there's no tomorrow. She was five-eight with brown hair. She wore a pale-blue dress with a lace collar. She wore little makeup. Her face was pretty, heart-shaped, and soft. Her natural expression looked to be a contented smile. She looked kind. I flipped through the hymnal during the opening songs. Since I couldn't sing anymore, I spent the time looking at the names of the composers and lyricists. There were tons of Ebeneezers. But wait! One hymn had been composed by none other than "H. S. Thompson." My first exposure to Hunter S. Thompson had occurred a few weeks earlier when I bought a copy of *The Great Shark Hunt* at a thrift store. And now here he was in the LDS hymnal. But no. The dates were wrong. The song was composed way back in 1770, stupid. It wasn't Hunter.*

When Janette started singing, I forgot about it. Her voice was a clear, confident, lovely soprano. I've never paid attention to a hymn the way I did to that song. I couldn't listen to her sing and be cynical or pessimistic. Suddenly life felt so precious and full of possibilities that I wouldn't have been surprised if a butterfly had landed on my wrist as a baby deer walked in to lick my face.

After, my mom raced up to tell Janette how wonderful she was. Then she nudged me forward and said, "This is my son Josh." I shook Janette's hand and nodded hello.

"It's really great to meet you," she said, and she gave me a

---

* Hunter S. Thompson's mom was a librarian.

smile that seemed genuine. I grinned like a fool. "You too," I whispered, jerking my head down and to the left, twice. Smooth operator.

"She's a folklorist," a mutual friend named Amy told me later. "She knows lots of stories. You'll get along great." We made plans to go to a barbecue at the home of some of Amy's relatives.

That evening I did push-ups until I collapsed. The next morning I ran two miles, then went to the gym in Elko to lift, the first time I had done so in months. I couldn't get myself back in shape for my date with Janette, which was three days away, but it seemed like a good time to get over the hernia and get back at it.

Janette picked me up in a white Buick Century, "the least fancy car in existence," she said. Now that I had her up close and could get a good look at her, she had the loveliest eyes I'd ever seen—a strange mixture of warm orange and icy green, depending on the light.

"Well, we can't all drive Honda Civics," I whispered.

She was easy to talk to. By which I mean, she was easy to listen to, since I couldn't say much. But she laughed at my whispered jokes.

"What do you like to read?" I asked.

"I just read a book by Mary Higgins Clark. I can't even remember what it's about, but it starts with this woman buried underground and she's supposed to have a string in her coffin. When she pulls the string the bell above ground rings so everyone will know someone's buried alive. It scared me because the bell didn't have a clapper. So I quit reading and all night I felt like someone was looking in the window at me."

I adored mysteries. Since reading Agatha Christie's *Ten Little Indians*, I'd read everything by her. "What does someone being buried alive have to do with your window?" I asked her.

"Plenty."

"What're you doing in Elko?"

"I started working at the Western Folklife Center as my first job out of grad school."

"Did you have to write a thesis?"

"Yes. I wrote about an old cemetery."

"Do men get intimidated by you because you're so smart?"

She blushed and smiled. "I bet you ask all the girls that."

Yeah. All the girls. "And you probably pretend you're not a genius with all the men you date."

"I don't date much." Had it been the wrong thing to say? Her shirt had an American flag on it. "Would you consider yourself insanely patriotic?" I asked, pointing at it.

"No. I like America, though."

"What do you like most about it?"

"Barbecues."

"Good answer. So let me just get this out there: Would you ever marry a twenty-three-year-old?" I would turn twenty-three later that year. "Just checking.

"There's no wrong answer," I added. "It could be any twenty-three-year-old, so don't think I was asking about myself."

"No," Janette said finally. "I think I need a man with a. . . ." She squinted into the depths of her soul. "With a . . . 401(k)." Then, horror-faced: "I can't believe I just said that. I don't know where that came from."

"Are 401(k)s the ultimate aphrodisiac?"

"Only for perverts. New subject. What are *you* reading?"

"You know the Harvard classics?"

"No. Should I?"

"When I thought I wouldn't be able to go to school any-more, I thought about how else I could get some education. I was getting addicted to eBay, but I never bought anything. I saw a listing for the Harvard Classics once. It's these fifty-two books that take up about five feet and if you've read them you're supposedly as educated as anyone, or something. I got them for Christmas and made this goal to read one each week this year and then I'd be done and a genius."

"How's it going?"

"Bad. I made it through the first three weeks. Don't read *The Autobiography of Benvenuto Cellini*."

"What's it about?"

"A guy makes some stuff out of silver. That's it."

"Hasn't there been anything good?"

"*Don Quixote*'s always good. I got through *The Inferno* by Dante. I nearly died trying to read Robert Burns. I'm not big on poetry."

"What about cowboy poetry?"

"I'm not sure. I got to recite a poem that I wrote in sixth grade with my best friend at the cowboy poetry gathering. It was about a feud. But I've never really read any of it. But the only other Harvard books I finished were two books of quotes. Something by a Quaker and a bunch of sayings from Epictetus. I just can't ever see myself getting into the science papers of Charles Lyell, but we'll see."

Janette turned the car into a driveway. When we stopped, I got my guitar out of the trunk as Janette went and said hello to Amy.

"What did she say?" I asked Amy when I got her alone.

"She said you're better looking than she expected."

"What does that mean? She saw me on Sunday."

"And she said she told you she wanted a man with a 401(k). I told her you don't have one."

"But she saw me at church," I whispered.

"She said the light was weird there. Are you going to play for us?" She nodded at my guitar.

"Uh, yeah, maybe. I told her I played and she said to bring it."

After we ate, Janette said, "Play a song for me." Suddenly everyone else was outside and Janette and I were alone. I'd been playing a lot of folk instrumentals from various countries. With the loss of my voice, my playing had changed. Without my vocals providing the melodies, my fingers had to. I was more interested in finger-style guitar with complicated melody in the upper register and bass notes played on the thicker bottom strings. The song was called "Sakura Variations."

"That's beautiful," said Janette.

"Yeah?"

"Yes."

"Thank you."

When I got home, my parents mobbed me. "Well?" said my mom.

"It was good," I said.

"How good?" said my dad. "Good as in—"

"And you're going to see her again?" said my mom.

"Yeah." My mom's not much of a smirker, but whatever was going on with her face at that moment said, "I *knew* it. I was *right*!"

My dad is a smirker. So he smirked. But he looked happy.

The next weekend Janette and I hiked around Silver Lake.

"You're as nimble as a mountain goat," I told her as we walked the shallow incline around the lake.

"I practice," she said. "At home I build little obstacle courses and I see how many hours I can spend without touching the ground. My best is four days."

"Really? Pippi Longstocking did that."

"No."

Thanks to the Botox, I didn't have to worry about whether I'd scare Janette with hoots and whoops. But without the noises to define the "real" me, I didn't know exactly who I was. At first, I exhausted myself whispering getting-to-know-you small talk into Janette's ears. The longer we talked, though, the more I listened. I wasn't just learning who she was, but also who I was when we were together. I thought, *We've already seen each other three times.* She was spending her free time with *me.* She could have been crocheting, which she loved, or reading Mary Higgins Clark, or practicing with that lovely Siren's voice. Instead, she was with me, laughing and talking about nothing.

At some point we started holding hands. We looked at our interlaced fingers. She smiled. I snapped my teeth together and whistled two notes. When I'm touching someone, the tic often molds itself to wherever I'm touching. Because I was holding her hand my own hand tensed up and gave her an abrupt, but not painful, squeeze.

"I like you," I said.

"I'm glad."

A week later I agreed to come to her family reunion that summer.

One night she said she'd "made peace with being alone." This is a very Mormon way to feel if you are a single woman past twenty-two years old, and she was twenty-nine. So many students at church college campuses are engaged or married by the time they're in their early twenties.

"There were always girls that looked better," Janette said. "My friends are all my age. They all look about the same way I do. They're all single. None of us has ever even been kissed."

It bothered me that Janette didn't see herself as being as worthy as all the other women out there. The ones who weren't "her age" or who "looked better" or who were getting kissed because they were better somehow. I knew that any guy who knew her like I did would be as smitten as I was.

The phone rang. It was her dad. With a worried look she gave me the phone. "He wants to talk to you."

"Hello?" I said.

"Hi! This is John Watts. I just wanted to say that we're looking forward to meeting you. Janette's a great woman. See you soon. You'll fit right in. I can tell." When I hung up, I handed Janette the phone.

"You won't be alone," I said. "It might not have anything to do with me, but I don't want you to feel that way." Before she could protest, I kissed her cheek.

The night before the reunion Janette asked if I wanted to play Phase 10, a card game in which players race each other to make ten different card combinations.

"I'll play," I said, "but we should play for something."

"Like what?" she said.

"If I win, you have to kiss me."

"I knew you were going to say that. Okay, but what if I win?"

"You won't. Ready?"

She dealt the cards. By the time Janette was on Phase 6, I was still stuck back on 3.

"Is it my imagination, or do you look slightly despondent as you win yet another round?" I asked.

"Don't flatter yourself."

Then followed a rally that had never been seen before, and will never be seen again. Somehow, by the time Janette was at Phase 7, I was on 6. By the time I got to 8, I had caught up.

"My willpower is changing your momentum," I said.

"Why would you waste your powers on something like this?"

"If you're really asking then you don't know how attractive you are."

I won. When I set the last card down and said, "I'm out," Janette stood and began pacing. I don't think I'd ever actually seen someone wringing her hands, but she was doing it.

"Oh," she said. "Ah." She looked at me. Wring wring wring. "So?"

"So?" I said, standing. "So now you tell me how you want it." She blushed and laughed. Her hands fell to her sides and I kissed her.

Just like that, things were different. We were something different, and she had been kissed. "How do you feel?" I asked.

"I feel nervous about you meeting my dad."

"Really? He seemed so nice on the phone."

"Oh, he's nice. That has nothing to do with it. Go. Sleep. I'll be ready when you get dropped off tomorrow."

I kissed her again. She didn't wring her hands this time.

Janette grew up in Sunset, twenty-five miles north of Salt Lake City. She was tense by the time we got to Wendover, the midpoint between Salt Lake and Elko. By the time we got to Salt Lake she was grinding her teeth.

"I need to tell you some stuff about my dad. He goes to these mountain man rendezvous ever year," she said. "He'll probably introduce himself to you as Flintstriker, which is his mountain man name." From what she said, his mountain man experience was limited to Boy Scout Jamborees; he'd been serving in Boy Scouts for most of his adult life. Every year he'd go to a Jamboree—a gigantic campout with scouts from the region—and wear his leathers and fire his black powder rifle.

"We don't call him Flintstriker," she said. "And he shoots his rifle in the middle of the night on New Year's. He'll tell you everything he's doing in church right now. He'll probably mow the lawn at five in the morning tomorrow. Our backyard's always covered with deer hides that he's tanning. And he goes to DI"—Deseret Industries thrift stores—"and buys snowmobile parts and then puts them in the backyard and they just sit there forever. Drives my mom nuts. And . . ." She looked to see if I was reaching for the door handle, but I couldn't wait to meet him. Would he greet us in a coonskin cap? Would he demand that we leg wrestle on the lawn? Would he give me some manly test to prove that he was superior to me, like asking me to locate the spark plugs in his car?

When she pulled into the driveway, the front door opened and John Watts stepped out. You can tell that some people are friendly from a block away. He was about five-ten with the roundest belly I'd ever seen. Suspenders pulled dark green pants up over the belly to meet a maroon T-shirt. He shook my hand and squeezed hard. "Welcome!"

Five minutes later I threw a tomahawk; it twirled end over end, and struck the "throwing stump" with its handle, which then splintered. John nodded. "Not bad." Then he threw his own hawk, which missed the stump and clattered against the fence. And, yes, stretched across the fence was a deer hide that he'd tanned himself. I retrieved our axes and returned to the throwing line.

I was delighted to be at Janette's parents' home, throwing pieces of metal at a piece of wood with a man who indeed called himself Flintstriker. He even showed me a wooden box with his mountain man name scrimshawed into its lid. I hadn't had a chance to say one word about myself. John jabbered on about everything while Janette caught up with her mom, Linda. Linda looked exactly like what you'd picture if I told you that she was sixty-five years old, with glasses and white hair, and looked really nice. She laughed after everything anyone said, including herself.

After her parents went to bed, Janette showed me my room. "This was my room growing up. It shares a wall with the bathroom. That was exactly as glorious as it sounds." There was a chest of her old toys. "I loved Strawberry Shortcake, but my mom never had enough money to buy me the accessories, so I made them." She dumped a few yarn-haired dolls onto the bed.

I recognized their faces—my sister Megan had loved Strawberry Shortcake. Someone had obviously made them new clothes. And each doll wore a backpack. "That's not even the best part," said Janette. "Open their backpacks."

Each backpack contained three books made of construction paper, bound with tiny stitches. "Open the books," she said. I opened one. My hands jerked. I let the book drop.

"It's okay," she said.

"I don't want to tear it," I said.

"You won't."

Every half-inch page, of which there were probably ten, had tiny scribbled lines on it. "I didn't want them to get bored," she said.

"Okay seriously, this is the greatest thing I've ever seen. *Moby-Dick*?"

"I know, I've never even read it. They have, though."

That Janette had spent her childhood sewing books so that her dolls could be literate was too perfect.

If we weren't meant for each other, nobody was.

I woke to the sound of the lawnmower. The clock said six A.M. After breakfast, John and Linda piled into their camper while we followed in the Buick. Janette looked at me and lifted her eyebrows.

"He's not bad at all," I said.

"Oh, I'm so glad. He did mow the lawn really early though."

The campsite was already full when we got there. I met Janette's brother, Jeff. Jeff's wife pulled me aside. "So you're going to marry my sister-in-law! What's going on?"

How in the world had she gotten that idea? Did Janette say that? Is that what Janette wanted? Was that what was happening?

"Uh," I said.

John appeared before I could answer and handed me a long, thick needle. "Help me sew up the cover on the camper." I stitched away while kids I didn't know yet laughed and ran through the trees.

I thought about what Jeff's wife had said. I didn't feel pressured by this intrusion from someone I'd just met. But now I *was* thinking about marrying Janette, which was wonderful and terrifying.

Throughout the day I shook a lot of hands and immediately forgot everyone's name. Everyone was welcoming and kind.

That night Janette came into my tent and laid down, her head on my chest. My chest immediately lurched and bounced her head off for an instant. She laughed. "You're not a great pillow."

"I love you," I told her for the first time. I'd met her only a few weeks earlier. And now I knew I loved her. How humbling to think that mere weeks before I'd been alone and unhappy, and now I was happier than I'd ever been, because of her.

"I love you too." She felt my face in the dark. She had to know I had the biggest, dopiest grin on my face. And now I was even happier. That night, alone in my tent, I listened. I listened to my body; it clanged with desire, but it hummed with love. I listened to my mind—I'd often been forced to fight for the privilege of introspection by the blaring coming out of my mouth. For once, silence was more galvanizing than noise. Maybe our Plans of Salvation were aligning.

The next day we went to Bear Lake. I found myself next to John, ankle-deep in muddy water, moss trying to pin our toes to the earth. "This lake's pretty nice," he said. "We like it."

"I like it too."

"I'm glad. You know, Janette's a good woman." He stopped,

looked like he had more to say, then jumped in the air. "I think a fish just bit my toes!"

Now was the time to ask him if I could marry her. We were alone. Now was the time.

But I didn't. Then the fish bit my toes too and I screamed and we laughed and headed in to shore.

After lunch Janette and I went for a walk. Eventually we tired and sat on a half-rotten log.

"What are you thinking?" she asked.

"I'm not sure," I said. "Well, that's not true. I'm sure. I guess I'm thinking we just need to make it official, right?"

She smiled. "Make what official?"

I started to get down on one knee, almost slipped, but caught the log and saved myself before falling over. I yelled when a beetle ran out of the log over my hand. After making sure the log was now empty, I took her hand in both of mine, kissed it, and said, "Will you marry me?"

The word "yes" is just a sound. It's nothing without context. It can signal the end of a life, an exultation after a scored basket or a vanquished foe; it can answer questions or refute them; it's an affirmation. Under the trees, leaning against a decaying piece of wood with the warm June sunlight filtering through the branches above, Janette's "yes" was the sweetest sound I'd ever heard. If there was a more exhilarating feeling, I didn't think I could have survived it. There was a woman sitting in the forest with me, agreeing to share our lives. We would bear each other's burdens. She would have our children and we would raise them together. Maybe we'd save each other's souls if the church turned out to be the one true way. There was a woman whom I loved deeply and profoundly, and with one syllable she'd changed our lives forever.

At dinner Janette said, "I have an announcement. Josh and I would like to invite all of you to come visit us in Salt Lake at the end of the summer because. . . ." Her voice broke. She took a deep breath. "We're getting married!" Cheers from the crowd! Slapped backs! Handshakes! I accepted them all and realized that my face was starting to hurt. I obviously didn't spend enough time smiling. When the furor died down John hugged me. "Janette is a wonderful woman. She'll be a wonderful wife." I realized that I never asked him for her hand. And I'd meant to! Why hadn't I done it?

We went home the next day. Outside my parent's house, Janette squeezed my hand. "Ready?" I was. My dad suddenly opened the door, took one look, and asked, "What's going on?"

Cheers! Hugs! Slapped backs!

That night we all went to dinner at Elko's one decent Mexican restaurant. How wondrous and unexpected to have something this special to celebrate after the previous year of such darkness.

At home, my mom came into the living room where I was reading *A Confederacy of Dunces*, which somehow I didn't hear of until 2001. "Sit with me." We sat on the couch. She said she was proud of me. That she couldn't be happier.

"I know, Mom. Me too. I can't believe this has happened."

"I knew it would. I always knew it would. You've got to start listening to your old mother."

"It's my New Year's resolution."

"Good."

"For 2002."

I didn't tell her that, happy as I was, I was scared. How could I say that I wasn't sure I'd be able to support Janette, or our family? How could I tell her that, although I felt like I was now strong enough to grit my teeth and move forward, all on behalf of Janette's love and support, that I still wondered if it would be enough?

Later, I did tell her about the 401(k) story. "Oh yeah. It's all we girls ever think about. Modest 401(k)s."

Janette was cooking dinner for us. This was a dangerous proposition; Janette cooks and bakes as if she's trying to fatten you up before eating you. It was two weeks before our wedding.

"There's a good chance that our kids would have it," I said. "You know that." Janette had a niece and a nephew with Tourette's. Having the disorder on her side of the family increased the chances that we'd pass it on.

"You don't understand how it can be," I said. "When it's really bad. I've had friends that just weren't able to be around me anymore. I lost my best friend. A girl I planned on marrying. They couldn't take it. You haven't seen it like that yet."

Janette smiled. "I'll understand once it happens. Then we'll deal with it. Now shut up about it."

"Are you sure you can do it? What if you can't? I don't want this to happen and then just be alone again."

"No, I'm not. How could I be sure?" she said. "But I believe in you. How can I be sure about any of that tonight? It hasn't happened yet. I don't think it will."

"But doesn't that scare you?" I jerked my head back and whipped it forward.

When I stopped, Janette touched my face. She looked at me just the way Fern looked down at Wilbur the pig when he was in the stroller in *Charlotte's Web*. "Committing to spending the rest of my life and more with someone is scary enough without guessing at all the things that might happen. So stop."

"But don't you—"

"If I did, I'd say so. Here's what I'm sure of: When I'm with you—when I'm with you and things are bad with your tics— it's hard. It hurts because I love you and I don't like to see your pain. But it's not nearly as bad as not being with you. I've spent most of my life without you and I know what I'm talking about. Now be quiet. I'm done with this conversation, which means don't bring it up tomorrow. We're getting married two weeks from now, so smile and deal with it. You proposed to *me*, remember?"

I remembered.

On the morning of our wedding I met Janette at her parent's house. Despite all of the doctrine that gets filed under weird and superstitious, nobody ever told me that I shouldn't see Janette before the service. We drove to the city of Bountiful. Janette grew up in the Ogden temple district, but it was closed for cleaning, so she chose Bountiful. I'd predict that even if you think the religion is the height of absurdity, you'd still find something to admire about Mormon temples. The Bountiful temple is a pristine white, with light shades of gray being the only other colors on the walls, both inside and out. It rests at the foot of the Wasatch Mountains. Gorgeous flower beds line the walkways to the doors, and the whole place is even cleaner than Disneyland. From the center of the towering building, a spire reaches upward, topped with the angel Moroni, blowing his horn to announce that we're in a sacred place.

Inside, we each went to our own changing rooms. We donned the traditional white robes of the faith, which are only worn in the temple. Soon we were seated next to each other in one of the eight "sealing rooms." These are rooms where couples are "sealed" together for time and all eternity. If you're sealed to your family, you've effectively achieved the pinnacle of what we're here to accomplish on earth. If you're sealed and then you both live righteously until you die, you'll be together after death. If not, well . . . that's more complicated.

Janette and I knelt on opposite sides of an altar and held hands. Behind each of us was a wall covered by an enormous mirror. Over each other's shoulder we could see endless reflections of ourselves, drifting out into eternity together. The officiator turned to me.

"Will you take Janette as your companion, for time and all eternity?"

"Yes," I said. There was that word again. That simple sound. It sounded like nothing and meant everything.

He turned to Janette. "Will you take Josh as your companion, for time and all eternity?" There was an endless pause. Janette was crying. "Yes," she said at last. I'm sure that people also get left at the altar at Mormon temples, but it's hard for me to picture.

The officiator smiled. "In the name of Jesus Christ, in the presence of these witnesses and the families who love you so dearly, I now pronounce you man and wife. You may kiss the bride."

"Are you okay?" I whispered to Janette after the kiss.

"Yes," she said. "I never thought it would be my turn," she said. "I love you."

In many ways, a Mormon ceremony isn't that different from a traditional wedding. The major differences are that we wed in the temple, wear peculiar clothes, and there's no "until death do you part." Janette changed into her wedding dress and I got into my tuxedo. A photographer took way too many pictures over the next ninety minutes. Oh, and of course, the luncheon afterward wasn't exactly a bacchanalia. As revels go, it was about as thrilling as eating a box of Wheat Thins with a glass of water. But Janette and I weren't there for the party.

We were there because now there was such a thing as We.

After ninety minutes of eating and laughing and reminiscing about That Time When Someone Did Something Funny, we got in the car and pointed it toward Moab, where we'd spend

our honeymoon. I quickly pulled in to a car wash. We'd requested that our families not toilet paper our car, or write on
the windows with soap, or tie cans to the bumper. They had
mostly complied, but there were some balloons glued to the
windows, and well wishes soaped on the windshield. As the car
was pulled along the conveyor belt and under cover of soapsuds,
we started pawing at each other as the brushes scrubbed the
windows and doors. "Do you want to go check into a hotel for
an hour before we go?" I asked hopefully. "Or do you think you
can make it to Moab?"

"Let's drive," she said. "Every mile can be like a
countdown."

"I want another car wash," I said.

"No, let's go."

When we got to the Archway Inn in Moab we learned that
my grandpa had paid for our room. It turned out to be the
handicapped suite. None of it mattered. We shut the door and
flew at each other. After that first energetic night I declared that
the theme of our honeymoon would be "For the strength of
youth." This was also the name of the church's youth progress
program. I thought this was hilarious. Janette didn't laugh
quite as much, although that night she proved herself to be a
quick study in extreme irreverence.

Over the next two days the seasons could have changed and
we wouldn't have noticed. We only left the hotel twice. Once
was to eat and then to buy food to take back to our room. The
other time was to recharge during a viewing of Tim Burton's
Planet of the Apes. We were so goofy and delirious and happy
that the movie actually seemed good. That's how perfect it was.

That's how perfect We were.

CHAPTER 8

153.6—Truthfulness and Falsehood
616.692—Infertility—Popular Works
636—Dogs
021.65—Library Science

We were at my family's house in Nevada. We'd gathered there for Christmas and were still there on December 31 for Janette's birthday. We'd spent the day trying to see who could eat the most junk and introducing Janette to "the Food Game," a childhood favorite. You blindfold someone and then feed him the most disgusting concoction possible. Anything in the kitchen was fair game, if it fit on a spoon. Janette refused to play, but laughed dutifully when my sister Lindsey bested a mouthful of peanut butter, clam juice, thyme, two jalapeño seeds, and the fat from a strip of bacon.

Later, I gave Janette her birthday present. She could tell it was, obviously, a book. She hid her disappointment well and chirped, in a bright voice a full register higher than usual, "I know what *this* is!" She tore the wrapping paper off and said, "Oh." I wondered if she was taken aback, but, no, she was smiling. On the cover of the blue paperback, two chubby babies sat on two blocks. She held it up for my family to see. *One Thou-sand and One Baby Names!*

"We're going to start trying," I told everyone.

"Name it Frank whether it's a boy or a girl," said my dad.

We were two years into our marriage. The first few months had been about as storybook as it gets. We'd wake up and smile at each other. She'd go to work and I'd go to school. When she came home we'd make dinner or go out, and smile at each other some more. We had weird upstairs neighbors: One, Ollie, spent his days in the shared basement laundry room, making wooden gargoyles. We enjoyed wondering when he would murder us. We'd go to the grocery store and buy trashy romances and read them to each other, trying to distinguish "anguished groans" from "urgent gasps." *Her Texas Ranger* was the first. I wasn't able to work much because of Misty, and my first semester of post-wedding school was unsuccessful—ultimately the tics were too challenging for me in the classroom. But for that first year being together was enough.

And I could talk! I decided to stop getting the Botox injections after we'd been married for eight months. I wasn't having verbal tics, but the physical tics were getting worse. I'd traded the obnoxious but painless noises for scratching my face and chest, slapping and punching myself more often, biting my tongue more severely, etc. I'd have chosen another hernia from screaming over hitting myself one more time. I hoped that if the milder vocal tics returned they would vent some of the pressure in a less destructive way. It was a thrill to talk to Janette with as many words as I wanted.

On Sundays we went to church. When I was voiceless, I couldn't use noisy tics as an excuse to stay home. But I found that worshipping with Janette made worshipping easier. I could pray when I prayed with her. I felt more sincere because she was *completely* sincere.

When my voice returned, it wasn't long before I was called

to teach lessons in elder's quorum. Two Sundays each month, I taught the doctrines of the church. My lessons always ended with my testimony: variations on "I know the church is true." And the more I said it, the truer it became. Any concerns I had about the differences between knowledge and belief faded. When I lived as if I believed, belief was easier to come by.

It gave me peace.

At the end of that year we started trying to get pregnant. We weren't honeymooning anymore, but we were still getting after it with a wonderfully taxing frequency. We designed a fertility schedule that looked fun on paper. Once we were a few months into the experiment, it was still fun, but the best part of sex is the spontaneity. It was never better than when we were overcome and just had to have at it. But we had to plan the pregnancy attempts. Nothing was less arousing than an X on the calendar; during that first year of trying we lived in a state of constant "counting down" according to a menstrual cycle. Always waiting. Always wondering. Now we had an unwelcome bedroom companion: trepidation.

A year of unsuccessful trying later Janette said, "If we ever have a daughter, I really hope she gets your calves and my personality." We'd moved from the sure thing to the distant and hypothetical: *If we ever . . .*

When I bought that baby-name book I thought the process was buy a baby-name book, have sex, baby wearing an adorable bonnet appears. But no.

"Your chances of conceiving a child are less than four percent," said the fertility specialist.

Janette sighed. "Four percent?"

"Yes," he said, "but there are options. I would propose starting you on a regimen of . . ." He talked, far away in Doctor-land. I held the test results, which said that my sperm spent their time cavorting, swimming in circles, bumping into one another, guffawing with self-effacement every time they lost their way and found themselves at another dead end.

Part of me was relieved. I hated that part of me.

If you're married, or you've ever been married, and you went into it with the hope that it would somehow fix your problems or bridge the gaps in your personal failings, you're a sucker. I suspect that you know it. All honeymoons, literal or metaphorical, end. After Janette and I got married, we moved to Salt Lake so I could finish school at the University of Utah. That semester I was a classics major for some reason. Within a month I told my Greek professor that I wasn't sure I could complete the semester. That morning I was fine in class, but I struggled in the hallways. Too many bodies. My arms flailed over my own head, to keep everyone else safe. I shouted my repertoire of nonsense syllables. I avoided eye contact as my right shoulder jerked up over and over with such force that I fell against someone.

I told the humanities advisor I doubted that I could finish the semester.

"Do you think it will get easier?" she asked.

"No. I'm not sure why it would." She helped me with a medical withdrawal, filing a form with the head of the College of Humanities and getting it approved. So I terminated my semester without receiving failing grades.

I wanted to work while I regrouped. Janette was working in the church office building downtown. It's a tall building where administrative church stuff happens and men grow rotund bellies. She was a secretary, and then became an editor. I looked for graveyard shifts at gas stations, or jobs at bookstores.

I entered a Barnes and Noble while someone was putting

up a "now hiring" sign. They interviewed me and I started a week later.

I thought that working in a retail store would be thrilling, amazing somehow, as long as the product was a book. I'd walk in, shelve a few volumes, and then sit around sipping a hot chocolate from the café while talking about books with my coworkers.

The reality, though . . . I arrived at 6:50, clocked in, and shelved books for four hours while musical abominations blasted from the store's speakers. If you've never heard the Beach Boys singing "Be True to Your School" at an unholy decibel level at 7:00 in the morning, I envy you.

On my first day I shelved for an hour before the morning briefing. We gathered around the information desk while our managers outlined the day. What was corporate pushing? What were the new releases? Yes, James Patterson really had another book out. And then our manager introduced me.

"Hi!" I said.

"Welcome, Josh," said our manager. "What do you like to do for fun? Tell us something about yourself."

"Well, I just got a literary agent," I said. *WHAT! No, I didn't!* What was I *saying*?

It seemed that some of the other employees' eyes widened. Others narrowed. What had possessed me? I wasn't above the occasional embellishment to tell a better story, but this was an absolute lie. Years later I would read Patricia Highsmith's *The Talented Mr. Ripley.* "Better an important fake than a real nobody," said Ripley, who was also a sociopath and eventually a murderer. It was like the scene in *The Karate Kid* where Daniel Larusso, the insecure new kid in town, lies about knowing karate to impress someone. Well, it starts innocently enough, but it's not long before he's getting his face kicked off by a dojo full of hooligans. But I wasn't some kid, I was a grown man! Except I wasn't, obviously.

Soon I was telling other would-be writers how to go about getting an agent. I received an imaginary offer and then flew on an imaginary plane out to New York for an imaginary meeting with imaginary publishers. Upon returning I announced an imaginary two-book deal with Viking. I can't remember why I chose Viking. At least it was a real company. As opposed to imaginary, like everything else about me. Every time I opened my mouth it got worse, because it was usually to answer a question about how great things were going for me and "how excited I must be." Each new lie was a bar in the cell I was forging for myself, and I didn't know how to let myself out of the cage. And I had no idea why I'd started building such a stupid cage. Soon, I'd repeated my publishing fable so often that I was barely aware that there was a cage at all. "You're living my dream!" said one teenage girl who worked in the café.

I returned from my imaginary New York trip to see an all-too-real banner stretched across the second-floor balcony. "Congratulations to our new author and bookseller, Josh Hanagarne!" I gladly/horrifiedly accepted congratulations from patrons and coworkers that day. It was only a matter of time before Janette came in and saw it. It might be an hour, or a month, but she'd see it. So I did the only thing I could think of.

"I've got some great news!" I said over dinner.

In the store, she looked at the banner. "Wow!" she said. Then, more quietly, "Wow." I didn't know how to interpret these "wows." She was either happy and awestruck, or she was onto me and couldn't figure out who she was with. I made it through one more day before breaking down.

"There's no book deal," I said. "I have no idea why I said it but now they all think this is happening and I don't know what to do!"

"What do you mean, you don't know what to do? You've got to tell them! Why would you do this?" She was angry, which was a relief. Better that than pity. "What's the matter with you? You've got to tell them!" More than anything, she sounded tired.

"But I'll get fired!"

She was quiet for a long time. "Josh, do you love me?"

"Of course!"

"How can I believe you if you can just lie like that?"

Ouch. "Okay," I said. "I deserved that. But I do. You have to know I do."

"Look," she said, "so what, your career as a bookstore shelver is over? So what! Go tell them, let's figure out how to get you back into school, and you can work on something you actually want to do."

"Okay." It made sense. The next day I went into work prepared to tell my boss the whole story. I wimped out. "Janette is really sick," I said instead. "I can't get into it but I need to quit. I paid back the book advance and called off the deal so I can spend more time with her." That was my last shift. As I watched my manager's face, it seemed like she wasn't quite as upset by the news of Janette's devastating illness, or my departure, as she should have been. Did she know? Was it that obvious?

"I'll find another job," I told Janette. I elided the conversation about her imaginary illness. There were still new lows for me. I decided that if I ever published a book it would be called *How a Despicable Person Became Slightly Less So*.

The next three years passed in a similar pattern. I'd enroll in school, then withdraw for medical reasons. Occasionally I'd complete a class and get a couple of credits. I'd get hired at menial jobs, then quit shortly thereafter. I told Janette that things would be okay, but they never were. And she continued to be patient and generous and kind and wonderful, although I think she'd tell you that if she didn't struggle with codependency issues she might have been brave enough to cut me loose.

Through it all, we kept trying to get pregnant.

One morning Janette woke me while it was still dark.

"Is everything all right?"

"Josh, I'm pregnant." It was the first week of October.

"What!" That afternoon I called my mom. She screamed! I called everyone in my family. They screamed! I told the few friends I had in our ward. They were thrilled! Janette did the same with everyone she could think of, everyone who knew that we'd been trying for so long.

It had been four years. Four years of trying. Now sex itself was almost odious. Sex on a schedule bordered on tedium. I'll never forget the non-afterglow of one uninspired bout when I realized that Janette was crying. *I wonder if it worked . . .*

But now! We couldn't look at each other without laughing. We threw out nonsense baby names all day. "We'll name it Headlock!" I said. "Headlock Hanagarne!"

"No," she said. "How about Hoth? Or Darth?" Janette's a *Star Wars* fan. "We'll ask Jim and Amy for suggestions tonight." We went to dinner to celebrate with our friends.

Janette had been in the restroom for several minutes by the time we ordered dessert. "There's blood," she said as we walked to our car. She called her gynecologist, who prescribed some pills, which I picked up that night at a gruesomely lit Walgreen's.

Janette bled all night.

The next morning we sat in the waiting room of her doctor's office. We didn't talk.

Janette's pregnancy officially ended that night. I lay on our bed for hours and held her. She shook with sobs. I cried, but it was nothing like what she was experiencing. I pictured oceans of tears filling up, overflowing the shores of Bleakland, and drowning unsuspecting peasants. When she had cried herself out and her breathing had steadied, we fell asleep.

We didn't talk the next morning. I tried to read. She stayed in bed. In the afternoon I went for a walk. Our apartment was a block away from a park. The sounds of a kids' soccer game reached me before I saw it. At one time, each of the children in the bright jerseys had been a mere idea. Someone's dream. Someone's accident. Planned or unplanned, it didn't matter: They were here in this world. More than anything Janette wanted to bring a child here to earth to play on a soccer field, or learn the piano, or get good grades, or wrap its little fingers around her own and squeeze.

I wanted Janette to have what *she* wanted but the responsibility of a child felt unreal. I hadn't made my peace with being an unreliable, unequal partner in my marriage and hoped I never would. Feeling like a sponge was bad enough. But worse was the fear that Janette would be so long-suffering that I'd never have to change. Staying the same would be easiest, though I wouldn't be happy about it and it wouldn't be fair to her. But the thought of disappointing a child . . . of being a bad or inept or reckless father . . . that was unthinkable. But I wanted a child. I wanted to have it both ways. I'd always loved babies. I'd always wanted a little boy. But there were always qualifiers. I was in the thick of my fight with Misty. A child would just give her a new plaything. I wanted a child; I didn't want a child with Tourette's. I wanted a child who could have all the chances that other "normal" kids had; I didn't want a child who would need to live with his mom forever or sponge off his future wife. I wanted a child I could be proud of; I didn't want a child whose love affair with couches would rival my own.

A boy scored a goal. Cheers erupted. I screamed and slammed my heels together hard enough to trip myself. I'd been walking in a circle around the soccer field, head down, and fast enough to make me pant.

A slobbery, rolling tennis ball stopped by my shoe. A long-haired red dog appeared and looked up at me. "Hi," I said. "*Woo!*"

The dog barked.

Janette and I spent the months after the miscarriage avoiding each other's eyes most of the time, offering small, pinched smiles when we did. All of our talk had the forced, false chirpiness of a sitcom. Without talking about it, we skipped church on Mother's Day, then again on Father's Day. But little by little, small talk, all talk, became possible again.

Janette never seemed angry, just sad. Church continued to give her the comfort it always had, but it wasn't helping me. I was angry, although I knew that whether God existed or not, being angry with Him wouldn't change things. Janette didn't deserve any of this. There was a clear difference between us: Janette was more likely to ask, "I wonder why God let this happen?" or "What is he trying to teach me through this experience?" while I had thoughts like "Hey! Are You up there? *Leave her alone!*"

Another year passed. I enrolled in school, then withdrew. I sold women's shoes at Dillard's during the Christmas season. It was as horrible as you think it was. I got a job at Salt Lake City's first Best Buy, worked for a few months, then quit when the tics were too much. I loaded a truck at UPS for four hours each night, frantically scanning and stacking boxes into a wall that grew endlessly. I reveled in the exertion of it. I quit the job at UPS so I could spend more time in yet another school. Then I withdrew from school and was back to having no job again. Back on the couch. Janette no longer tried to hide her frustration. But she managed to be more frustrated by the situation than with me. When I pressed her to tell me how she was feeling about everything, she would always say, "I know who you'll be. I'm just not sure when. We'll get there."

But if I couldn't go to school and I couldn't work, what was I going to do? Where were we going?

My dad once told me about a guy who said there were finite amounts of misery and happiness in the world. Meaning there was only so much of each to go around, so if you were happy it meant someone was sad. "Dumbest thing I ever heard," said my dad. "The easiest way to forget yourself is to help someone. Your mom said that to me once. I don't always do it but I believe it. And if it's true then there's no reason to think that any of us should be sad forever, unless everyone gets everything they want and there's nobody left to help."

I remembered that discussion during a long, sleepless night. Helping other people was something I hadn't tried yet. But who? Janette was the obvious answer, but helping her meant school and/or work, and I wasn't ready for another try yet.

Janette left for work.

That was when I heard the children across the street and, before I could second-guess myself, I put on my clothes, went outside, and walked across the street to the brick building. The building spanned the block and at certain times of day it sounded like a wild puppy pen: the joyful sounds of recess. It was a special-needs school. I never really thought about these challenged kids in terms of their disabilities when I'd see them on the street, but having so many kids around did keep our struggles with infertility fresh in my mind.

"I'd like to volunteer," I told the woman at the desk.

"Oh, honey," she said slowly, "if you're going to be here, you'll want to get paid. I'll take you on a tour. We could use someone with the older kids' program."

During the tour, I saw kids in wheelchairs. Kids rocking back and forth to silent music. Kids playing basketball. Kids speaking English and kids jabbering away in what may not have been any recorded language. Kids smiling, laughing, crying, and playing tag. A boy hugged me around the waist, then ran away before I could say anything.

Two weeks later I'd been fingerprinted, background-checked, and was an assistant in the class with students in the nineteen-to-twenty-two-year range. The goal was to help them acquire "life skills." My first week we took them to the state fair. I was in charge of eight kids with eight different disabilities. As soon as we got off the bus at the crowded fair park they all ran in different directions. I rounded them up by the time we had to go back to school, but just barely. What "life skills" had they learned at the fair? I don't know. We bought elephant ears, and posed for sepia photographs that were then plastered onto a giant novelty button that I wore on my shirt for the rest of the day. One young man asked if he could ride the Zipper, but I said no when he threw up halfway through his elephant ear. But most of the day I felt like I was chasing kids around, hoping they wouldn't get hurt or lost. It was fun, in a nerve-wracking type of way.

During my first week we had an assembly. Suddenly the Jazz bear—the mascot from the Utah Jazz, Salt Lake's NBA team—ran into the room. It was like someone had detonated a bomb of distilled joy on the students. I have never seen such unrestrained happiness. Everyone was screaming and laughing and trying to get close enough to hug the bear. As usually happens in noisy places, my tics were intense. I shouted and jerked, but nobody noticed! Or if they did, it just didn't matter. There were so many symptoms and conditions in that place that nobody would ever look in my direction twice no matter what Misty compelled me to do. This realization gave me goose bumps. I could stay here forever and be at ease.

I was patient enough for the work. I was capable of changing adult diapers. I played games, led field trips, took the students to a vocational training center once a week, and did more puzzles than you can imagine. One day I was invited to play a game with "the King of Games." The boy who asked was nearly as tall as I was, with dark hair and darker eyes. He was very serious. He would draw game boards on construction paper. We would roll dice and advance around the board. Each square had a command written in it.

"Do it," he said as I landed on a space that said, simply, "Sharp your foot."

"What does sharp your foot mean?" I asked.

"Do it. Sharp your foot."

I tried but, unsurprisingly, couldn't get it right. "When I landed on "Dance like a jackass," he was more accepting of my efforts. I got it right on the first try.

Then it was October again. Another normal morning interrupted by a positive sign on a pregnancy test. Once again we were elated and terrified, but this time the celebration was muted and tentative. "We'll tell everyone in three months," said Janette. She visited her gynecologist who said that everything looked great. Two weeks later we were in a room with a doctor who looked like Gene Wilder. He manipulated the sonogram equipment and squinted. "Can you tell what we're looking at here?" he asked.

I looked at the gray blobs in that alien environment. It looked like the negative of a bowl of Rice Krispies and sea monkeys. "No," I said, sure that he was about to say, "I'm sorry, but it's happened again. October is simply not your month."

"Right"—he tapped the screen—"here. That's a heartbeat. It's as healthy a heartbeat as I've ever seen at this stage."

Janette made a noise between a laugh and a sob. I leaned closer. A tiny beacon of life blipped and flickered on the screen, a pulsing bit of darkness in the graphic tumult of the womb. And it was everything.

"It's going to be okay?" I said. "It's okay?"

Janette grabbed my hand. "Oh, wow," she said. "Oh, wow. *Josh.*"

We shook hands with Gene Wilder and went out to lunch. "Maybe it's just time," she said. "Maybe . . . maybe we're just better this time and it'll work."

I kissed her across the table. "I'll do anything to help you with this. I'll do everything." I meant it. It was true. My job was going well and I was considering a career in special education. We had more money. I had more confidence. It was time. It had to be.

The next two weeks passed in a tentative euphoria. We were happy but we tried to be cautious and humble; what if we celebrated too hard and wrecked everything?

Another quiet morning. "Josh, I need you to drive me to the doctor." Janette sounded like she was choking. The drive was only fifteen minutes away, but it felt like it took years. We didn't talk. She shook in the passenger seat of my truck. I yawned and realized how tightly my jaw was clenched when the effort of opening my mouth actually hurt.

We sat in the same waiting room.

No Gene Wilder this time. We were taken into a dim room where Janette, quietly crying, removed her clothes and slipped into a dressing gown. She lay on the table and stared at the ceiling. A young female sonogram technician entered the room and began applying the cold clear jelly to Janette's stomach. I couldn't organize my thoughts, but one surfaced, cutting through the chaos. *They're going to give her another ultrasound and we are going to have to sit here and look at the screen and try to see if there's still a heartbeat and if there's no heartbeat then that means it happened again.* I wanted to lift Janette in my arms and carry her out to the truck. If I could just get her out of here before they started the procedure, we could escape the result. We could return to the book of baby names and laugh, and the next year wouldn't have to pass with me blaming myself for my wretched, insubstantial seed and she wouldn't have to lash herself with the guilt that her body was an inadequate vessel. If we could just—

"Hmm . . . ," said the technician. "Maybe I'll—let me try a few more angles." I stared at the screen. Where was it? Where was the small dark disturbance in the fluid? The pulse that had made the past two weeks a joyous dream? Where was the life we had made? Janette looked, then turned her head back to the ceiling. She closed her eyes.

"Janette, it's going to be okay," I said. "She just has to try another—"

"I'm so sorry," said the technician. "I can't see a heartbeat." She left us alone. Alone with this terrible silence and this blank screen. A pin-sized change.

I watched my stricken wife remove her dressing gown and dress herself. Things can change so quickly. As we left, we passed a young couple and their daughter, a girl who couldn't have been more than three years old. "See!" said the mother, pointing at their hot-off-the-press sonogram. "That's your little brother!"

We walked by and scheduled Janette's D and C surgery.

A week later, my brother, Kyle, sat with me. Minutes earlier Janette had been wheeled into surgery. I hadn't eaten all day so we walked to a Subway across the street. "I know that I haven't always been able to get things done, and that I break down, but this is something different," I said. "This isn't part of that. This actually *is* this hard, it's not just me."

Kyle nodded. "I know, Josh. We all know. Want me to cheer you up?"

"Yes. Please."

He drew back his arm and held his hoagie like a football. "See that old lady over there? I'm going to throw this right into her mouth."

I laughed. I had to. I was cried out.

Janette recovered slowly. We were heavy and dull and the

world was cobwebs and leaden air. Her emotional state, her entire psyche, became its own delicate fontanelle. Every happy
word within earshot, every laughing child, every piece of evidence that someone else's life was going how that person wanted
it to . . . it was unwelcome, destructive pressure. We were walking emptiness, a patchwork of living voids stitched together
from fissures and rifts.

Three weeks later I was on the couch. Our apartment was
empty, but the building wasn't. I heard a baby crying through
the floor. Two sisters and their mother lived below us. One of
them had a two-year-old and was pregnant. The other talked
constantly about getting pregnant and spoke of a child that no
longer lived with her. They each said they were battling meth
addictions. They often knocked on our door with no particular
goal in mind. "Hi," they'd say. "Hi," I would say. Then we'd
stand there and blink and after a while I'd close the door.

We couldn't have what they had—children—and what
they had, they dishonored with recklessness and drug use.
Maddening.

I fled outside. The sun made me self-conscious, as did the
sound of my footfalls and the fresh air. And of course, the tics.
As I walked, the noises ripped out of me as I flailed like a
puppet.

People stared. Even holding the gaze of another person was
too heavy. I screamed. I walked. I screamed. I scratched myself.
My arms waved about, striking at invisible swarms of bees. *Tic
tic tic tic tic.* I slapped my face and chewed my lips until my eyes
watered. I could barely remember where my house was. The cold
air hit the heat of my face and seemed to create its own wind. I
was crying in frustration. I walked faster and watched my feet,
dragging them over another crack in the sidewalk, then another.

I found myself alone on the corner of an intersection. Over the sound of my ragged breathing and my convulsing body I reached out and tried to find something still. Something calm.

Across the street, two golden retrievers ran back and forth behind a chain-link fence, barking at me. They weren't the only ones. Every single dog for what sounded like a square mile was barking its fool head off. *They think I'm some big weird dog.* I felt exactly like one of Kafka's hapless characters, stumbling onto a new path and realizing that I'd lost my way. The dogs were barking at me.

Dogs always look so happy. So pleased with themselves. "Huh!" I shouted. "Huh huh!"

They barked and jumped and one of them spun in a tight circle.

I started to laugh on the street as everyone else hurried by, bent into the wind, grim-faced and lashed. I went to the nearest convenience store and bought the biggest bag of dog treats I could find and walked around the neighborhood, doling out those treats to every dog I saw. By the time I passed the school where I worked, the bag was empty.

"Janette," I said when I walked in, "I'm going to go to the gym.

She stuck her head out of the bedroom. "Is our membership still good?"

"I don't know. I'll find out."

The membership had expired. The last thing Janette had wanted to do after the miscarriages was exercise, and I'd stopped going too. I signed us up again and went into the weight room.

I had a decision to make. My suspicion that I could stay at the school and be totally at ease, hidden among the other noisy kids, had been right. It was easy to be there, but it wasn't challenging in the way I needed it to be.

"Janette," I said that night, "I want to find another job."

"Why?"

I explained that I felt like I was hiding out in the school, and that even though I enjoyed it, I wasn't ready to commit to decades of work in special education. I needed a job that would keep me honest. A job that would prove that I had toughened up and could handle more stress. And of course, I wanted a job that I'd love. What sort of test would be ideal for a man with noisy, disruptive Tourette Syndrome?

"A convent?" said Janette. "A monastery? I don't know, why don't you just find a job that you like and not worry about whether it will be hard enough to make you miserable?"

The next day I walked into the quietest building I knew of. A building that, incidentally, I visited almost every day: the public library. I dropped off my books. The silence was heavy and thick. Someone cleared his throat. It sounded like a shotgun blast in the stillness. My mouth went dry and my heart started its familiar pattern: What *if*? What *if*? What *if*?

"Woo!" Whoops. Sure enough, everyone looked at me, including the staff members.

"Can I have a job application?" I said.

I got hired. I wasn't doing anything super-important. I checked in the books that people returned. When someone wanted to borrow books, I ran their items under a scanner and got them a bag if they wanted one. If they wanted to chat about books, I'd chat. It was a tough, tic-filled four hours, but I did it. There was one moment of absolute panic when a woman approached the desk carrying an infant in a car seat. The baby's neck was crooked at such an impossible angle that I thought, *It's dead. She has no idea that the baby she thinks is only asleep is dead!* This was followed by an even worse thought: *It's dead and SHE KNOWS and she's in here smiling and checking out Nora Roberts books!*

The baby opened its eyes and saw the horror on my face.

That night Janette and I went out for dinner and celebrated.

I had to laugh. "Some celebration, huh?" I said. "Another first day at work."

"Don't think like that," Janette said.

"I'm trying."

"Good. What else was on your mind as you served the needy public today?"

"Honestly?"

"Of course."

"I think we should start our adoption paperwork."

CHAPTER 9

613.7—Kettlebells
362.734—Adoption
306.874—Fathers and Sons
291.13—Greek Mythology

The young mother stares at a computer screen. Her infant girl in a car seat screeches while her little boy plays on the floor nearby. Other patrons are staring, frowning, shaking their heads. I kneel by the mother.

"Could you please keep your children more quiet?" I whisper. "I think they might be bothering other people. Can I help?"

She begins sobbing. "Do you have kids?" She wipes her nose on her sleeve. "These are my kids. I have no idea where their dad is. I haven't known for about two years. I have to give them up for adoption. They . . ." Her shoulders shake and she folds forward, crying into her lap. The boy toddles over and pats her on the back, concern on his little face.

She sits up and whispers, "They don't know. I don't know how to tell them. I don't know if I can tell them."

I hug her and now I'm sniffling and I can't imagine what

anyone must think we're carrying on about. I think about that woman a lot. I never saw her or the kids again.

LDS Family Services didn't look like a place where dreams came true. It just looked like a building. I don't know what I'd expected; maybe that we'd be meeting in a giant crib, or that the employees would all be wearing baby bonnets. Or that they'd pass out babies as party favors. Janette and I were there because as members of the LDS Church, we could take advantage of what we called afford-a-baby. This meant we'd only shell out four thousand dollars or so for our adoption, versus the ten to twenty thousand that other agencies might charge. And of course, it being a church-led agency, God himself was at the helm. If creating perfect families was the goal, surely He'd know how to handle things.

During our intake session Janette and I sank into a plump leather couch as a pleasant, slender, white-haired woman explained the process. She spoke so quietly that we almost invited her to sit on our laps so we could hear her. The breakdown: We'd attend six weeks of adoption classes. We'd prepare a mountain of paperwork that, while she avoided calling it our "sales package," was exactly that. An employee would visit our house and make sure it wasn't a meth lab. We'd write a personal statement to whoever would birth our child. We'd participate in interviews, both jointly and alone.

"Isn't this exciting?" whispered the woman before embracing us. It was like hugging a sweater full of twigs.

"This is going to be a lot of work," said Janette afterward. "I don't even know how to start."

"Let's talk to Shaun and Maryanne." They were two friends from the ward who had recently adopted a child from this office. I arranged a dinner date for that weekend. After dinner

Janette went upstairs to talk with Maryanne while I stayed with Shaun.

"So how were the classes?" I asked. "What were they like?"

He moaned. "Worse than church. You sit around and everyone sniffles while they tell you how lucky you are to be adopting. There were people in our classes who'd been coming for years and still hadn't filled out their paperwork. That was actually one of the only reasons I got our papers done so quick— I didn't want to do another round of classes."

"What do they ask in the interviews? How should we handle that?" I asked.

"I'm not kidding: Lie through your teeth. Say whatever you have to to look like the ideal candidate." Shaun looked at something I couldn't see and frowned. "When we got John, I hadn't believed in the church in years. I was unemployed. We didn't have health insurance. Our marriage wasn't going that well, either."

"So why'd they give you a kid?"

"Because I said the opposite of everything I just told you. I lied like crazy. I had a job. I had insurance. I had faith. All that. You don't want to get into an argument with these people that you can't win. Say whatever you have to."

"Oh."

"Well, that was encouraging," Janette said when we were alone. "Maryanne felt like it couldn't have gone better. She loved every step of it, apparently."

"Well, here's what Shaun said." I couldn't get through it without laughing.

"Oh. Well. But Maryanne said . . . Well."

"Let's just start the classes and see."

Classes took place upstairs in the agency. Maybe eight rows of beige chairs, the kind you instantly know will be the inverse of agreeable, lined an aisle that led to a pulpit and microphone. Maybe eight people, the kind you instantly know are not your kindred spirits, rose to meet us. We shook hands. We smiled. They smiled.

"So what are you guys here for?" said a ruddy man whose white shirt and tie made me feel like a mucky hog in jeans. I thought this was a dumb question—what else would we be there for? But I found that many of the couples were there to learn about the process, or to support loved ones going through the process, and, yes, there was one couple who'd attended the classes for three years without completing their paperwork, and that I couldn't process at all.

"We want to adopt," I said.

In chorus: "Congratulations!" Everyone wanted to hear our story, which was this: Our bodies won't do what they're supposed to so we can't have our own damned kids.

"Tell us something about yourselves!"

As always, I couldn't manage to introduce myself without talking about books. This time out I mentioned my man-love for Mark Twain. You could feel the room deflate. Twain had famously called the Book of Mormon "chloroform in print" and in *Roughing It* he referred to Mormon women thusly:

> Our stay in Salt Lake City amounted to only two days, and therefore we had no time to make the customary inquisition into the workings of polygamy and get up the usual statistics and deductions preparatory to calling the attention of the nation at large once more to the matter. I had the will to do it. With the gushing self-sufficiency of youth I was feverish to plunge headlong and achieve a great reform here—until I saw the Mormon women. Then I was touched. My heart was wiser than my head. It warmed toward these poor, ungainly, and pathetically "homely" creatures, and as I turned to hide the generous moisture in my eyes, I said, "No— the man that married one of them has done an act of

Christian charity which entitles him to the kindly applause of mankind, not their harsh censure—and the
man that married sixty of them has done a deed of
open-handed generosity so sublime that the nations
should stand uncovered in his presence and worship in
silence."

Twain wasn't a fan of organized religion and I'd brought
him to LDS adoption class. Oh well, he could keep me company while Janette paid attention.

And so began our night of extreme tongue-biting. Our instructor spent the next ninety minutes talking about how grateful we should be that we were adopting. It's not that I wasn't
grateful that we could adopt, but by the end I felt like anyone
who wanted their own biological kid was a sucker. The others in
the class, beaming faces every one, whooped and clapped and
teared up here and there. Someone made a *Family Circus* reference and everyone in the room laughed. When someone makes
a *Family Circus* reference and everyone in the room laughs, I'm
in the wrong room.

"Look around you," said the instructor. "These are your
peers. Spend as much time together as possible. Picnics. Holidays. Go to the temple together. Get to know each other. These
are your friends. This can be another family."

What did we all have in common? Our bodies didn't work
together with our spouses' bodies the way we'd assumed when
we yoked ourselves together. But that was, of course, part of the
Plan of Salvation. We had purpose. Our path involved adopting, along with all the heartbreaking epiphanies that paved the
road to this classroom. The whole point of polygamy back in
the day was that Mormon families could bring forth *more* kids
than anyone else and play theological strength in numbers. I
talked to one guy who literally had tears in his eyes as he said he
"just felt so guilty" because his desiccated loins weren't helping

"build the kingdom." What was I supposed to say to *that*? He really felt guilty and I didn't know any *Family Circus* jokes to perk him up.

Peers? Just because?

"How do you feel?" asked Janette in the parking lot.

"Like an asshole," I said. "Seriously. I was annoyed by everyone. By nice, sad people. Did you ever read *No Exit* in school?"

"No."

"Well, the short version is that three people are in a room and it turns out that they're in Hell. One's a lesbian postmaster or something, one guy is a war deserter and cheated on his wife, and I can't remember what the other woman's deal was. They're in this room expecting to be tortured, but nobody comes, and they finally realize that they are one another's punishments. If you've ever heard the quote 'Hell is other people,' it's from that play."

"Okay."

"Well, tonight was like being trapped in *No Exit*, except that 'Hell is other people' was 'Hell is other people who are probably very nice and are just here trying to be brave and reassure one another.' They wouldn't have chosen this. Nobody did anything wrong. I don't know. Just the situation, maybe. I'm just annoyed that we have to be here at all."

"I get it."

"Do you care if I go to the gym? I know it's late."

"Go ahead. Take your time."

The Iron never lies to you. You can walk outside and listen to all kinds of talk, get told that you're a god or a total bastard. The Iron will always kick you the real deal. The Iron is the great reference point, the all-knowing perspective giver. Always there like a beacon in the pitch black. I have found the Iron to be my greatest friend. It never freaks out on me, never runs. Friends may come and go. But two hundred pounds is always two hundred pounds.

This was the final paragraph of Henry Rollins's essay "The Iron." Rollins had been the singer of the punk band Black Flag, an equally reviled and adored spoken-word performer, an author, an actor in several movies that required a man with a fierce scowl and a thigh-sized neck, and obviously, a man to whom lifting weights was a transcendent experience.

For the past year I'd gone to the gym, or trained in my home, nearly every day. It was 2006. When I wasn't training, I was often thinking about it. When I wasn't thinking about it, I was probably reading about it.

When I descended the steps at the gym in Sugar House, my hair stood on end. When I heard the clink of the weights, my skin warmed. Despite being in a basement, this gym was no dungeon. It made an extreme effort to be trendy and inviting.

I didn't yell, grunt, or swagger. I didn't slap backs. I didn't give advice. I didn't know enough.

Few people spoke to me, probably because I didn't spend any time in front of the mirrors, grimacing as I searched for veins in my forearms and amplified my exertions to the point where nobody could ignore them. I didn't have an exercise "outfit." I wore a sweat suit with a hood. I walked down the stairs, put on my headphones, went to a corner, and tried anything I could think of to get stronger. I might be the only person whose first three-hundred-pound bench press was accompanied by the Recorded Books production of *Don Quixote*.

Henry Rollins said that half of life is fucking up. The other half is dealing with it. Like Rollins, I was no gym bunny socialite. I was there to smother the parasite inside of me. To deal with the other half of my life. I didn't work out. I *trained*. I wasn't a bodybuilder. I was building an obelisk that would commemorate the end of Misty's dominion. I didn't want muscles—at least, that wasn't the priority. I wanted exertion. I wanted to pant and tremble with the strain because if I couldn't breathe, then Misty couldn't breathe. If she insisted on living inside me, I'd make her regret it. If, after a session of heavy squats, five minutes passed before my legs could climb the stairs, she had to wait with me. If I burned, it seared her.

Within months I was stronger than many of the regulars. Training was hard. Because of that—or at least that's how it felt—everything else became easier, including school.

After attending many colleges over the previous decade I needed four more semesters at the University of Utah. I'd decided on an English degree. I was impatient in my classes. I didn't want to sit around and theorize. The action and results-oriented mania of my gym life didn't fit with the philosophical meanderings of academia.

I didn't enjoy my studies but every class period behind me was a step toward a goal. Wanking around about Hegel and Louis Zukofsky's *"A"* and seeing affable young men who looked like hobos nearly come to blows over the implications of a semicolon in George Oppen's *Discrete Series* felt wasteful. It led nowhere. It produced nothing. I couldn't measure my progress beyond my grades, which were always good.

I was in a class once where, after discussing, if I recall, a cyborg opera, a man with fingerless gloves (in July) somehow turned the conversation to George Romero's zombie films.

"Because when you really think about it," he said, stroking beard stubble that he seemed to wish he had, "zombies are essentially just vegetative nonlife commodities."

Yes. When you really think about it . . .

Graduation crept closer.

One of the adoption classes was about foster care. This was essentially a crash course in "fast-track adoption." In cases where a foster child's biological parents have vanished or died or couldn't get it together, the foster parents often receive first crack at the adoption. "This will be the hardest thing you'll ever do," said the leader after relating yet another case of a broken child who nearly broke his new home as well.

I couldn't imagine nobler work than foster care. It also seemed too hard. We left feeling like hypocrites. We wanted a child "more than anything," but not enough to invite a potentially damaged child into our home.

Shortly after that we had our joint interview with a twenty-three-year-old, giggly blond intern from Brigham Young University. "It is *so awesome* to meet you both!" she trilled.

There's nothing wrong with being twenty-three, or blond, or giggly, but we were uncertain about her qualifications in representing us to prospective mothers. *They're so awesome you've totally got to give them your baby!*

"So how would you describe your parenting style?" asked the intern.

"We don't have kids," said Janette.

"Kind and supportive," I said.

"Right, right," she said, making marks on her clipboard. "That is totally why I love doing this work. You've really got to see it to believe it."

"See what?" I said.

"How would you describe your marriage?" She stared into my eyes.

"Good. Good?" I looked at Janette. "It's good. It's not always perfect. It's—we're trying, just like everyone else. Ha-ha. We."

"It's good," said Janette, patting my leg. "It's the smartest choice he ever made."

"Janette, what is your dream job?" This felt like a trick, but Janette aced it.

"To be a stay-at-home mom," she said. Luckily she could say this and mean it.

"Josh, what can you tell me about the Tourette's?" As I stumbled through a lengthy answer, I could tell I was nervous: I made too many jokes about it. But even though the Tourette's was horrible, I didn't want to scare the intern away. Surely it was better to make light of it than to frighten off the mothers.

After each answer she'd nod as if she'd heard something of great significance. Scratch went the pencil. At the end of the "awesome" meeting we went out to eat.

"How do you think that went?" I asked.

"I liked her boots," said Janette. "Other than that, I have no idea."

An odd book crossed my desk at work: *The Naked Warrior* by Pavel Tsatsouline. Pavel, aka the "Evil Russian," was allegedly a trainer for the Spetsnaz, a Russian special forces unit. The cover showed a contemplative, muscle-bound Greek warrior in bronze. The subtitle trumpeted, *"Master the Secrets of the Super-Strong— Using Bodyweight Exercises Only."*

The Naked Warrior was about dominating your body and achieving maximum strength. It also contained an ad for kettlebells, and the challenge: "Try it if you think you're so tough. You'll wish you were dead."

I was conditioned and strong, but my first session with the kettlebell—essentially a cannonball with a handle—drove me into the ground. Kettlebell marketing has some of the shrillest, shriekiest ad copy you'll ever see, and much of it focuses on "gaining strength without size." Meaning, use kettlebells and you'll never get that grotesque bodybuilder look. Never mind that nobody is capable of That Bodybuilder Look without drugs—these ads were TYPED IN ALL CAPS! They were full of SOVIET STRENGTH-TRAINING SECRETS!! You could now LOSE FAT WITHOUT THE DISHONOR OF DIETING!!!

The kettlebell world is an incestuous realm of back-slapping and defensiveness, but it was free of the grunting, glaring, overly tanned bros filling most of the gyms I'd used. I aligned myself with fitness zealots who were every bit as dogmatic as the priests of any religion. We were the anti-bodybuilders. We were the hard-living comrades. Nobody cared, but so what? "Kettleballs? What are those?"

"Oh, well, all you really need to know is that they're so much better than _____" and here you'd insert dumb-bells, barbells, sandbags, Atlas Stones, and anything else not sold by the kettlebell companies. What was lost in this evange-lizing was the fact that most people don't care about exercise. You could argue with a bodybuilder about your superior method, but someone who just wanted to watch *Mad Men* and eat Cheetos wouldn't care.

I trained obsessively with the kettlebell for the next five months. It didn't help with my tics. Actually, it made them more frequent, louder, and the physical tics had greater force behind them. Kettlebell movements are big and fast, and often done for high numbers of repetitions. Performing three hundred snatches in a session was common. The snatch is a movement where you swing the kettlebell back through the legs, then propel it over-head by snapping your hips forward and guiding the bell to a locked-out position overhead. I'd never panted like this or trained this hard. When my breathing got erratic, my tics worsened and persisted with a duration determined by how hard I trained. I knew it made Misty miserable because it was killing me.

These workouts hurt worse than any Tourette's symptoms and made me feel like a very sassy comrade. And I was proving to all those "wish you were dead" guys that I could WORK OUT IN ALL CAPS!!!

Also, kettlebells were portable. I let my gym membership expire and trained at home. When I needed advice, I'd buy another of Pavel's books, watch someone on YouTube, or jump into Dragon Door's online forum, where it felt like every single person who used kettlebells was. Many of the posts were either people telling one another, "Good job, comrade!" or mocking other training systems. There were lots of questions like:

"I'm doing Pavel's Enter the Kettlebell program. Can I substitute . . . ?" And then they'd ask whether they could do push-ups instead of kettlebell presses, or something like that. And then everyone in this crowd of user names would jump in and say, "Comrade! The party is always right!* Yes, you can substitute, but then it would no longer be the program!" Or some outlander would say, "Kettlebells are for pussies, lift some real weights."

But even in this largely anonymous group of cyber-comrades, there were some standout personalities. I quickly got bored with most of them, but I read every post by a guy named "Unbreakable" Adam T. Glass. It seemed important to him to always have that T. in his name, because he never left it out when referring to himself.

Adam usually logged in to post videos of his latest strength feat, offer advice to anyone asking for it, and excoriate anyone who claimed magical levels of strength but never offered proof. He was, in his words, "brusque as fuck" with people whom he felt were wasting his time and asking questions just for attention.

I started following his blog, "Walk the Road Less Travelled," despite the fact that he had spelled "Travelled" with two

---

* In 2012, citing "differences of vision" with Dragon Door's CEO, Pavel abruptly left the Russian Kettlebell Challenge. From the resulting online hysteria, you'd have thought this was an event akin to Martin Luther nailing his ninety-five theses to the door of that church. The great schism of our time!

ls. I learned that he was a tech sergeant in the air force, stationed in Minot, North Dakota.

He said things like, "If a bully approaches you, do not rob him with words. Do not bow to the rude and insane. Reward him with the face he deserves."

And, "No, I don't hunt, but if I did, I'd hunt mountain lions with a pistol. I won't hunt anything that can't hunt me."

And, "If you're claiming to be a fat-loss expert, don't point at me with a finger that's dripping with cake batter."

And, "If your boot camp didn't involve combatives training, you might consider taking it off your gym's promotional material. Exercise does not give you PTSD. Perhaps some respect is in order?"

And, "I'm a real fucking handful if you fuck with me. Ponder that before continuing this line of questions."

He was into some weird strength stuff he referred to as "old-time strongman." Think of the vaudeville guy in a leopard-skin suit, but substitute a massive guy in karate pants and a T-shirt with a shaved head and an eternal scowl. Adam bent wrenches with his hands. He bent railroad spikes. He pulled chains apart. He could lift four hundred pounds with one finger. He tore phone books in half. He could take a deck of playing cards and tear them into four pieces, sometimes without even opening the box first. He bent horseshoes into the shape of hearts. He could take kettlebells that most people couldn't even press, turn them upside down, and press them like that. He had a heavy, stupid sledgehammer with spikes on the end that he called "Big Danger." He would hold the hammer at arm's length, then let the spikes drift back toward his face, supporting it with his wrist strength. He was also an expert in hand-to-hand combat and marksmanship.

The feats of strength were strange, but they looked fun, minus the spiked hammer. The problem was, seeing the finished feat of strength gave few clues about how to work up to it.

If you see someone bench five hundred pounds, you know that he got there with a lot of benching. But if you see someone roll up a frying pan like a tortilla, all you can do is try to mimic the feat itself. When that didn't work, I didn't know how to start developing that kind of strength, because I had no idea what kind of strength it really was. Wrists? Hands? Fingers? Pain tolerance?

After I'd read all of Adam's forum posts, I reached out, very, very tentatively with a private forum message that was the equivalent of "Gee, mister, you're super cool, can I ask you some questions about how to get big and stwong like you?"

He replied by saying, "Yes, do this, this, and this, and don't ask again until you can show me that you actually did what I said."

And so I started doing this, this, and this, and working on my hand and wrist strength. It would be a while before we'd interact again.

"So today I'm just going to ask you some questions, kind of like the interview when you and Janette were both here, okay?" The intern looked serious.

"Okay," I said.

Janette was right: The intern's boots were impressive. Black, shiny, almost knee-length, with a heel of such slight diameter that it could have punctured concrete.

First, she asked me the identical questions that she had asked the two of us. Then it changed.

"How do you and Janette resolve arguments?"

"Well, we don't argue a lot," I said. "But sometimes I think that might be part of the problem." I heard myself thinking aloud but couldn't seize my attention. "What I mean is, I don't love any sort of conflict, but Janette absolutely hates it. She's more like my mom. She'd rather lose an argument than argue, if only to make it stop. So I wonder if sometimes I get my own way without realizing that we've actually been having an argument and she's just shut it down early . . . but again, we don't argue much. We're at a good enough place that we can actually have discussions like this without hurting each other's feelings. That's taken some work and we're proud of it."

"Mmm-hmm." She wrote something. "What do you guys do for fun?"

"I love to write. And read, of course. I've been working at the library for about a year now, so yeah, I love to read. And I like to lift weights, but I don't really work out. I train."

If she cared about the difference, she didn't ask for clarification. "What are you reading?"

Oh no! I tested various truths in my head. This was my favorite question, but it tended to prompt only one follow-up: What's that book about?

I'm reading Blood Meridian *by Cormac McCarthy. It's about this band of scalp hunters and there's this giant hairless albino named the judge. He might be Satan. Or War. It's hard to tell, but he and his gang just go out and slaughter everyone. And there's this great scene where they make their own gunpowder out of bat guano and urine, and then they kill all of these Apaches who thought they didn't have any ammunition, and—*

Wait, can I start again? *Actually, heh-heh, I'm reading* The Day of the Locust. *It's about Hollywood, sort of. West wrote the bleakest stuff. He said, "Not only is there no one to root for in my work, there aren't any rooters." This girl writes this letter to an advice columnist about how everyone makes fun of her for not having a nose and it's really funny, but—*

Okay, I can do better. *I'm rereading* Choke *by Chuck Palahniuk. It's about this sex addict who goes to sex addiction support groups to meet women. By the end he has started to think he's the second coming of Christ, but then his friend, a compulsive mas-*

turbator who has to keep stacking all these rocks up so that he can keep his mind off his—well, it turns out that he's not actually Jesus, but—

There was only one way out: "Stephen King."

"Oh? Which one?" Damnation! One hundred out of one hundred Mormon moms hate Stephen King.

"*Cell.*" I shut up. I waited.

"What's it about?"

"Well, it's kind of silly, not his best, but you've got to understand how long I've been reading his books. But if you read Stephen King looking for realism you're probably just—well, it's about this event called The Pulse, and when The Pulse happens, everyone who's on a cell phone at that moment turns into a crazy zombie. There's a great opening—maybe the most frantic forty pages King has done—and right up there with the opening of the final *Dark Tower* book for sheer craziness and pace. Or even *It*, which is the book about the clown that kills all the kids. So this guy in the city is just walking around and suddenly everyone around him starts attacking one another. This woman attacks a dog! And he starts hearing cars crashing and then a plane crashes somewhere else in the city. Then of course he has to meet up with a few other people and they get the group together, which is something King always does really well. And later there's some bad guy called the Raggedy Man who might be killing people in a stadium but I'm not sure what to make of him yet. But the beginning, it's just—" I stopped.

I don't remember the rest of my interview. My love affair with Stephen King had potentially undone me again.

"How did it go?" Janette asked.

"Great!" I said. I did think it went well, other than the King fan letter I'd improvised. I'd been honest. I thought I'd been charming. I'd sold our strong points without shying away from the challenges we'd faced.

"Okay, so the director of LDS Family Services just called and they want to meet with us next week! I guess our interviews went okay!" Janette said.

"Oh, that's great!" The paperwork was done. The home visit had gone well. Our interviews and classes were over. We had apparently prayed enough. We would be "in the system," meaning that our profile would be available for pregnant mothers to pore over before bestowing their precious gift on us.

Now we'd wait. Who knew how long? But waiting would be easier than selling ourselves. Waiting isn't humiliating.

LDS Family Services felt different on the day of our meeting. Shiny and new and full of hope. The receptionist smiled, asked us to have a seat, and eventually ushered us down a hallway. At the end of that hall I shook hands with a plump, middle-aged man in a white shirt and dark tie. The director. I smiled my most winning smile at him. It seemed like he flinched, but that was surely my imagination.

"So you'll finally be graduating next week?" he asked.

"Yes! I'm so excited! It's taken ten years but it's finally done!" It was true! A decade of pecking at classes had gotten me my relatively useless English degree, but I'd finished what I'd started.

"Yes," the director said. He ushered us into an office. An unfamiliar woman with white hair and a fat Cosby sweater—despite it being June—sat inside. She rose, shook our hands, and we sat.

The director cleared his throat and took out a familiar-sized piece of paper. "I'm sorry," he said, "but at this time we cannot endorse you as candidates for adoption. We will of course refund the thousand dollars that you paid at the beginning of the process." The check stretched toward me.

Janette issued a harsh bark of a sob.

"What are you talking about?" I said.

He shifted in his chair. "There were some red flags in your conversations. Your interviews with our staff."

Stephen King, you mean. "You mean the intern that we each spent thirty minutes with?" I said.

"Yes, that's correct."

I tried to unclench my fists. I couldn't. I actually couldn't. Shaun and Maryanne had told us that in the six months before their adoption, they'd had two visits per month with various workers. More or less constant contact. I have no idea if that was true, but that's what they told us. Beyond our joint interviews, our solo interviews, and the time when someone visited our apartment to make sure that it wasn't an S and M dungeon, nobody had visited us. Maybe we should have reached out, but we'd had the impression that the process couldn't be forced. That *they* initiated the proceedings and we waited at their pleasure.

I gestured at Janette, who was shaking her head and examining the ceiling. I wondered if anyone had ever grabbed a worker in this nice little office and dashed his brains all over the walls. Things were happening fast, but not so fast that I couldn't feel *afraid* of how intense the emotions were. "Can't you give us an example of these red flags?"

"I think . . . that if you're both honest with yourselves . . . you'll admit that you have some work to do. Before we can consider you suitable candidates."

"But we did everything right! I finished school! I'm working! I've never gotten this much done! I'm starting grad school next week!"

"Yes, about that," he said. "Do you really think that's fair? After all the time Janette has spent supporting you. Now you're going to do *more* school?"

"That isn't any of your business," said Janette. She was pointing at him! She sounded pissed. I loved it. Maybe she'd be the one to murder them. They were, after all, standing between her and her child.

"That's right," I said. "And we've explained my health to you. If I could've done it quicker, I would have."

"Josh, you can't have it both ways," he said. "You don't get to joke constantly about Tourette's—as indicated by our assessments—*and* claim that it is the source of all your troubles." He leaned in front of me and placed the check in Janette's lap. "I understand that you handle the finances," he said, "so I'll give this to you." It was as if he'd planned on being as emasculating as possible.

"Can't you . . . can't you at *least* tell us something we could do better?" I asked. I was close to tears. The anger was receding.

"We just don't feel that you're right. Not right now. And if you're both honest with yourselves, we think—"

We don't feel. There it was again. That word. "Feel." There was subtext here, but given the pristine and pure location, it was pretty much all just text. *We've prayed about this and received confirmation that meth heads and your insurance-less, lying friends who we gave a baby to, and all the other broken, reckless, irresponsible people who don't even always want to have kids but get pregnant anyway—they're all more deserving of this than you.* It said that if we had a problem with their decision, we had a problem with God. They worked for God. They received inspiration from God. Were we going to argue with God if God said that we weren't fit parents?

I remembered the photo collage we'd made as part of our "sales package." One picture haunted me: Janette, smiling as I tried to hold the camera still. *Does it look like a fake smile?* she'd asked. In the picture she's wearing oven mitts, taking cookies out of the oven, offering a cookie sheet to whoever looks at the picture. *See how many cookies your baby will get to eat!* "I feel stupid," Janette had said. "It feels fake."

We ate the entire sheet of cookies that night.

The hoary vassal in the sweater spoke for the first time. She patted Janette's knee. "Janette, you don't seem comfortable. You haven't said anything and it feels like you're not comfortable talking in front of Josh. We'd love to have you come back and tell your side of the story. Alone."

Janette—Janette, I love you more every time I remember this—took the woman's hand and tossed it aside. "What are you talking about? We're here *together*. I'm not talking because I can't. Stop. Crying. Because you won't explain!" She handed the check to me and we stood. The man offered his hand. I don't know why I shook it, but I did.

"Feel free to try again when your situation is better, Josh," he said.

"Our situation has never *been* better. Get out of my way."

In the parking garage Janette put her arms around my neck. "I'm so sorry," she said. "It's my fault." She was shaking.

"Why would you say that? What could possibly even make you think that?"

"I messed up in my interview. I told them that sometimes our marriage wasn't perfect. I told them that it's been hard sometimes."

"So did I. That's the truth and that's why we said it."

"We should have lied."

"No. Not you. Never you."

I called my mom. She cried. "That is huge news, I'm so sorry," she said. She didn't ask what had gone wrong, or how we (I) had slipped up. She just listened and offered condolences. I didn't tell her about Stephen King.

I called my dad. "WHAT! I'm going to go punch my bishop in his fat face and tear up my temple recommend! Call me back later. I'll—"

"Dad! Calm down." My dad was living in Canada that year after taking a short contract with a mine. I can only guess what his bishop would've thought when he roared into the room and knocked him about, raving about babies and grandchildren.

Janette smiled when I told her. By the next evening we were talking about it rationally. I think. We justified our rage and despair. We mocked them and their office. We imitated the intern. But it was all superficial and obviously so. It wasn't even sour grapes. It just felt like we were at the mercy of a process breakdown. They just hadn't asked us enough questions or spent enough time with us.

It didn't matter. Nothing changed the fact that we couldn't have our own baby. Our last option—a service that provides better lives for unwanted children—had rejected us. We wouldn't be a better option for a child. We would ostensibly make a child's life worse. Or so God thought, maybe.

The day of my graduation was sunny and traffic was hellacious. I rode the bus to the university with Janette, my mom, and my sister Lindsey. After ten years, I was done.

"I knew you could do it," said my mom when we arrived.

I almost said, *It didn't impress them at the adoption agency*, but I stayed cheery. After all, I had a mortarboard on my head. My dad said once that it's impossible to be pessimistic with a breast in your hand. The mortarboard wasn't as good, but it helped.

After a speech by a former mayor that was too long, and after the presentation of some awards that went on for too long, and after the applause that went on for too long, I walked down the steps in a line that was too long.

Someone with gray hair put a diploma in my hand and then I stepped off the stage toward the photographer. Jeff Metcalf, my favorite professor, appeared at my elbow. We'd spent his Young Adult Literature class reading the *Alice* books and *The*

White Boy Shuffle. "Smile, Josh!" he yelled. "This took you ten damn years!"

I broke out of the line and hugged him. Then I elbowed my way back into line and stood before an American flag to have my picture taken.

"Uh . . . ," said the photographer. "Can you maybe kneel?" Apparently my head, far above the madding crowd of fellow graduates, was out of the frame. You can't tell in the picture that now sits on my mom's hearth, but I'm on my knees in the photo.

I found my family. I hugged my mom, took off the red sash I'd bought at the bookstore, and put it around her neck. Then I grabbed it back and said, "Oh, wait, you have to read it."

In black magic marker: *To my parents, who held me up when I couldn't hold on. I wish I knew how to say how much I love you.*

That was in June. During the next year I finished a master's degree in library science through the University of North Texas. We made our peace with the fact that we couldn't have kids and we couldn't adopt.

"We can travel anytime we want," I said.

"We can go to the movies without trying to find a sitter," she said.

"I'll never have to get a vasectomy."

"I'll never lose my figure."

And so on, until July 4. "I'm late," Janette told me that morning. I'd been joking for a year, or trying to joke, that I should write a bestselling book called *What to Expect When You're Expecting a Miscarriage.* But I didn't joke now. We went to a barbecue at her parent's house and, strangely, we didn't talk about it again until that evening when we were deciding whether to go see the fireworks.

"Let's go to Walgreen's instead and get a test," she said. By eleven P.M., we knew that she was pregnant. I laughed. She laughed. We stopped laughing and practiced looking worried. The next day her doctor confirmed what that portentous pink cross on the test had said: Here we went again. Janette was seven weeks along.

"You know," I said, "we went on a roller coaster a couple of weeks ago, so the baby would have been five weeks old at that point. That means if it's still in there, it's tough."

"I don't know about that, but it's not like it's October, so I guess that's something. I only miscarry in October."

"I get it."

"I'm just joking."

"Okay. My turn. Whose kid is it?"

In October we were back in the ultrasound room with Gene Wilder. He got out the gel, the wand, and fired up the monitor as we stared at the screen. "Do you want to know?"

"Josh? Do you want to know?" asked Janette.

"Seriously? You know I want to know, but it's up to you."

"Okay, tell us."

The doctor squinted, moved the wand around, and set the alien gray landscape of the womb a-churning. He'd performed all of the ultrasounds for us except for the one where the heart-beat had stopped. Maybe that was that poor technician's only job: telling people it was over. "Give me a second. Okay, do you see that? Can you tell what you're looking at?"

"No," I said. "It all just looks like . . . wait." There, relaxing as if it hadn't a care in the world, was a tiny body. Now that I'd seen it, I didn't know how I'd missed it. It wasn't a blip or a blob. Not a gray speck or the absence of a heartbeat. It was a tiny body, with a head, two legs, two arms—well, one arm that I could see—and—

"It's a boy," said the doctor.

"Ow!" Janette was pinching the fleshy part of my thumb between her own thumb and forefinger. I yanked my hand away, then gave it back to her. "It's a boy! We've got a boy!" I yelled. We laughed like idiots and she cried and I shook the doctor's hand harder than he liked and then he said, to distract me, "Did you see that?"

"What?"

He tapped the screen. "He moved."

He!

Then I saw it. The little body curled up its legs and turned its head slightly, abruptly. "That was a tic," I said without thinking.

"Josh," Janette said.

I looked at her. "I just . . . he might— We don't know."

"Josh, it's a boy! That's your *son*."

"He looks like a strong one," said the doctor.

I wanted to name him Ajax, but I couldn't tell Janette why. She knew Ajax Hanagarne was badass, but she wouldn't have wanted to hear me say, "Ajax was the only one in the war who didn't need the help of the Greek gods."

This was the weird thing: I was grateful that a pregnancy had finally taken, but I didn't know whom to thank. I think my sporadic church attendance and apathetic attempts at prayer over the last year had more of an effect than I'd realized. Sometimes I felt that this pregnancy had worked because I *hadn't* prayed for help. That didn't make sense, but I couldn't keep it out of my head.

About the labor itself I'll say only this: That is serious business. I'm glad I was there but I don't know how women can handle it. The nurses kept watching me as if I was going to faint or something, but I was fine. I just held Janette's leg up in the air, did what they told me to do, and marveled at how much she was sweating.

And there he was, being placed on Janette's chest.

Max had only been out for about five minutes before I couldn't imagine life without him. Nothing before that moment when the nurse placed that pointy-headed little boy in my arms felt real.

"I'm your dad," I said.

Everything before that moment felt like another person's memories.

"I love you, Max." There was something in my life that I knew I would die and kill for without hesitation. It was empowering and terrifying and humbling.

"Thank you for this," Janette said to me.

Four weeks later we took Max to church for the first time so I could give him a blessing. This involves male friends or family members—at the proud new father's invitation—standing in a circle as the father holds the child and ad libs a map of the child's life. Between me, my dad, a couple of uncles, and my brother, it was a huge circle of massive men.

"Max Lewis Hanagarne," I said, "in the name of Jesus Christ, I hold you in my arms to give you a blessing." I said a bunch of things, but only remember this:

"I bless you with a mind more agile than mine. I bless you with the courage to be whoever you want to be, and to do whatever you want to do, and know you'll have our support. When you need guidance, I bless you with the ability to look to the women in your family, not the men. We love you more than we can say"—now my voice was shaking—"and we're so happy you're here."

I noticed that my dad smiled. He knew I was right. There are good men in my family, but we're more erratic and impulsive and unreliable than the women.

Back home, in my armchair, holding my tiny boy, I realized that I was sitting completely still so that he wouldn't wake up. I knew that I could sit still for hours without twitching just to watch him sleep.

Max was another place of sanctuary. Misty couldn't come near him.

CHAPTER 10

027.8—Libraries and Education
92—Strong Men—United States—Biography
006.7—Blogs
828—George Orwell

Now that I was assistant manager at the Day-Riverside branch of the Salt Lake City Public Library, I'd attend two community council meetings each month. I didn't know what community councils did, but my boss said that I'd love the meetings. He was positively gleeful about it. My only hint of what might lie in store was a rumor: *And the manager didn't set the chairs up right for community council and the Council Chair, a nice little old lady, slapped her good.*

The first meeting I attended was in the art room of a local high school. The chairperson, an elderly, energetic woman, stood and read the agenda. She spoke so enthusiastically that the enormous cross dangling from the chain around her neck disrupted her balance as she emoted. "Now, if we can please have the crime bulletin."

A policeman in uniform stood and introduced himself. He handed out a sheaf of papers that we passed amongst ourselves.

Each district in the city was broken down on a spreadsheet by various crimes committed the previous month.

"Something I know that you've all been concerned about," the officer said, "is that we've finally stopped the old woman who's been selling corn out of her cart."

A cheer from the crowd. His other reports were less interesting but more practical: Carjackings were down, but keep locking your vehicles. Graffiti was up, so call the hotline. And once again, if you saw the old lady selling corn, let him know and he'd assemble a team to vanquish her.

"Okay then," said the chair. "Is there any business from the previous meeting to revisit?" An elderly gentleman in green pants raised his hand, stood, and offered a ten-minute disquisition on event-controlled versus time-controlled traffic lights, and could we please get event-controlled lights because the traffic on North Temple during the morning commute was horrendous, just horrendous.

More people drifted into the room. Most had a story to tell. It was like they'd wandered into an amateur storytelling festival and realized they'd also get a chance to heckle a city council member. "I used to live in Idaho. A one-light town. But that light was *event* controlled, not time controlled! Are you telling me that we can't get *event*-controlled lights out on North Temple Street while I'm going to work? It's taken *way* too long. A one-light town! One light!"

Or: "I knew a man in Springville, Illinois. Jared Ellenberger. He was a fine citizen and never really got his due. I was proud to know him. Have any of you ever heard of Jared?"

"Where would we have heard of him?" asked the chair.

"In Springville."

Or: "I've been hearing that the lights from the soccer field are making it harder for some people in that neighborhood to get to sleep at night. Can't we turn them off earlier? I don't even live in that neighborhood, but I'm getting tired of hearing about it. Thank you."

By the time the chair announced me, several people were dozing off. My manager wanted me to report on the exciting things we were working on at the library. Because there weren't any, I said:

"Can I ask you all a question?" I took their stares as a yes. "One thing I've never seen at the library is all of you. I might have seen your kids, but I never see you. Why is that? What could we do better?"

"It doesn't even feel like a library in there." "The computers are too old." "I'm scared to walk through the parking lot at night." "I saw someone with a gun in the garden."

The chairperson raised her hand. "Are you aware that there is a soccer field behind the library?" I was. And it was too brightly lit, all night long. "That soccer field gets used all the time by people who don't even live in this county."

"Or even this country!" I couldn't tell who said it. "They come over from other areas just to mess up that field. They don't come to clean up their own garbage, that's for sure. But I understand why they don't get it. Why, I saw a kid the other day just pull down his pants and pee right on the ground. That's how they do it in their country, anyways. Right there on the ground."

I sat down.

The next morning I was on desk when a wrinkled hand skittered over my own. "I'm sorry if I rattled you last night," said the chairperson, "but I'm here to talk about something else right now. Those restrooms you've got are absolutely atrocious. I mean there's just a mess *every*where you look."

That was true. We had some messy patrons.

"But I've got a solution for you," she said. "I'm not just some complainer. It's because of the Mexicans. They don't have to clean up after themselves back home, so we can't really blame them for not doing it here. So what I did is, I went and made a big sign and put it in the ladies' room. It says, 'Please clean up after yourselves.'"

"Ma'am, we can't put that sign up just like—"

"Oh, I know, don't worry, I made one in Spanish too." She was gone as soon as she had come, rustling out the door. I went to the ladies' room and knocked. When nobody answered, I went inside.

There was no sign in English or Spanish.

Library school was uninspiring. I spent the first twelve days of it in Denton, Texas. The rest was online.

The professor arrived late to the first class. She looked like she'd spent the entire night rolling downhill in a car, after which someone had pushed her out onto the steps of the school and said, "Now, get in there. You've got a lecture to teach. Braless. In a green crocheted sleeveless top that can only just encompass your fulsome gifts. And keep your energy up."

To stay stoked and regather her wits, she swigged from a one-liter bottle of Dr Pepper while lecturing about how neat databases were. She interrupted herself periodically to eat a Pop-Tart straight from the box.

I didn't sleep well in Denton. My pillow was stiff and it smelled rubbery. I stripped the pillowcase. The blue rubber underneath was stamped with the words "Texas Correctional Institute."

Oh, and I read *Maus* by Art Spiegelman in a Graphic Novels class during my library school studies through the University of North Texas. Besides a great hamburger place I found in Denton, it was the most worthwhile part of that expensive program.

If you don't look up when you enter the Main Library in Salt Lake City, it's easy to miss the enormous hanging sculpture dangling between floors 3 and 2. The many thin black wires hanging from the ceiling form the shape of a large head. This is the sculpture *Psyche*, a creation of two Boston artists: Ralph Helmick and Stu Schechter. "Psyche" is the Greek word for "butterfly"; it literally means "spirit, breath, life, or animating force."

Each wire terminates in a small sculpture: nearly fifteen hundred butterflies and books. Some of the butterflies actually flutter their wings, prompted by a mild electrical current. Many have writing on their wings, in twenty different languages, quoting phrases from the Universal Declaration of Human Rights.

> Article 18: Everyone has the right to freedom of thought, conscience and religion; this right includes freedom to change his religion or belief, and freedom, either alone or in community with others and in public or private, to manifest his religion or belief in teaching, practice, worship and observance.

> Article 19: Everyone has the right to freedom of opinion and expression; this right includes freedom to hold opinions without interference and to seek, receive and impart information and ideas through any media and regardless of frontiers.

> From Article 26: Everyone has the right to education.

> Article 27: Everyone has the right freely to participate in the cultural life of the community, to enjoy the arts and to share in scientific advancement and its benefits.

If your Greek mythology is rusty, here's the least you need

to know about Psyche: She was the Greek goddess of the soul. Eros, at the behest of his lovely but insecure mother, Aphrodite, snuck into Psyche's bedchamber one night, intending to shoot her with one of his amorous arrows. When she woke, she'd fall in love with the first thing she saw: a hideous creature that Aphrodite would place in her room. But Eros accidentally scratched himself with the arrow and fell in love with her instead.

Eros had entered Psyche's room with a vengeful mission, but exited with a soul. An appropriate starting point when walking through these doors.

The Main Library owns over one million items. At any time half of those are on the shelves, and half are checked out. If patrons returned every item at once, we'd be in trouble. But that won't happen: The Main Library circulated over four million items in 2011—books, CDs, DVDs, VHS tapes, and art prints.

One million is a number so big I can't visualize it. And I know what five hundred thousand items looks like, because that's how many are here with me at work. Among the books, movies, and CDs, let's imagine that every item takes up, on average, half an inch of space on the shelves. The Empire State Building is 1,250 feet tall. That's only thirty thousand items from the library stacked on top of each other. That means that if you stacked everything this library owns, you'd have a stack the height of approximately thirty-three Empire State Buildings.

I love to tell kids that everything in the library is theirs. "We just keep it here for you." One million items that you can have for free! A collection that represents an answer to just about any question we could ask. A bottomless source of stories and entertainments and scholarly works and works of art. Escapist, fun trash and the pinnacles of the high literary style. *Beavis and Butt-Head* DVDs and Tchaikovsky's entire oeuvre within ten feet of each other. Every Pulitzer Prize–winning book and National Book Award winner. Picture books for children. An enormous ESL collection for learning English as a second language. Art prints you can borrow and put on your wall for a month. A special-collections area of rare books. Full runs of ephemera from *The New York Times* to the original Black Panther newsletters.

If I could bring my bed, expand the fitness room, and kick everyone out, I wouldn't need to pursue Heaven in the next world. I'd be there. But since the circulation statistics keep rising, our patrons are probably here to stay.

Not everyone who visits borrows something. We try to hook them with programs and classes instead. In July 2011, the six Salt Lake City libraries put on 138 programs. In June, it was 162. Three hundred programs in two months. Our publicity department says the library system has approximately twenty-two hundred programs a year, from tango lessons to computer mouse usage to a travel lecture by Rick Steves or a program about Tourette Syndrome (I'll give you one guess who hosted it). The staff of three hundred creates these programs with the community in mind. What do they want? What do they need? What would they want to learn? What would they enjoy that they may never have heard of? What would just be fun?

And once you're here, if you start asking questions, you'll probably find a librarian you'll bond with. The employees are too smart, strange, and interesting to resist.

Those four million circulations represent people taking action. Four million acts. Four million times that someone got something from the library. Even if the circulation simply means that someone requested something on her computer, came in and picked it up, then left right away, she still came. She still used the service. She still took a chance on getting distracted by something else in the building.

The four million small acts lead to members of the community gathering in the same place. People who might never lay eyes on one another elsewhere. In this digital era when human contact sometimes feels quaint to me, this is significant. If libraries themselves become quaint because they house physical objects and require personal interaction at times, so be it. For that reason, I believe physical libraries always need to exist in some form.

Recently a man approached the desk. He dragged a dolly behind him, his possessions fixed to it with bungee cords. His gray beard was a mad tangle. He reminded me of one of the ancient, shambling seers prognosticating on so many pages of Cormac McCarthy's novels. He wore a look that I didn't recognize as wonder until he said, "I never could have imagined a place like this in Nicaragua. I've been traveling for a long time, to this country. I hope you know what you have. In my towns, we had nothing like this. And if we did, we had to pay for any information. And just because we were willing to pay for it didn't mean there was anything there worth reading. It just wasn't allowed. It took me a long time. It was worth it."

I shook his hand. "That'll certainly be the best thing I'll hear today."

He smiled. "I hope you know what you have here. It's a miracle."

In *A Prayer for Owen Meany*, the hapless, doubt-plagued, stuttering Pastor Merrill tells the narrator, John Wheelwright, "But miracles don't c-c-c-cause belief—real miracles don't m-m-m-make faith out of thin air; you have to already have faith in order to believe in real miracles." The man from Nicaragua was right. I had faith in the library long before he walked in and told me what I already knew: A library is a miracle. A place where you can learn just about anything, for free. A place where your mind can come alive.

In George Orwell's essay "A Hanging," he describes his experience as an imperial policeman in Burma, walking a prisoner to his execution. As they approach the gallows, the prisoner, a small brown Hindu, sidesteps to avoid a puddle.

> When I saw the prisoner step aside to avoid the puddle, I saw the mystery, the unspeakable wrongness, of cutting a life short when it is in full tide.

This was a man, like him. A man of tissue, organs, bones, muscle and, one would hope, a man who had dreams of something better for himself. Then comes the line I can't forget:

> He and we were a party of men walking together, seeing, hearing, feeling, understanding the same world; and in two minutes, with a sudden snap, one of us would be gone—*one mind less, one world less.*

For Orwell, the loss of a life was the loss of a mind was the loss of a world, and the world we inhabit is poorer for each loss, for the contributions that mind could have made.

As a librarian, saving lives and worlds isn't in my purview, although if I could put those on my résumé with a straight face, I would. Saving minds, however . . . perhaps it's not as farfetched. A mind can be lost without its owner's death. A mind that no longer questions only fulfills the rudimentary aspects of its function. A mind without wonder is a mere engine, a walking parasympathetic nervous system, seeing without observing, reacting without thinking, a forgotten ghost in a passive machine.

The mind that asks and experiments and evaluates will die one day, but will provide a richer life for its owner. The mind that does nothing but rest inside the brain doesn't sidestep the puddle. It's sitting in it.

I inhabit my own world. You inhabit yours. We still share space on earth and so, in some small fashion, have the potential to alter one another. To better one another's lives. At its loftiest, a library's goal is to keep as many minds as possible in the game, past and present, playful and in play.

But the road to that happy thought is blighted with ruts and twists. Most reality is harsh; it's easy to lose sight of the Big Picture nobility of libraries in light of the small picture.

I loved my job from the beginning, although any romantic notions of being a purveyor of knowledge were soon interred beneath the duties of community council meetings, monitoring of the mentally ill, surrogate parenting, gang and drug activity tracking, and the myriad other realities of being a librarian (at least in this library) today.

The surrogate parenting scares me. When I was managing the Day-Riverside branch I had several parents who worked two jobs ask if they could leave their kids there for "seven or eight hours." These were generally eight-year-old kids or older but too young to be dropped off during a work shift. And sometimes these poor kids had toddler siblings with them.

"I'd prefer you didn't," I'd tell the parents. "This isn't a safe place."

"What! What do you mean?"

"I mean it's for the public, and that means everyone. We're not cops or babysitters and sometimes there are going to be people in here that you might not want your kids hanging out with. But it's up to you. I'm not telling you what to do. I just want to make sure you know how it is. We can't watch your kids."

Reactions vary. "But I have to work, what am I supposed to do?" "Oh, you just don't want to help us." "I'm not *asking* you to babysit, just help them find some books today while they're here . . ." (For an entire day?) If the parents insist, there's nothing we can do, unless the child's behavior becomes an issue, which can happen when the poor kid doesn't eat anything for seven or eight hours.

As far as gangs, it's been hard for me to know what we should be concerned about. I don't know who's in a gang and who's not. Between patrons whose equanimity deserts them when it's time to talk about race and talkative security guards who love inserting themselves into tales of heroism, it's easy to think that I work in a city-funded version of Don Pendleton's action-packed Executioner novels. From my extensive experience watching *The Wire*, I suspect that the real gangsters are probably out on corners somewhere, or asleep while I'm working . . . not in the library watering their Farmville crops.

But then a patron will say, "There's a guy in a red bandanna over there and he said he's going to stab me—oh please where can I hide?" and then a guy in a red bandanna appears and stalks around looking angry, and I'm wondering if I should err on the side of caution or outright paranoia. (That time, I did what we always do: called security. I don't know what else happened). We aren't trained to deal with those situations; the guards are. Unfortunately, with the five floors, hordes of patrons, and two security guards, they're harried and hectored and overworked. I'm sure they're also underpaid. They should make twice what librarians make. I recently talked to a guard who was bitten on the thigh by a patron we all thought was very sweet. This was a week after that same guard had asked a man to stop talking so loudly on a pay phone. The guy threw scalding coffee at his crotch. It took both officers to get him into cuffs. His pockets were full of drugs. And so on. Most of the libraries' training programs involve things like "smiling warmly," "going the extra mile," "being approachable," and "oh no, call the guards!" There's nothing about knowing where to get an AIDS test after a soft-spoken patron bites your thigh so hard that your fluids mingle.

We deal with these situations—which are rare, but too disturbing to forget—by wrapping ourselves in the mantle of the "public" part of "public library." It's for everyone. And all of their multiple personalities. There's nothing funny about mental illness but being scared by disturbing behavior doesn't make me insensitive, either. Until a behavior escalates to the abusive or biting or scalding-coffee level, we have little actionable information in terms of getting people that scare us out of the building. The guy who has now called me a "tall bigot" or "fucking Jew" twice in the last two years still comes in every day and asks me to find books for him.

I don't know if people realize that it's nearly impossible for librarians to avoid looking at the books they check out. I was in a training session once where the instructor encouraged me to unfocus my eyes when dealing with patron's items.

If I started unfocusing my eyes to avoid everything I shouldn't see here, I'd never get a clear look at anything.

Part of my job is watching the computers, all twenty of them within thirty feet of me. I make the rounds, glancing at every screen to see if anyone is viewing something illegal. It's against the law to view pornography—we're not allowed to call it porn, since the Supreme Court can't define it—in the presence of children, so you can't be looking at gyrating nude people on the public computers. We all still call it porn. Nobody's going to accuse someone of "viewing objectionable material" and expect to be taken seriously. This conversation is not fun. Picture yourself at your desk. A patron approaches and says, "I'm sorry, but you need to see what that guy is looking at." So you look. Sure enough, there he is—I've never had to talk to a woman about her porn in the library—leaning toward his monitor. Maybe his hands are playing nice. But maybe you can't see where they are. All you know is that your mission is to startle him out of his sexual reverie and hope that when he looks up at you with eyes that haven't blinked in far too long, his pants will be buttoned. Then you have to get close enough to whisper—for his privacy—*There's been a complaint about what you're looking at. No, I'm sorry, I'm not going to weigh in on how attractive she is. You need to get her off your screen.* This is what you say even if your gut wants you to whisper, "Seriously, man, you're in a library—put your cock away."

The first time I catch him, it's a warning. He can stay on the computer and do whatever he wants, unless he was looking at something illegal like child pornography. In that case we call the police.

As strange as the porn discussion is, it's equally surreal to wake someone up who fell asleep in the middle of an *Andy Griffith* episode on YouTube and is snoring in the midst of twenty other people.

How do we deal with *that* situation? Oh, we tip their chairs backward and blame it on someone else as they topple to the floor.

Just kidding. We tap on their table or chair and say, "You're not allowed to sleep in here. Please stay awake." But I won't stop dreaming about tipped chairs and smelling salts. But these are usually adult problems.

I'd estimate that 80 percent of the library patrons at my branch were under sixteen years old. Of those, the majority was Hispanic, but there were several ethnicities: Vietnamese, Polynesian, Somali, Sudanese. This also makes it so hard to figure out the gang situations. There *are* gangs. But it's not always obvious, like, "Oh, they have blue clothes and the others have red clothes, so they're enemies." And it's not as simple as white skin versus black, or brown versus black, or whatever. I had a man run up and throw a wallet into my lap because he claimed, "That Arab bastard over there is trying to steal someone's wallet, but I grabbed it from him!" The "Arab" was a refugee from Ethiopia who was there to attend a job-search class with the International Rescue Committee. He was done using the computer and had picked up his own wallet, which he had set on the desk while he worked.

One day I spoke at a local elementary school. I was there to get those kids into the library. Three times I stood in a circle of fifty kids and asked them what their favorite part of the library was. Computers and comics, every time. When I gave my standard "books aren't boring, you've just been reading boring books" line, many rolled their eyes.

"Do you guys have a favorite TV show? We've got DVDs of TV too."

Jersey Shore was the clear favorite.

"How many of you speak a language other than English?" I said. Nearly everyone raised a hand. "How many of you speak Spanish?" Lots of hands. "How many of you speak Vietnamese?" Lots of hands. "What other languages do you all speak?" The only kids who didn't answer spoke no English, and even they perked up when I mentioned *Jersey Shore*.

Several times, a white woman asked me to walk her to her car because she was scared of the brown kids outside, harmless thirteen- and fourteen-year-olds that I knew well. "I always feel like they're about to start fighting," she said. How do we solve this conundrum?

The short answer is: I don't know. But while we may never find specific, actionable solutions, a good library's existence is a potential step forward for a community. If hate and fear have ignorance at their core, maybe the library can curb their effects, if only by offering ideas and neutrality. It's a safe place to explore, to meet with other minds, to touch other centuries, religions, races, and learn what you truly think about the world.

One of the profession's buzzwords is "relevant." Libraries must stay "relevant." I disagree. There's nothing relevant about this place. It's so much more. A community that doesn't think it needs a library isn't a community for whom a library is irrelevant. It's a community that's *ill*. It doesn't know what it needs. Maybe that's the librarians' fault for not proving their worth, or maybe it's a proverbial sign of the times in the Internet age.

Libraries can't be all things to all people. At the Internet Librarian Conference in 2009, I spent three days sitting in rooms of "innovative" librarians and heard only one thing that made any sense to me. Stephen Abram, past president of the Special Library Association, said, "You're making a mistake if you're trying to give people things that they can get somewhere else. We can't innovate through being derivative—that's just trying to be relevant." I remember this when I see librarians deciding whether we need to have teen video game night. Or more public PCs. Or fewer books. A truly bizarre former director once told me, "People no longer want information from libraries. They want . . . transformation." This inane homily would eventually appear on a PowerPoint slide that the entire staff sneered at. The text captioned a slide of a butterfly on a dewy leaf. The next slide was of a woman's glaring eyes as they stabbed out through the slit of a burka. I can't remember the caption for that one. Or the point.

Many librarians—I've done this myself—lament the idea that we might simply be competitors for Netflix or iTunes. I'm past caring about that. I want people walking through the doors. I don't care what their reasons are. That kind of makes me feel like a carnival barker*—that my job might just be to get people in a building—but I still think it's worth it. Once they're here, we'll work on why they return. Once they're here they've entered an institution dedicated to fighting ignorance and providing a space without ideology. Is it too lofty to hope that a library could curb the poison of racism? That it could create a reality usually expressed by treacly expressions like "a sense of community"? Even if someone believes that the library's primary function is as an expensive homeless shelter or as a place to rent free movies, even if they believe it's a waste of taxpayers' money, even if they think that all of the goofy stories I'm telling in this book are the norm . . . well . . . what patrons use the library for doesn't change what it offers. Anyone could enrich

---

* Thanks to the sublime Annoyed Librarian for the analogy: blog.libraryjournal .com/annoyedlibrarian.

their life by spending some time here, if only they were willing to look around.

Nothing rivals this library for its sheer variety of humanity. During one forty-eight-hour period:

I counseled several homeless people who were fighting a bedbug outbreak at their shelter. While being solicitous and keeping my distance, I found some articles about bedbugs and how to recognize their bites.

I watched a man chew on his own ponytail with such boyish exuberance that it gagged him. Then he asked me if we had any tissue paper. Then he wiped his mouth and walked away, presumably to wring out his hair.

I shepherded a dozen kids through their homework assignments. If they're writing papers, homework help usually means helping them find books or other sources, but these kids wanted me to do their problems for them with a calculator on the Internet. I didn't.

The next morning I witnessed the immediate aftermath of a bloody suicide. Someone screamed as I walked past the phone books. More screams followed. I heard something break. From the balcony I saw a broken body, far below. I ran downstairs to see if I could help, exited the wrong door in the basement where she had landed, and nearly tripped over the first dead body I'd ever seen outside of a viewing. I went home haunted by the questions: *Why at the library? How could this have been her best option?*

The next day a blond woman in her late thirties said, "Yes, can you make me a computer reservation?"

"Sure."

"Good, because the computers are picking on me. They know me."

Ah, trapped in a Philip K. Dick novel, huh? "I'm happy to make the reservation," I told her. "Did you have trouble getting on before? Sometimes the PCs make—"

"Whoa! Get your director down here right now." She scowled at me.

"Okay . . . what should I tell her?"

"Young man, I'm not sure if you're aware of how often you use the *m* sound, but it sounds highly sexual to me and I don't come here to be sexually harassed by you."

I was flabbergasted. "By the letter *m*?" It's not like I'd said, "While we're at it, might I massage your mammaries, ma'ammmmm?"

"Or by anyone else, no offense. Actually, you know what? Just make the reservation, but maybe this is a good time to get rid of Computer M over there as well . . ." Her voice dropped to a whisper: "*For the same reason.*"

She fled into the stacks before I could apologize for coming on too strong with such a lurid consonant. The letter *m* came from a hieroglyph used to represent the word "water." Perhaps it was the ancient etymological wetness of it that sent her pulse a-racing.

Librarians are required to be social workers, janitors, baby-sitters, researchers, e-mail-account-setter-uppers, and more. We make ourselves feel better by saying that we provide an "essential service." If we were as essential as the police or fire department, then we wouldn't always be first up for budget cuts. Libraries are essential to people like me, but that's my parents' doing. And in my opinion, we *deserve* to be first up for budget cuts, unless we start putting out fires or arresting criminals.

When I started taking Max to the library, he was too young to want to do anything but jump on the couches. But I'll never forget the first time I took him in and he said, "And I can take any book, Daddy!" He *quivers* when we walk into the library. I was that kid. I'm still that kid at heart. That's a definition of "essential" that works for me.

I want people to agree with Luis Borges, who said, "I have always imagined that Paradise will be a kind of library." Or

Thomas Jefferson, who said, "I cannot live without books." Tom Clancy, a writer who has made millions writing sentences like, "But a man had to hold his woman at a time like this," still wins my heart by making statements like "The only way to do all the things you'd like is to read." In *Something Wicked This Way Comes*, when the kids were investigating the unholy provenance of Dark's carnival, who found the origin story? Charles Halloway, the librarian!

Bill Gates said, "I'd be happy if I could think that the role of the library was sustained and even enhanced in the age of the computer."

And here's Warren Buffett: "If past history was all there was to the game, the richest people would be librarians."

I think I've read every movie review Roger Ebert has ever written. My favorite thing he's ever said is that "doing research on the web is like using a library assembled piecemeal by pack rats and vandalized nightly."

To see the value of a library, ignore the adults. Find an inquisitive child who doesn't have an iPhone yet, take them to the library, and tell them that they can learn anything they want there.

One Saturday when Max was about two, I awoke to see him by my bed. His hair is still blond, like mine used to be. His eyes are deep blue. He's as skinny as Gollum from the *Lord of the Rings* films, has the same wiry strength, but is adorable and has healthier obsessions: puppies and kittens and mud and climbing. He held a calculator to his left ear. "Yeah, Daddy, I'm just calling to let you know that I need a graham cracker."

I nodded.

He cocked his head, listening. "Oh yeah, okay, I'll tell

him." He patted my head. "And then we're supposed to go get some stories at the library."

"Says who? Who called you?"

"Adonis." Adonis is a dog that lives across the street.

At least twice a week I take Max to our neighborhood library. Sometimes he wants books. I give him a basket and let him wander. Sometimes he wants books from the kids' section. Sometimes he seems more interested in dense books on socialism. Sometimes he just wants to put the library's chinchilla in the basket, but he's finally getting that we can't take it out of its cage.

We play a game to teach him words. I point to a book's cover: "What's that?" *It's a horse. An airplane. A shark. That's Snooki. It's a truck. That's a lady crying. I don't know why she's sad, but that book's probably too big for you.* Once when I asked if he was ready to go, Max gestured at his stack of books and said, "No, I have too much work to do." One minute later, he put a book down and did a somersault on the carpet. Then he got back on his chair as if nothing had happened and kept reading, holding the book over his face. I couldn't see his expression, but I knew from his quaking shoulders that he was laughing, wondering what I'd made of his somersault.

My time with him has been the happiest of my life.

Misty has been content to watch him from a distance, but she still jolts me constantly. Max has noticed.

I inhaled, bent, and lifted the heaviest stone in our garden, a three-hundred-pound behemoth with jagged edges. I crushed it to my chest and walked. At the other end of the grass I dropped the stone and tried to catch my breath. I turned to find Max standing next to me, clutching a small stone to his chest. He looked very serious. I don't think I've ever simultaneously been so moved and laughed so hard. How surreal, this little person in my backyard who was learning how to be a person by watching me.* "Okay buddy, set it down," I said between breaths. I stopped laughing when my hand crashed into the side of my head. Misty. It didn't knock me down, but I lost my balance and stumbled. I caught myself with one hand and lowered myself to the ground. Max was still holding the stone. He put it down. Then he put his arms around my neck and squeezed.

"You okay, Daddy?"

"I'm okay," I said. "Thanks."

"What happened?"

"I just fell."

I was chilled. *Will this be his story?*

Shortly after Max's birth, Janette asked me what I wanted for my son. The Hopes and Dreams discussion. I knew what I did not want.

Max has my eyes. Will he inherit the broken teeth?

He has my long fingers and toes. Will the joints hold?

He has his entire life ahead. Will he experience his own share of squandered years? His narrow torso is barely wider than my hand. Will a hernia break it?

He chatters and sings constantly. Will he ever submit to voicelessness so he can be out in public?

During my lunch breaks at the library, I trained desperately in the small fitness room downstairs. I'd pound away at the weights until I was on my knees. As my breath returned, I'd try to figure out where Misty was. If she'd had enough. In the evenings, I trained in our backyard. Because it took enormous effort, I'd put Max in the back of the truck and literally push it

---

* In 2012, I would speak at a camp for kids with Tourette's in Gettysburg, Pennsylvania. You could literally watch the tics jump from kid to kid. Really weird. This is one reason I try to keep my tics from Max: I have a fear that he'll start having tics *just* because he sees me having them, and then suddenly he'll have Tourette's too.

around our cul-de-sac while Janette steered. Anything and everything to keep Misty at bay. I collapsed into bed at night, hoping that I'd exhausted myself enough to banish her.

I continued with my kettlebell obsession, collecting a nice little family of them in our backyard. The largest weighs 106 pounds. The smallest belongs to Max. It weighs two pounds. It could've been the prize in a box of cereal.

In 2009, in a fit of madness, I sold my set of the Oxford Mark Twain to defray the cost of attending the Russian Kettlebell Challenge, aka the RKC, a three-day certification for instructors. It was put on by Dragon Door, the publisher of Pavel Tsatsouline's book *The Naked Warrior*.

Twenty-nine volumes of Mark Twain. My favorite author. More than fourteen thousand pages, not all of it great, but great enough. Each volume contained an introduction by a noted author. Kurt Vonnegut wrote the introduction to *Connecticut Yankee*. That intro alone was almost worth the price of the books. My mom got them for my college graduation present for three hundred dollars on eBay, but I would've paid more. I smiled at those books every time I saw them on my shelves. In many ways I still felt like an incomplete person, but at least I had those books; I was more complete than anyone unlucky enough *not* to have them.

So, yeah, it was madness to sell them. Why did I want to go to the RKC? As I've said, I'm susceptible to both advertising and challenges to my ego, so there was that. But also, I was enjoying the online kettlebell community. I went to the Dragon Door forum every day and wrote and read about training with kettlebells with other people doing the same thing. It was fun to belong. It also gave me a chance to get friendlier with Adam T. Glass, an ever-present and domineering force on the message boards.

I wasn't interested in being a kettlebell instructor, but didn't think the certification would hurt. People often asked if I would train them with kettlebells, but I didn't feel qualified without certification. Before that, training someone would be irresponsible. This was, of course, false—any worthwhile certification will be the *beginning* of your qualifications—but the fitness industry's driven by our convictions that we can't train ourselves. Like most people I know who exercise, I went through a phase where I thought that unless I did exactly what "professionals" said I should be doing, I would exercise myself right into a wheelchair or decapitate myself somehow.

A few months and two thousand dollars later, I was sharing a hardwood basketball court in Minneapolis with martial artists, a Hollywood fight choreographer, personal trainers, high school strength coaches, and more. Some of the brightest strength minds in the world—or so the legend went—were there, including Pavel, the Evil Russian, who had introduced me to kettlebells. The marketing goes like this: In 2001, Pavel swam the ocean with a kettlebell in his mouth, arriving in America to declare war on weakness. He had one goal: to help Americans train with honor, using super-duper secret Russian strength techniques and tools. And quotes:

"Just do it. The party is always right!"

"Power to you, naked warrior!"

"Strength is a skill."

Applied to various concepts: "If you have a hard time remembering this . . . get it tattooed on your arm!"

Everything was done the "Evil Russian way."

This was all shtick. Some of the marketing had to be hyperbole. On the other hand, I'd read many blog posts and articles about how kind and generous and intelligent Pavel was. Those would all prove to be true.

Pavel isn't a large man. About six feet tall, maybe 180 pounds. He has thinning hair and a fierce scowl when he wants it. Nobody says, "I want to be built just like Pavel." But I didn't care. I wanted in.

I ate in the hotel's restaurant on the morning of the certification. Pavel sat nearby, reading a newspaper. Everyone snuck glances at him and worried about how hard the next three days would be. "I actually don't think it'll be that bad," said a big guy who talked nonstop about being in the Marines.

"Be afraid," said a deep voice. Pavel, despite his mere seventy-two inches, loomed over us. He walked away. We were afraid. We'd paid to be afraid.

A bus took most of the candidates to the gym. I was stupid enough to walk the two miles prior to a ten-hour day of brutal workouts.

Most of the people at the certification were fit. Tank tops must have been on sale somewhere, but I wore a white T-shirt and black sweatpants. We stood in a circle and passed a microphone around as we each introduced ourselves and gave our reasons for attending.

"My name is Josh Hanagarne . . . I'm a librarian in Salt Lake City." There was some laughter, and I laughed too. "I've got Tourette Syndrome, and I've let it cripple me for the last ten years. I'm here to celebrate getting control of my life. Dragon Door's been a huge part of that." My voice shook and everyone clapped. I nearly added, "And I sold my Mark Twain books to get here."

The next three days were among the silliest of my life, but I was too much of a zealot to know it. The RKC certification is like fantasy camp for personal trainers. There's no getting around it: You paid upward of two thousand dollars to learn how to do (and teach) six exercises. You paid to be beaten into the ground with excruciating workouts by enthusiastic instructors who'd forgotten that they're part of an absurd quasi-militaristic fitness academy. On Day One we were told that we would be "bonding with our kettlebells." You took a kettlebell everywhere! To the field. To the lunchroom. To the restroom. Failure to comply resulted in punishment for the entire squad: extra swings or burpees, aka squat thrusts. When it was time to listen, an instructor would scream, "Down!" If someone dropped to their belly with insufficient haste . . . swings or burpees. To teach us to brace or flex our abs, we "comrades" would drop into a plank position (picture a push-up held halfway down) while instructors in khaki pants and black shirts and black shades got to pretend they had evil black hearts while they lightly kicked us in the ribs.

We poured onto the large grass field for our five-minute snatch test. My comrades were consumed by self-doubt. People seemed to think that they'd fail the snatch test, despite their own admissions that they'd trained for months specifically for said test. A refresher: snatching a weight is moving the weight from the ground to an overhead lockout (meaning you lock it out overhead with your arms straightened) without pressing it. Think about grabbing a dumbbell, swinging it back between your legs, then swinging it forward and up your torso until your arm is straight overhead. That's a snatch. I had to do one hundred snatches in five minutes with a fifty-three-pound kettlebell. I passed easily, but was surprised to see several people fail the test, including the loud-mouthed Marine. I couldn't imagine shelling out the money and then coming unprepared. They could send in videos of their passed tests later, but they wouldn't be certified that weekend.

People's hands were shredded into hamburger by one P.M. This was held up as a glorious exhibit of "getting our money's worth." After the instruction portion for each exercise, an instructor led us in a brutal workout. These were unnecessarily difficult and arbitrary. For instance, after learning how to squat, we were ordered into the bottom of a squat by an instructor. "Ten!" he shouted. We had to squat at rock bottom, holding a kettlebell to our chests, until the instructor yelled, "Up!" After the tenth squat we did ten kettlebell swings—swinging the weight between our legs, then popping it out in front by snapping our hips. Then: "Nine!" We started over with nine squats and nine swings, and so on. By the end we were screaming our fool heads off. It hurt! I couldn't decide if I'd gotten any quality practice or not. But as we collapsed on the grass we were delirious with happiness over how much we were "learning."

As we practiced, the instructors stalked about, hands clasped behind their backs, eyes invisible behind their shades. "Do it again! Focus!" My team leader was a police officer. Another was a massage therapist. Some of them had their own gyms or worked as personal trainers, but many of them had other jobs. They were there because . . . well, you'd have to ask them why.

The night before the third day, Adam T. Glass called me. He was, to put it lightly, a disillusioned RKC instructor, well on his way to total apostasy. "Have you figured out that you could have just watched kettlebell videos on YouTube for ten minutes yet?" he said. When I didn't say anything, he said, "That doesn't mean you shouldn't enjoy it. But do it for fun. Don't listen when they say you're going to get strong doing this. It's fun, and it kind of feels like family when you're there, but it's not useful."

I passed the course. After the final workout everyone ran around and screamed and hugged. I was as excited as anyone and it was easy to lose sight of the fact that we had all just paid big money for the privilege of having someone blow a whistle and give us light kicks in the ribs so that we could feel like we were preparing for war. Or that we had *been* to war. Or that we were now martial artists, or ninjas, or black ops specialists. Big dreams. Big nonsense. And yet, I felt as if they'd done me a huge favor, that I owed them some unpayable debt. So I evangelized for them, spreading the good word.

But I kept studying various systems of strength training. I had to. Progress in strength training gave me control over the rest of my life. More progress meant more control, but I couldn't spend much time on Dragon Door's forum without noticing that most comrades weren't making great progress. To have more control, I needed to follow the people who were the strongest, not those who were simply friendly and willing to discuss strength training.

"Yes," said a harsh voice on the phone. There was yelling in the background. Lots of it.

"Hi, Adam," I said. "It's Josh. Josh Hanagarne."

No answer.

"Josh from the librarian blog," I said. "You called me at the RKC."

As enriching as the strength progress was, I couldn't keep track of it; I'd write down a week's worth of training and then lose the notebook. After complaining to a friend, he suggested that I "start a free blogger blog" to record my training. I can't remember why I chose to name the blog World's Strongest Librarian beyond the fact that it made me smile.

"I know," said Adam. "What do you want?"

"Oh, sorry," I said. "I thought we'd agreed to talk tonight."

"We did," he said. "And now we're on the phone. I'm out on maneuvers tonight. I don't have much time. What do you want to talk about?"

"Uh, okay," I said. "I guess we'll just get right to it?"

He said nothing. Then, to someone in the background: "Hey, asshole! If I have to tell you one more time to—hold on, buddy," he said to me. Incomprehensible yelling in the background.

"Okay, it's sorted," he said. "Go on."

"What happened?" I said. "Is everything okay?"

"Someone owed me an apology," he said.

"Okay," I said. "I'll just get to it."

"Yes, so you said."

Good grief, he was weird. "Okay, so I'll—well, look, with the Tourette's, I just, it's better if I'm stronger, so I'm saying that—well, I'd like to be able to do some of the strength stuff. Perform. I don't just want to be strong. I want to be as strong as I can possibly be."

Silence.

"You know, like the stuff you do," I said.

"What are you proposing?"

Before I could backtrack, I said, "Could I come up to Minot and train with you for a week? Have you show me some stuff?"

I flinched away from the phone, waiting for a bullet to fly through and strike me dead.

"Yes," he said. "That would be useful for you. I have some vacation coming up. Book your tickets and I'll take the time off in September. I've got to go. And by the way, good job on your blog. Those Tourette's people need you. I have some ideas. Your life can change."

"Thanks! I—wow, thanks! I—man, you're not going to be sorry. I'll work hard, I promise. I'm not one of those guys who asks just so they—"

I'm not sure when he hung up, but he wasn't there when I finished thanking him.

At this point the blog was about five months old. I found that I couldn't *just* write my training numbers without putting some commentary in. Soon I was finding reasons to mention H. P. Lovecraft after recording my training. I started writing book reviews and enjoying the resulting conversations with readers. Soon I was writing about anything that interested me because I knew that I'd be able to discuss it with people who were actually reading what I wrote. And that was really the key to it all: the social aspect.

Misty no longer kept me home from work. I met my obligations, but didn't have the energy for much socializing after a day of trying to stifle the tics. Being in public was still hard, whether it was on the reference desk or at a friend's dinner table. The people I was "meeting" online through my blog were becoming my friends. They wanted to discuss ideas and books and questions. I chatted with them way more often than with pals I'd grown up with. I looked forward to the online group every day; I wasn't lonely.

Eventually I started writing about Tourette's. That's when the comments and e-mails really increased. There were apparently a lot of people out there with Tourette's, or with Tourette's in their families.

We don't know what to do.

We don't know how to help our son or daughter.

How worried should we be?

How did your parents handle you? How did they help you?

I'm afraid my boy will kill himself.

My daughter keeps running into the restroom to scratch herself. Please help.

Nobody understands me.

I hate myself.

I'm smart and funny but I feel like everyone gets to enjoy my good qualities except me.

It's all a show. I'm a lie.

Do you ever feel like you're a waste of space?

I am going to hook my daughter up with you. Thanks for sharing.

I am excited to learn from you. What can you teach me?

I want to die.

Josh, life is easier when you don't care if people look at you weird. I believe that, even though I can't make it feel real. This sucks.

I had no answers. My responses usually included something trite like "Hang in there. Let me know if you'd like to talk."

I didn't even know where to look or what questions to ask. My brain didn't know what to think.

But someone else's brain did. Someone whose brain *couldn't* think like anyone else's. That brain was being carted around inside of a damaged skull on an air force base in Minot, North Dakota.

CHAPTER 11

612.82—Neuroplasticity
306—Peace—Psychological Aspects
616—Pain

"Sir, can I ask you something?"

It's closing time. Hopefully this won't take long. "Of course. Please, call me Josh."

The man drags a massive green duffel bag. His beard is chest length, red and gray. "Thank you," he says. "I know how this looks. I'm homeless. I won't deny it." His speech is slurred. Alcohol on his breath. But he's nice and I hope he'll ask for something that I can help with. "I've got to ask you . . . are you looking for a training partner? I mean, I can tell you work out. I was in a wreck a couple of years ago and I've got terrible pain. I'm losing my strength. Hurts to move. I could work out with you two or three times a week, as long as it could be at your house. I don't have the money for a membership." Then he stumbled forward and hugged me. Then he wouldn't let go. I patted his back. He patted my back.

"I usually train alone," I say. "And I live in West Valley. But we can talk whenever you want. Just come see me and I'll always give you as long as I can."

We close at six o'clock. I am still trying to get out of the hug at six oh five.

I waited on the curb outside the Bismarck airport, shifting my weight from foot to foot. Despite our many phone conversations and online interactions, I didn't know Adam. And our conversations were so abrupt and odd that I was nervous.

A Chrysler Magnum pulled up. A massive forearm beckoned from within. I stowed my bag in the now-open trunk and hurried into the passenger seat.

Adam didn't look at me. Or at least, he didn't turn his head. His eyes were hidden behind mirrored aviator sunglasses.

"Hi," I said.

"Hi."

We left Bismarck. He didn't say anything else.

I'm not used to feeling small around people, but Adam had a presence that felt *heavy*. Like if you knew how to look, you'd see space bending around him. He's not tall compared to me, maybe six-two, but he was thick and broad. His arms stretched out a blue T-shirt that would have billowed off me like a windsock. His hair was clipped short. He was pale. I surreptitiously studied his tattoos. Either flames or thorny vines crept out of his left sleeve.

I'd never paid attention to anyone's forearms before. Probably because most people's forearms just look like the typical real estate between the elbow and hand, just holding things together. Adam's forearms were about *all* I could see. They were as big as my biceps.

If you hired a master sculptor to create a statue of the most intense face imaginable, when the dust settled, you'd be looking at Adam. When he stares through a windshield, you think it's going to shatter. I held him responsible for every pothole on the road.

I've seen a lot of serial killer movies where the initially friendly killer offers the hapless victim a ride. After ten or fifteen silent minutes, when we reached the grassy plains, the city behind us, I felt like we were at the point where the victim would say, "Hey, you just passed my turn." But he'd get no response and then he'd get massacred with a claw hammer.

At last Adam spoke. "There are more nuclear weapons under these innocent little acres than just about anywhere else in the world," he said. "What do you think when you think about North Dakota?"

"I don't really think about it," I said.

"Exactly," he said. A small airplane zipped by and dwindled ahead of us. "You know where that plane's going?"

"Back to the base?" I said. "Isn't your base out past Minot?"

"Afghanistan," he said. "With a load of bombs. He'll be back later tomorrow. They're fast."

There was nothing left of the plane but the vapor trail.

"So tell me about your Tourette's," he said.

As I recapped my life with Misty, he interrupted: "No, we'll fix this. You're not seeing it. Let me guess, your doctors are all about managing it, right? I suppose nobody's ever suggested that you could reverse it?"

"No."

"We will discuss it," he said, before lapsing into another lengthy silence.

We eventually pulled into the driveway of a small gray house. The house next door was bright pink. "Ha! Too bad you don't live in the pink one!" I said.

"Why is that too bad?" he asked.

"No reason," I said.

He stared at me. "I'm going to change, we'll grab Casey, and then we'll go eat," he said.

Dinner with Adam and Casey, his tiny blond wife, was a

nightmare. Every time I touched my fork my hand got squir-relly with tics. I'd stick the fork into my food and then have to psyche myself up for the brief trip up to my mouth as my fist gripped the fork tighter and tighter until my whole forearm shook and the fork tried to dart around. When the fork was two inches from my mouth, I'd have to either rush it into my mouth, trusting that it wouldn't accelerate too much, smashing into my mouth or cheek, or I'd set it down and regroup for another bite.

"This is the weirdest thing I've ever seen," Adam said. "And I've seen some shit." He stared without incredulity or pity. He didn't grimace when I told him about the worst of it. I wouldn't even have thought he was curious about it except for his questions.

"What makes it worse?"

"What makes it better?"

"What do you think causes it?"

"What do doctors think causes it?"

"How the fuck have you not gone insane?"

After a couple of drinks, Casey started bragging about how good she was with a shotgun—she'd also served in the air force. As they debated who was more lethal with a scattergun, I was suddenly able to eat without any trouble.

"Hey!" said Adam, after seeing me take an uneventful bite. "What just happened? What was different about that time?"

"You weren't looking at me."

He stared. "I see. Very interesting." Then he stared some more.

Hey, you just passed my turn . . .

Maybe this had been a mistake.

Back at his house, Adam showed me to my room. "I tried to put you in the room with the most books, but Casey said you couldn't sleep down in the basement, so this is the room with the second most books," he said. The bookshelf also held scrapbooks with newspaper articles about Adam's strongman performances.

"Glass bends steel," read one headline. Adam showed me his military ribbons and awards, telling me what each stood for.

Two fat brown-and-white bulldogs waddled in, then flopped onto their bellies.

"This is Brutus and Julie," Adam said. He got down on the floor and stared at each of them in turn. He tickled the dogs behind their ears and growled playfully. "What did you goofs do today?" It was like he forgot I was in the room. He might have stayed there all night if I hadn't whooped and startled him.

There were pictures of the dogs everywhere, far more than of Adam or Casey.

"I'll show you something," he said, leaving the room. I sat for a few moments before realizing I was supposed to follow him. In the kitchen, he stood at attention next to a counter on which bottles of supplements stood in a row. Fish oil. Calcium. Flaxseed.

"Okay, here's what I would like you to do," he said. "Touch your toes."

Was this a trick? If I started leaning forward, would he club me over the head?

"Lean forward," he said, "but don't stretch. Just let your arms drop and hinge at the waist. Stop just *before* you start to feel the stretch. Stop at the point when going farther would mean you were stretching."

I did it. My fingertips dangled just below my kneecaps. "Like this?"

"Now tap your shins with your fingers. Just to remember how far down you went. It doesn't have to be exact." I tapped at mid-shin and stood.

"Now pick one," he said.

"One what?"

He pointed at the bottles. "A bottle."

"Based on what?"

"Based on whether it's one bottle. Just grab one, not three."

I grabbed the zinc pills. "Okay?"

"Now do the toe-touch again, same as before, while holding the bottle."

"Why?"

"Because."

I did it, feeling stupid. But this time my knuckles scraped the floor. I'd either gotten more flexible in the past ten seconds or I'd stretched with too much effort. But I hadn't stretched at all—hadn't felt any tightness in my hamstrings or calves.

"So," he said. "What did you notice?"

"I went down farther?"

"It didn't resist you as much, did it? Not while you were holding the bottle. The brakes are off." I thought of Dr. H and those stupid bottles of water and minerals in Elko, Nevada. "Resist me!" he had said.

"No," I admitted. "I don't think so."

"Try it again. See if anything changes."

I did, with the same result. My knuckles hit the floor. "But I'm sure it's just because I'm getting more warmed up each time I do the toe-touch."

"Then drop the bottle and do it again."

"Okay." This time I tightened up at mid-shin, just like the baseline test. "What's this all about?" I asked, intrigued and weirded out.

"Would you say that an increase in range of motion is a good thing, generally speaking?"

"Sure."

"So, a couple of things. More mobility is a good thing. Why wouldn't you take every chance to gain mobility?"

"Okay."

"If you can tell if a food increases your range of motion with this test, would it make sense to say that food is good for you?"

"I have no idea."

"We'll talk about it more later. Get ready for tomorrow. Go rack out."

"What does that mean?"

"Sleep." Adam went into his room and closed the door.

We drove to the gym in the morning. Eyes boring straight ahead, Adam said, "What's the worst thing one person can do to another person?"

"Uh. Kill them?"

"No." He ran a hand over his scalp. "I've got a big dent up here from where my head got crushed in a riot with a tent stake. Big gash somewhere else too, somewhere I won't show you. Now I get migraines. Constantly, acutely, ninety-plus-hour migraines where my eyes fill up with blood, and it's the least convenient thing in the world. And people say, 'Wow, you're tough.' And I want to say, 'Yeah, okay, so what?' I don't want to be tough. I want my head to stop hurting, that's what I want. Toughness is severely overrated."

"So that's the worst thing someone can do to you?" I said, pointing to his head.

"This happened because people weren't where they were supposed to be and I had to fight my way out of an unnecessarily bad situation. The fact that I literally can't elaborate on the particulars—I'm not allowed to and I don't want the DOD breathing down my neck—is bad, but it's not the worst thing. The worst thing is that I got let down and part of me is still stuck on that day. I can't let go. I can't let it go." His voice was a mixture of pleading and fury and what sounded like a great loneliness.

We passed a store called Sophisticated Man of Minot. "Hey, do you ever shop there?" I asked.

"Oh, you know it," he said. "I'm nothing without my bowler hat. But listen, take some of the so-called 'friends' in my life. Facebook friends, military acquaintances, fitness industry punks who want me to mail for their products . . . they're part of the problem, they're why I have a hard time making it back from that day. Stuck. They want me to do shit for them, but do they ever return my e-mails? Phone calls? Let me tell you something, the people who tell me they'll e-mail and then they don't, well, that matters. The people who abandoned me in that riot probably started their career in not following through by not returning e-mails and phone calls like they said they would. But I knew you were different." Suddenly he laughed and pointed out the window. A tall thin dog was walking down the street. "Look at that dog walk! My dogs can't even walk two feet without needing a nap. Those goofy fuckers. Eighteen hours of sleep every day. You think you'd feel better if you had eighteen daily hours of rack time?"

"I'd have fewer tics."

"Yes. But it's not time to sleep." We were at the gym.

Mirrors lined one wall. On the mirrors were written, in marker, various poses and forms of knife combat that Adam drilled on his own. Black rubber mats lined the floor, and bent horseshoes—part of Adam's strength-building protocol—hung from pegs. A banner on one wall showed a silhouette of a man's face and the words "POW/MIA: Gone but not forgotten." Upstairs, a children's karate class was in full swing. Grunts and "hi-yahs!" and the sounds of stomping feet drifted through the floor. I glanced at a stainless steel rack of tools that I knew were for strengthening the grip and my hair stood on end. I was itching to lay into everything around me.

"Today you're going to press that bell. With your right arm."

He pointed at one of the many kettlebells lined up like prisoners against another wall of his gym, Unbreakable Fitness.

I looked at the kettlebell and laughed. Press ninety-seven pounds? That weight was four pounds heavier than my best press. For months, nagging shoulder pain had kept me from pressing more than thirty-five pounds.

"Maybe with both hands," I said. A year of on-and-off physical therapy, Ibuprofen, ice, enthusiastic cursing, and rest hadn't alleviated the pain in my right shoulder. I had all but stopped using it.

"We'll fix it when you come up," Adam had said on the phone. "Just don't make it worse until I can deal with it." Like Mulder, I wanted to believe. I was sick of the pain.

Adam scowled. He had many scowls. I classified this one as mildly affectionate. "You'll do it in five minutes. Get on the stairs. Let's fix your shoulder."

I'd been to two doctors and an osteopath. Each had sent me home with a pamphlet and a large rubber band. I'd tie a knot in the band, slam it in the door, then waggle my arm back and forth. This never helped. "Of course it didn't help!" Adam said when I told him. "Doing those fucking rotations only makes you better at doing those rotations. The goal isn't to do those rotations. The goal is to press something overhead."

"The doc said I shouldn't do that."

"A doc told me that once. You know what I told him? I said, 'I *want* to do it, so give me the right answer or *imshi*.'"

"What's *imshi*?"

"Don't worry about it." (I looked it up later. It meant "go away" in Arabic.)

Adam had me stand sideways on the bottom stair and dangle one foot over the edge. "Push your heel at the floor like there's a pencil on the bottom. You're trying to draw a perfect circle. Keep your chin level. Don't look down. Relax." Echoes of Dr. H. *A perfect, perfect circle.* I followed these instructions and would have rolled my eyes if he hadn't been so close, glaring.

After some reps, he had me wiggle my jaw, open my mouth as wide as I could, and walk around on the balls of my feet for thirty seconds. What did this have to do with my injured shoulder? Adam pointed to the ninety-seven-pound kettlebell. "Now press it." When I stalled, he said, "Go do it. Quit thinking. You won't die, I promise."

I walked over to the kettlebell, grasped it in my right hand, cleaned it to my chest, and pressed it with less effort than any press I'd ever done. It fell out of my hand from the top position and hit the ground with a thud.

"Yes!" he said. "Damn, I'm good!"

"What just happened?" I said. Adam opened his training log and ignored me. "What just happened?" I repeated. I was ecstatic, confused, curious, pain-free, and slightly freaked out.

"The same thing that will happen with your tics," he said without looking up. "It's fun to be smart. You're lucky you've got me."

Ninety grueling minutes of kettlebell training later, Adam said, "I want chicken wings." We passed a young woman walking on the side of the road. Her hair was blond, with black roots. "What is she, a bumblebee?" he said. "I'll tell you what you just saw, Josh. A lack of personal excellence. You know who could use a good old-fashioned public shaming? Just about everyone, including you and me sometimes. Ponder that."

We talked about Tourette's over lunch. "Honestly, I don't know how you do it," he said. "Having control of my body is one of the only things that keeps me this sane, and I'm pretty wrecked."

"It is what it is," I said.

"Look me in the eyes," he said. "Men look each other in the eyes."

"It is what it is," I repeated, looking him in the eyes.

"No. It isn't. That's stupidity right up there with 'failure is not an option.' Of course it's an option or there wouldn't be any sort of adventure to it, would there? The word 'adventure' means undetermined outcome, did you know that? So failure would have to be an option, right? I've seen people blown up right next to me. I've watched people hop around after losing their limbs, and this shit you deal with is just as bad as any of it."

"No, it isn't!" I said.

"I saw a kid with rebar sticking out of him after a bomb. He had it worse than you, definitely. But this is as bad as some things we went through. Maybe worse, because you don't understand it. Someone whose arm gets blown off by a bomb knows why his arm is gone. Someone who hits himself in the face without warning—"

"There's kind of a warning," I said.

"What do you mean?"

"Well, I usually know that something's coming."

"How?"

I think this was the first time that someone actually asked me to think about what was happening to me. My doctors, as knowledgeable as they were, never asked how I felt. They treated symptoms. Well, they tried.

"Okay, if I have a tic where my shoulder jerks up toward my ear, there's a sensation in my shoulder before it happens. I know my shoulder wants to move. It's like the buildup to a sneeze, it just happens faster and the urge doesn't really leave once I have the tic. It starts building again."

"Okay, here's the mind-set I need you to be in so we can cure you," Adam said.

I didn't roll my eyes, because now that we were making eye contact he'd have seen it.

"Change gears," he said. "What makes a good trainer? Someone who gets results *and* shows clients how to figure something out for themselves. I'll give you an example of a bad teacher." He mentioned a kettlebell instructor who uploaded technique videos to Facebook and YouTube. "This guy, and I'm not saying he's a bad guy, but he's a terrible trainer. Terrible presentation. He's got these dead eyes and this dead voice. Here's how uncomfortable watching his videos makes me. Picture an endless row of urinals in a public restroom. You come in and see me urinating at one of them. I'm the only one there. You have your pick of the place. But you choose a toilet next to me. Then, as we relieve ourselves, you lean over and softly start batting at my penis."

I started to choke on the celery I'd been chewing. When he saw that I would live, he said, "Watching his videos makes me more uncomfortable than that scenario would. The only ethical way to train people is to help them understand how their bodies can teach them."

When we finished eating, he drove to Best Buy. A couple of helpful workers approached him while he was browsing the CDs. Each time he looked up and smiled before they opened their mouths. Each time, they smiled and walked away without saying anything. In *War and Peace*, during one of the many drawing room scenes that open the novel, Tolstoy describes Sonya Rostova as wearing a "company smile." I'd made ten runs at *War and Peace* before finishing it, and each time I noticed this phrase. And in *American Gods* Neil Gaiman describes the enigmatic Mr. Wednesday as smiling "as if he learned to smile from a manual." Adam didn't remind me of Sonya or glass-eyed Mr. Wednesday, but his smile did. Being smiled at by Adam feels more like being smiled at by a predator than welcomed by a friend.

Adam picked a CD and walked toward the cashiers. My right hand smacked my cheek with that familiar, hideous thwack. Adam turned and saw me shaking my fist out. "Now *that's* a sound I'd know anywhere. Are you fucking *kidding* me?" I felt like I was in a zoo. But he nodded slowly, a smile creeping onto his face. "I see it."

"You see what?"

"Not yet. We'll talk about it later."

"You know what?" he said as we got into the car. "I like you. I do. So I'm going to tell you a story. Someone was giving me the eye in a bar once. Alcohol is fucking phenomenal when it comes to creating stupidity. If you were going to start shit with someone, would it be with me, I mean, based on looks?" He laughed. "I'm amazed that there's enough alcohol in the world so that *I* start to look like someone who's going to put up with your eye, or your finger in my chest. Anyway, I stood up, I walked over, and I sniffed, real obvious and slow. 'I don't like that aftershave,' I told him, and then I gave him the eyes. You've seen me do it, right?"

"Yeah."

"'I'm not wearing aftershave,' he says, and his voice doesn't sound as tough as he wants it to."

"'Wipe it off anyway,' I say, 'because I don't like bullies and I feel like you were trying to bully me. That was a poor decision.'"

Adam really started to laugh now. "And so he says, 'I'm not sure what I was thinking.' And I say, 'We can start over, but first wipe off the aftershave you're not wearing.' And he *did* it!"

"Wouldn't you have done it too?" I asked. "If you'd been in his position?"

"Well *yeah*, but if I'd been in his position I wouldn't be giving the troops the crazy eye, but what do I know about what I'd do? It obviously made sense to him. For about ten seconds." Adam paused. "But let's get back at it. So how do you know if a movement is good for you?"

"I'm not sure. If it doesn't hurt?"

"Let's consider something. A man lifts weights on Monday. What does he do?"

"Bench."

"Correct. Most programs dictate that you will bench press on Monday. Who knows why? Now, would you consider the bench press a good movement or a bad movement?"

"Well, wouldn't it depend on your goals? I'd ask why you thought bench was the right—"

"Wrong starting point. Lifting weights is an activity. Forget about right and wrong here. This isn't church. It's pushing a weight off your chest. So—good or bad?"

"Okay, I'd say it's good if a heavier bench press is your goal."

"Yes. Specifics. But what if benching hurts your shoulders?"

"Well, I can't think of a good reason to do it if it hurts you."

"It doesn't always feel good, does it?"

"No, some days feel better than others as far as that movement."

"Why?"

"I don't know. A lot of things can change the way a workout feels."

"Such as?"

"Sleep. Injuries. Food. Time of day. Is why even the right question? It seems like you want me to ask something else."

"Let's say that I can demonstrate exactly how you could know whether bench pressing today—no, let's get even more specific—what if I could show you whether benching in the next *hour* would be positive or negative for you? Would you try it?"

"You mean a way to learn whether it's right or wrong?"

"Those terms don't apply. Just treat it in terms of better or worse in terms of the associations it causes in your body. Worse means it puts you in distress."

I wasn't sure what we were talking about, but I wasn't bored.

"What should the purpose of a movement be?" he asked. "Now I want you to really think about this. 'Should' isn't a word I use often, but it applies here."

"I'm not sure."

"You think you're not, but you know this. How would you define fitness? Start there."

"Being in shape?"

"Meaning?"

"Well, it means you don't get out of breath when you run, or that you can lift without it killing you, or—"

"There's more to movement and sport than running or lifting or being in shape. What's a better question? About being in shape, what's a better question?"

"I don't know."

"Look, being in shape to do what? That's what I want you to think about. Fitness has lost all meaning in this industry. Nobody asks, what is fitness? Fitness is the ability to perform a task. If someone is 'unfit for duty' in military terms, what does that mean to you?"

"Unqualified to lead, or perform the task that's required by the office or the job, I'd guess. A guy in basic training wouldn't be ready for Colin Powell's job. Like that."

"What made you think of Colin Powell? He's not in combat, but correct. So why would physical fitness be any different?"

"I'm still not sure what you mean."

"Fitness is the ability to perform a task. If you can do the task, you're fit to perform the task. Does that make sense?"

"Yes."

"So how do we decide which brand of fitness to pursue? Which is superior? If fitness is task specific, is it logical for an organization like the RKC to say that they will take care of all of your fitness needs?"

"No, probably not."

"Using kettlebells makes you better at using kettlebells. It doesn't make you fit enough to paddle a surfboard against the current for ten minutes. Or to swim. It doesn't mean you can bench heavy weight or that your tennis serve is more explosive. It means that you're fit—that you have the requisite fitness to perform that movement."

"Okay."

"So, again, how will a person generally choose the sport or fitness activity that they perform?"

"Well, I think they'd listen to what someone else says they should be doing, like a magazine, or do something that they like. Or maybe they're required to do it, I mean to improve at it, for some reason, like being on a sports team."

"Exactly. Remember what I said about movements making you better or worse at any given time?"

"Yes."

"Would you predict that a movement you enjoy makes you better, or worse?"

"Better. Anything I enjoy makes me feel better when I'm done."

"Well, that depends. Doing a bunch of heroin might make you feel great short term, but it's inferior in terms of its benefit to you. Okay. Let's consider that a clue as to how one could or should choose an exercise. The enjoyment they get from it."

"Okay."

"How can you make a movement more enjoyable?"

"I'm not sure. Uh . . . I like it when I can lift heavier. Are you talking about adding weight?"

"No. I'm talking about movements that make you better. More mobile. It starts with a movement that *makes you move better.* Now, once you know what movement that is, how can you improve the movement that's already doing something good for you?"

"I don't know."

"Yes, you do."

"No, I really don't, and I don't do well when I'm put on the spot like this. I'll keep giving you answers just to be saying something, but that means I'll be saying things I haven't thought through that really won't tell you anything. This really isn't how I think. I usually have to write something down before I really know what I think about it."

"Fair enough. But you do know. So here's what you already know. Increasing fitness—one's fitness to perform a task—means making the movement, or movements, involved, more efficient. Let's say that efficiency means the quickest, smoothest way to pass between two points—point A and point B. Consider the bench press. Think about a military campaign, like Hannibal leading those elephants from start to finish. Or someone playing a piece of music on the piano. What do all of those things have in common?"

"I can't think of *anything* they have in common."

"They're all just movements," he said. "It's all just movement. Lifting, thinking, running, swimming, having a go with the wife, breathing, swallowing. It's all just movement. And the big movements are made of small movements. Anything that is a movement can be made more skillful. What do I mean by skillful?"

"That you're good at it?"

"Not just that. Would you go see a concert pianist who made every song look like it was really difficult to play? Like she was just barely holding it together?"

"I guess not." I'd seen Tori Amos live. She made it look pretty easy, even when playing two pianos at the same time.

"No, because you don't have money to waste on things that aren't worth seeing, and you don't pay to see someone make a difficult task look difficult. Anyone can make hard things look hard. We pay to see mastery. To see people doing what looks impossible, and it's impressive when they make it look easy. So tell me how this could apply to Tourette's."

I opened my mouth, closed it, then sort of waggled my fingers in the air as if doing the hula while sitting down.

"Haven't you been listening?" he asked. "I'll tell you something Frankie Faires said. He said, 'There's no off switch to adaptation. Everything you do catches up to you. We get better at what we do. If your body is your biography, then you are, at any given time, a perfect representation of all of your resolved and unresolved stresses. *You're* always getting better at having tics. It's not your fault, but that's what's happening, in my opinion."

"Who's Frankie Faires?"

Frankie was a Texas-based martial artist who had apparently taught Adam about the things we were discussing.* Testing weights, testing foods, testing movements. "So, when you started moving away from the RKC stuff, was Frankie telling you to?" I asked.

"Nobody tells me to do anything, but he helped me ask some different questions and decouple from some poor assumptions. But enough about him for now. You've got the pieces to start with."

We went to a grocery store. In the nutrition aisle I tested various supplements, trying to ignore the people watching me touch my toes while holding a bottle of zinc. Some of the bottles definitely seemed to change the toe-touch test. But when I tested a bottle of pills that promised to increase my estrogen naturally, and my range of motion greatly increased, I decided that I wouldn't test any more supplements. It made me feel stupid and I wasn't interested in taking estrogen or birth control because of a toe touch.

"But how do you know the test works?" I said. "The toe touch?"

"I could ask you the same thing about religion," he said. "I just don't get how anyone could believe in a church," he said. "You can't test it."

"What, you mean like with a toe touch? What, would you pray and then see if it increased your range of motion?"

He snorted. "You say that like it's a stupid idea. I can believe in the test because my results strongly suggest that it

---

* Frankie would eventually compile his ideas into a system called Gym Movement.

works. I've got the numbers to back it up and you know it. What results can you show me that are going to convince me that any church is worth going to? Results that you couldn't get in any other way? I mean, do you still go to your meetings?"

"I go for an hour each week, mainly to help Janette with Max. He gets fussy."

"I'd get fussy too. So that's the only reason you're going? Someone else's convenience?"

"I don't know. Maybe."

"But what do you get out of it?"

"Not much anymore. I don't hate it, though. And honestly, it's not worth the heartache it would cause the rest of my family. It's not a bad thing for me to be there. They're good people."

"But doesn't your family know how you feel?"

"You know, I'm actually not sure. I haven't really talked about it, except for with Janette, so unless they have put it together on their own—no, they probably don't know. But again, I don't hate going."

"That's like praising something because it could have been worse. Like saying, 'I went to the zoo and the monkey only hit me with one piece of shit.' That's not a win."

"You asked! Settle down."

"But it's all based on feelings, right?"

"Yeah, pretty much."

"And that's supposed to convince me?"

"It's not supposed to do anything to you. You asked."

"But if it's not doing anything for you, why are you doing it? That's all I want you to think about. What you believe makes no difference to me, but don't you think your faith should make a difference to you, if you really have it?"

"Honestly, it's just easier not to talk about it. If it ever comes out, it's going to break my mom's heart."

"Why? I don't get why it would be such a big deal."

"Well, because for her, me not believing in the church

doesn't just mean I'm not there on Sunday, it means that when we die, I won't be with them. I don't know if she'd ever say it to me that bluntly, but that's how people who really believe see it. And I can't fault her for that. I love her as much as she loves me. If it turns out that she's right about the church, believe me, not being with them in the afterlife would break my heart too."

Adam stared at me. "See, this is why I like dogs. They don't make things more complicated than they are."

I spent five days in Minot. I listened more than I talked. Adam asked questions. We trained at the gym once or twice each day. Then it was time to go home. We ate a final dinner at Red Lobster.

Adam stared at his plate.

"Are you okay?" I asked.

He looked up. "I—" he said, staring with his eyes wide open, all lit up and alert. Based on the look on his face he was about to say:

"—am going to kill you, I hope you're ready to die!" as he placed a forearm over my throat.

"—am so disappointed."

"—surprised."

"—hungry."

But what he said was "I'm proud of you." If this were a Bette Midler song, this is where the strings would swell. But even though Adam was complimenting me, it was unnerving. I felt like I'd been lined up in the sights of a rifle. His eyes were *piercing.* You'd understand if he was complimenting you with all the intensity of a mean dog who hopes you're about to run.

Praise, threats, lifting weights, or drinking—the guy commits. Maybe that's what was so unusual about Adam; he spoke with total conviction. With eyes that made me think I'd wandered inside an unseen blast radius. As David Foster Wallace said, "Psychotics, say what you want about them, tend to make the first move."

"Why?"

"Because you could have offed yourself a long time ago. I've seen guys turn out the light for less than you're dealing with."

"Well, I don't know about that," I said. "I—"

"Stop," he said. "Learn how to take a compliment, Josh. Don't argue, don't joke at your own expense, and don't tell me I'm wrong. One of the problems I see with civilians is that they've never been forced to rely on themselves. I'm not saying you've got to go to war to know what's up, but you learn things about yourself. You *really* know what you're made of. You *really* learn whether you believe in yourself. I don't think you're half as confident as you act like you are. So you know what I think you should do about that?"

"No," I said.

"Forget about what you think about you. You just take action and let someone else be right about you. Me, your parents, your wife, I don't know, my dogs. They like you. Let someone else be right."

"Okay," I said. "Okay, I will."

Then he rhapsodized about a helicopter whose guns fired bullets the size of Red Bull cans.

On the way to the airport Adam asked, "What did you learn this week?"

"I learned that there is a store called Sophisticated Man of Minot by your gym. And that's where you can buy bowler hats."

"Anything else?"

"Well, okay, if I remembered one thing you've said, what would you want it to be?"

"Two things. Remember how bad that woman's haircut was, and don't let that happen to you. Second: Test everything that can be tested. As soon as you think you know something, that's when you stop questioning it. Understanding kills curiosity. It's—I won't say it's a problem—but it's common with religions. Understanding kills progress. That's not ideal. Here's your mission. Pick a movement, preferably one that you do constantly—I'm not going to give you more clues—and improve it. Make it easier. Make it more efficient. Test it out often. See what happens with your tics. Then report in in a couple of months."

"Why do I have to remember her haircut?"

"Are you serious? Because that shit was comedy gold, that's why."

I got out of the car at the airport, took my bags out of the trunk, and nearly screamed when I turned around. Adam was right behind me. Somehow he'd left the car and snuck up on me in complete silence. I put out my hand. He shook it and pulled me in close, delivering two emphatic whacks to my back. "You did good, buddy. Keep going. This is about one thing: How many questions you're willing to ask."

Then he got in his car and drove away.

"Good-bye," I said to the car.

"So how was it?" said Janette when I got home.

"I'm not sure."

Pick a movement and improve it. I wanted to improve my dead lift. A dead lift is simply picking something up off the ground. But I couldn't deadlift constantly without paying a price, not if the weights were heavy. My back would give out, or I'd burn myself out with fatigue, or or or . . . Adam couldn't have meant dead lifts. I took out a sheet of paper and listed movements that I performed on a daily or near-daily basis.

Kettlebell presses, snatches, and squats.

Dead lifts with a barbell were already ruled out, but anytime you lift anything off the ground it's a dead lift, so I put a question mark by it.

Bench press—no.

Running. No.

Walking? That seemed possible. I walked every day and I knew it could be more efficient. My feet have always everted to ten and two. Not ideal. Maybe I could focus on that while I walked. Was that what he meant?

What else? Sitting, standing, lying down, getting up from various positions.

Eating was a movement. Hands and arms and fingers involved in the manipulations of food and utensils. The mouth, jaw, and tongue involved in chewing. I could probably eat more efficiently, but what would that have to do with my tics?

Breathing.

Swallowing.

Blinking.

Squinting.

Scratching my itches.

Brushing my teeth.

As I wrote, my eyes returned to "breathing" over and over. The pen slowed.

Breathing.

I listed the times when my tics were almost always better. Talking. Playing the guitar. Sleeping. Reading, if I could get absorbed in something. Writing.

What did they have in common? I always assumed that these activities pushed the tics out because they took too much processing power in the brain. They used up my mental resources so there was nothing left for Misty.

But sleeping didn't fit that list. What if it had nothing to do with how complex the tasks were? What else could they all have in common?

And there it was. The breathing. It was the breathing. It had to be. These were the only times where I was completely un-aware of my breathing; this was when my breathing was least likely to be interrupted by tics. Did that mean the lack of air caused the tics? I didn't know, but now I could experiment.

Was breathing a movement? Yes. It was lots of movements. More things were involved in one inhalation and exhalation than I knew. Did it have a point A and point B? Yes. If standing at rest was point A, couldn't a full inhalation be point B?

The next day at work, I went into the fitness room at lunch.

What would breathing *better* mean? If nothing else, I could examine how I breathed. I tried to relax. My arms hung at my sides. My shoulders, neck, and jaw all settled. I tried to focus, to draw my attention to any part of my body that moved with my breath, or that was involved in any way.

How often do I breathe? Well, duh, "constantly" was the answer, but could I change it? It seemed like I was taking a lot of breaths per minute.

How quickly do I inhale? It took less than two seconds. The exhalation was just as brief. This seemed fast.

How deeply do I breathe? I inhaled beyond my usual stop-ping point and kept expanding my lungs. It felt so good that at some point I started holding the air in. I expelled it with an abrupt cough. Why had it felt so good? As epiphanies go, "breathe more" seemed kind of lame. Too simple.

I had inhaled for four seconds. More than double the length of my typical breaths. I tried again but was interrupted by Misty, who didn't like this. Annoyed, I reset, tried to calm my-self for another go, but it was no good. I opened my mouth and snapped my front teeth together. It would be a while before I could attempt another breath in a ticless state.

That one deep breath felt too good to be insignificant.

The next morning, before the library opened, I went into the stacks and tried to prepare, to calm myself, to ask.

One . . . two . . . three . . . four . . . and done. I managed a four-count exhalation and was still. I listened to what was happening inside me. Had anything changed? I tried three more times that day. One perfect breath, each time. Each time was satisfying, a relief.

I called Adam that night. Before I even told him about the breath he said, "It's too early to talk about it, buddy. You've got a month of experimenting before I'll weigh in."

I had a laboratory now: the restrooms at the library. They have hair-trigger motion sensors for the lights. If you stand perfectly still for about fifteen seconds, the lights go out. But so much as snap your fingers and the lights come back on. My goal was to breathe, focus, and see if I could stay still enough for the lights to go off. Once I could do it, I would see how long I could stay in the dark before triggering the lights.

The next day I managed twenty full breaths, each one delicious.

Physical relief and release soaked me at each attempt. Of course it did! What if all this time I'd simply not been getting enough air?

If you're not getting enough air you're in distress, but perhaps I'd simply adapted to distress. It made sense, the euphoria of oxygenated blood. Every tic, whether motor or vocal, was an interruption, disturbing my thoughts, my speech, my body, my heart rate, and my confidence. Every tic interrupted a breath. Try this: For the next sixty seconds, stop every breath you take at the halfway point of the inhalation. Do it by either tensing up your abdomen or clearing your throat. You'll feel slightly desperate at the end of the minute. But if you did it for the next year, the desperation would become the baseline. Your distress would become normal. You'd forget how good you can feel.

"Janette, this is going to change everything," I said. "I really think this is it."

She was supportive, but tentative. "I think it's great, and I'm glad that you guys are working on this, but I'm not sure I understand everything you've told me."

I'm sure that was true. Adam and I had talked so much, and he was so strange, so unlike anyone else I'd ever met, that it was impossible to re-create our conversations in a way that anyone else could picture.

"I don't either," I said. "I know it sounds confusing, but I'm probably not explaining it well. But at least . . . doesn't it make sense that if I could practice not having tics, then I could eventually swing things back so that I had fewer tics in a day? I think . . . I don't know, but if this works at all, I think I could scale it up."

"Okay. Let's see what happens. You know I want that. I just don't want you to work too hard and then be upset if it doesn't pay off."

"But that's the whole point! It's not about effort. Effort is what I've been doing, and it hasn't worked."

"Okay."

"I mean, think about it! If Max starts to have tics, maybe by that time I'll know how to help him! Maybe I'll be able to give him a way out."

And that, above all, was the reason I was so desperate to figure out my own Tourette's. Max had shown no tics, no signs of anything unusual, but the worry consumed me.

There's an idea in the bodybuilding world that to make a muscle grow, you have to torture it, to convince it that it's dying: It swells to protect itself from the onslaught next time. New tissue forms in a million micro-tears. The lifter forces the adaptation. "No pain, no gain."

That had been the equivalent of my attempts to stifle the Tourette's. I would simply bear down and see if I could outlast it through force of will. And it never worked, which made sense to Adam.

"Think about it, man," he said. "Think about the people you work with. You all spend your whole day in a chair, right?"

"Pretty much." This seemed like a very roundabout way to make a point.

"Those people's bodies will adapt to whatever it is they spend their time doing. They'll wind up shaped like chairs. They can't will their bodies back to normal. They can't try harder to have better posture; they just need to sit less, until that becomes normal again. Adaptation never stops. You can't turn it off and you can't turn it on. The best you can hope for is to divert it into paths that reward you instead of punish you."

I worked on my breathing for the next two months. I tried to practice in a totally ticless state. Stopping before the urges to have tics overcame me was a key. Have you ever seen a weight-lifting competition? Or watched one of the World's Strongest Man competitions that I always get sucked into when they broadcast fifty episodes every Thanksgiving? Have you ever seen someone in a gym struggling against a weight, freaked out as every single vein in their neck emerges like the arms of an octopus streaking toward the surface?

I'm guessing you have. Maybe you've even *been* that guy. I have. Let's call that distress training.

Let's say that guy spends most of his time lifting in that state. And let's say he never does anything but biceps curls and bench press. Doesn't it make sense that his body will start associating those movements with that physical state? If every time you bench it feels incredibly difficult, your body and your neurology remember that. But what if you could receive all of the benefits the "no pain, no gainers" are always chasing, and you didn't have to become overly tense to make it happen? Would that interest you? Do you think your body might feel better if you never turned purple and ground your teeth to pulp in the gym?

This is why I didn't want to struggle as I tried not to have tics while practicing my breathing. I wanted the association to be that when I took a full breath, there were *no urges to have tics*. I didn't want to write on the motherboard in a way that signaled that deep breaths were connected to the psychogenic urges. I didn't know if it was possible, but I wanted to find out. The evidence would be anecdotal, but for the person in pain, it would be enough.

In December, two months after my Minot trip, I was ready for the experiment. The goal? Sixty seconds of perfect, beautiful stillness. No gimmicks. No straining. No distracting myself by playing the guitar or doing multiplication tables in my head. I wanted to feel what a minute was worth. What it was like for everyone else. What it felt like to live without feeling as if whatever room you were in was a waiting room where nothing but bad news would be announced, whenever it came.

One of Pavel's maxims that I still love: Strength is a skill. You don't work out. You practice. I'd been practicing for this minute.

It worked! It was the most perfect minute of my life. There are over five hundred and twenty-five thousand minutes in a year. In 2009, after more than two decades of twitching frustration, I had a minute all to myself.

I paid for it. I spent the rest of that night getting lashed by Misty. But I didn't care because I could do it again. I could turn one minute into two. Maybe two would eventually become five.

I called Adam and reported.

"Sharper than a razor, brother," he said. "Was it the breathing?"

"What! How did you know?"

"I pay attention. Most people don't. It was pretty obvious, but I wanted you to figure it out. I knew you'd get there. Hey,

I'm eating dinner, but one more thing before I go: The dogs say
hi. They miss you."

I laughed.

"It's not a joke," he said.

Adam would later tell me that he had autism. It had taken
someone whose brain didn't work like anyone else's to ask me
questions that nobody else had.

CHAPTER 12

121—Belief and Doubt
155.432—Mothers and Sons

"Hey, man, there's some psycho back there talking to himself. If you don't deal with it, I will." He points back toward the cookbooks. This guy is big.

I nearly tell him that I've just finished reading Jon Ronson's *The Psychopath Test*, which led me to read *Without Conscience: The Disturbing World of the Psychopaths Among Us*, and that, while it was unlikely that the man talking to himself is actually a psychopath, I'll go check it out anyway.

I ask a coworker to call security and have a guard come find me, in case we have a situation.

Once I start walking, it's easy to find the guy by the sound of his voice. I turn a corner to see a man in the cookbook aisle, gesturing wildly at something in front of him.

"Is everything okay?" I ask.

He startles. "I'm so sorry, I know how loud I'm being, they just won't leave me alone." He's approximately my age, a nice-looking man with curly blond hair and clothes that look new. But his face is gaunt and several scabs dot his forehead. "I don't mean to be loud but they won't . . ." His head whips to the left. "Did you hear that?"

He turns and hurries to the end of the aisle.

"I don't hear anything," I say, catching up with him. "What are you hearing?"

"There are three women harassing me," he says, talking faster with each word. "They just won't leave me alone, and if you just—ohhhhhh—if you could just *hear* the things they're telling me, you'd—I don't know, you'd—"

"Can you show them to us?" says the security guard who now stands beside me. "It's helpful to have a description."

"See, the problem is that I've never seen them," says the man. "They've been following me for years, and, the thing is, they're always just ahead of me, around the corner. So I run, and I tell them to stop, and I'm sorry about the noise, but I can't get them to stop, and they're *always just around the next corner.*" He's near tears, desperate.

"You've never seen them?" asks the guard.

"They're real. They are," he says. "They're so close, but I can't show you. I can't catch them. They're laughing. If you could hear them . . . I'm not just talking to myself. They're real. It's real. You *really* don't hear that?"

"Have you been drinking tonight, sir?" asks the guard.

"No."

"Any drugs?"

"No."

"Do you take any medication?"

"Yes, but not right now. I don't like it."

The guard encourages the poor guy to come to his office and set up a plan for catching his tormentors.

Before they leave, the man says, "I wasn't always like this. I'm so sorry."

The more I practiced the breathing, the more I examined other things that seemed associated to the tics.

I learned that when I entered a new room, the change in lighting made me want to have tics. But if I walked into a room with my eyes closed, the urges diminished.

I learned that I could alter the speed of certain tics with some success. Especially with the big whiplash tics, this was a revelation. Sometimes having tics at half speed released me from the urges. That would save huge amounts of wear and tear.

It was the basic scientific method. Form a hypothesis, design an experiment, evaluate the result, confirm or refute your hypothesis, and then keep going or perform a new experiment. Whatever movement I wanted to test, I'd perform the baseline toe touch Adam had shown me. If something increased my range of motion, it was a "good movement *right now*." That status could change—in a week, day, or hour—but I could always test it again. I'd practice the movement up until the moment *before* it felt challenging, because I didn't want my brain to make an association between a good movement and effort; that was a recipe for a tic. If the movement felt noticeably harder than the one before it, if the speed of a rep decreased, if I panted or held my breath while doing it, if I tensed my jaw or any other body part, if I got pulled out of alignment, or if I felt pain— these were signs that I'd gone too far. I had no idea how much tension I carried in my body until it began to let go of me.

Every tic began to feel more like a challenge and an opportunity, rather than a sock in the guts or a kick in the balls or a reinforcement of my flaws. The more I asked, the more I could ask.

That was in January. By March I went for two minutes without tics. Two minutes became five. Then an hour. A day without tics. A month where I didn't notice any tics, although Janette said I was having some mild ones. But she was astonished at the progress. All apparently from the breathing, and from testing out the movements I used when I exercised, avoiding anything that made me more rigid.

I worked at the library.

I loved my wife.

I played with my son.

I read, trained, and wrote.

I loved my life.

"I told you, man," said Adam. "I think you're getting close to actually knowing something about all this. Have some faith." He laughed and hung up.

Faith was about the only thing in my life that *wasn't* going well. Now, in the midst of my track-and-measure-everything phase, I was more aware than ever that gauging spiritual progress was difficult. *On a scale of one to ten, just how righteous do I feel today? I have no idea. What does righteous mean anyway?* But I kept my doubts to myself—except for when I was with Janette, who knew I was struggling with faith, but said she'd never force the issue—and things carried on just as they had for the past few years.

Then my mom came to visit us for a week that summer. When Max and I picked her up at the airport, he rushed into her arms and forgot I existed for the next seven days. That night, Janette and I read on our bed while my mom and Max played in the backyard.

The back door opened and footsteps pounded over the floor as Max appeared in our room. "Come watch the show!" he said, before running back outside.

We went to the sandbox, where my mom was sitting in a chair next to several overturned buckets. "Okay, Max," she said, "show them what's under the buckets."

Max lifted the buckets one by one, revealing three goats from a toy farm set, and a grumpy-looking plastic lion. "Dad, are you ready for the show?" he asked.

"I'm ready," I said.

"One day," my mom said, "the three Billy Goats Gruff were hungry. But . . ." She looked at Max, who was positioning the three goats at the foot of a bridge. The bridge was made of a large stick and spanned the gap between two mounds of sand.

"But they ate all their grass," he said. "And the bridge—"

She leaned down and stage-whispered, "The bridge comes later, remember?"

"The bridge comes later," Max told me.

"So they'd eaten all their grass," she continued. "And so they looked on the other side of the bridge and . . . what did they see? A green field of delicious grass! So the first, smallest Billy Goat Gruff went to the bridge, but when he walked out—*pitter patter pitter patter*"—Max made the goat dance onto the bridge—"a mean old troll came up from under the bridge and said . . ."

Max put the lion—standing in for the troll—under the bridge quickly, then pulled it out and set it before the startled goat. "You can't have my grass!"

Janette laughed.

"Well, no, he didn't want the grass," said my mom. "He said, 'I'm going to eat you!' So what did the goat say, Max?"

"He jumped over his head!" And sure enough, the plastic goat jumped over the troll's head and landed on the other side of the bridge.

"Well," said my mom. "That's not exactly—"

Max was spinning the goat around on the other side of the bridge, drunk on delicious grass. "And he ate it all and got so fat that he never moved again!"

My mom persuaded Max to help the other two goats across the bridge like they had practiced. If you don't know the story, when the biggest goat comes to the bridge, he throws the troll off the bridge, into the water, and, if memory serves, the troll is never heard from again. Max put the troll under the bridge.

My mom said, "Okay, do it!"

Max ran behind a nearby stone and returned with a bucket that brimmed with water. He poured it onto the ground, at the mouth of a channel they had dug in the sand. The water rushed down the furrow and, sure enough, taught the troll a harsh lesson as he drowned in agony.

Janette and I cheered.

My mom stood and took Max's hand. "Remember?"

They bowed deeply.

"Josh, do you remember how we used to do this?" she asked me.

"Of course," I said. "How could I forget?" Her storytelling voice was like a time machine, dropping me right back into our living room, thirty years earlier.

"Okay," my mom said, "now tell Mom and Dad to go inside. Say, 'We're not done playing.'"

"You go inside." Max pointed at us.

I'm never more aware of what a lucky kid I was than when I see my mom playing with Max.

The next day I looked up from a book to see my mom smiling at me. "What?"

"I just can't believe you're able to sit still like that. You haven't had one tic in the last few minutes. It's such a blessing."

I laughed. "If you ever get to meet Adam, I want to be there when you tell him that he's a blessing."

On Sunday, we all went to church. After sacrament, the first hour, she leaned over and said, "Let's take Max home. I don't really care about going to other meetings in a ward with people I don't know." I was delighted to skip out early.

"You didn't fight to stay very hard," she said as we drove home.

"When I go now, I hardly ever stay after the first hour."

"Why?"

I sighed. Maybe it was time. "Mom, I'm just not getting anything out of it anymore. It's not for me. I'm sorry."

"What are you apologizing to me for?"

"I don't know. For keeping it from you, I guess."

"You think this is a surprise to me? I've been watching this happen for years, Josh."

"Well, aren't you mad?"

"It doesn't make me happy, you know that. It breaks my heart. But I'm not mad. You're making me feel like the grandma from *Flowers in the Attic*. What did you think I was going to say? 'Go cut me a switch'?"

I'd pictured a maternal rebuke. Disappointment and tears. "I raised you better than this!" Incredulity. A guilt trip. We'd never be able to have another conversation that wasn't about how concerned she was about me. She'd mobilize my father and siblings and the thought of the imminent, endless, sorrow-soaked interventions had made me squirm.

Instead, she said, "Well, kid, the older I get, the more I see that people just have to live their own lives and make their own choices. I'd be lying if I said I like this. I don't. If you've really lost your testimony, it breaks my heart. But you're my son and whatever happens, we'll all still love you and that won't change."

When you believe in the LDS Church, when you "know it's true," we say you have a testimony of the gospel. When you lapse in your beliefs, you have "lost your testimony." I love this idea; it makes it sound so simple to get it back. That you can retrace your steps and find your faith, or maybe if you close your eyes and concentrate, you'll remember the last time you saw it. Now wheeeeeere did I put that thing?

I don't so much feel that I've lost my testimony as that it's broken and scattered. When I scrutinize my life, turning over the proverbial stones, all I find are pieces of myself. Under one stone is the memory of my dream about Alan walking with Christ. Another stone covers the memory of the boy at the end of a dark road in Idaho, crying out for help, then believing he received it. Here are the people I taught on my mission. Here are the many Sundays spent in church, the countless times I heard someone say, "I know this is true." Here I am, offering the prayers of the past, kneeling, again and again, asking, pleading, and sometimes, feeling as if I'm merely speaking to an empty room. Here are the beliefs of my parents and their parents and theirs . . .

When I take the pieces of my faith, of the testimony I had, they don't fit together anymore. They don't create the bigger picture I used to fit into. I don't know how to make them *mean* what they used to mean.

"Max," she said, "did you tell Daddy what I taught you to say?"

Max leaned forward in his car seat and looked at me. "I love you with all my circle!" He made a circle with his hands.

"You too, buddy," I said.

We got back to my house, changed our clothes, got Max some lunch, and continued talking.

"Josh, do you know what my favorite thing is?" she asked. "I mean, my very favorite thing?"

"I'm not sure."

"It's when the whole family comes for a holiday and you kids just sit around and laugh together. You don't have any idea what that feels like for me. There's nothing I look forward to more."

"Yeah. I feel the same way." So did the mother in *The Corrections*, I thought, but things didn't go that well for her. "But just because I want us all to be together forever doesn't mean it's possible. Believe me, nothing would make me happier, but I just don't think I believe that."

"That's okay. We're not going to change each other's minds today."

"I really thought you'd be more upset."

"Why is it that you think you can't believe?"

"See, that's what I mean. I think I might be able to believe, but you don't say you believe, you say you know. I see it differently. I don't trust my emotions like you do, and so we've got very different ideas about what it means to know something."

"Well, maybe . . . would you say you love Max?"

"Of course!"

"You know that, right?"

"Yeah."

"And that's based on feelings. No, let me finish. All I'm saying is that there are different ways of knowing things. You know you love Max, but can you prove it? Not unless you make sure everyone has the same definition of love. But you know it. You do. Would you ever say, 'I believe I love my son'?"

"Of course not."

"Well, neither would I. We *know*. And when I say I 'know' the church is true, I'm speaking from a feeling that's as real to me as the way I love you kids, and the way you love Max. I don't go around telling people what they should do with their lives, but I *know* the truth of this well enough to know how I should live my own life. And you're one of the most important parts of my life, and that's why this matters so much to me."

"I believe you, Mom. I just don't feel what you feel. I'm not even saying I'm right. I'm just saying I'm not sure what it's possible to know. I've never been more uncertain than I am right now, and it scares me if I think about it for too long. It's kind of embarrassing, honestly. I feel like I'm a thirty-five-year-old man learning how to think clearly for the first time."

"Unlike me, right?"

"See, you think this is hard for you, but you have no idea how painful it is for me. It's lonely to be in this position. I can't say things like 'I finally feel like I can think clearly' without implying that, because you still believe, you're *not* thinking clearly. So it's just easier for me not to talk about it at all, even with you, and that's lonely."

She laughed. "Well, the good news is that you're wrong, so what do you think about that, sonny boy?"

"I think you're old and rickety. And probably senile."

She held up her hands in the familiar karate chop position. The left hand flashed out at me. I ducked.

She faked again and I flinched, which allowed her to rush in and hug me. "Well, if I'm not senile yet, I certainly will be, and I'm depending on you to take care of me. I love you, Josh, and I'll always be proud of you. Whatever happens, we're going to be happy when we're together. There's no sense in letting the Big Picture destroy the small picture. You really don't need to feel defensive about this, although I'm sure that's not as easy as I'm making it sound. It takes guts to take a stand the way you are, so don't think I'm not proud of you doing what you think you have to do."

"I'm not taking a stand, Mom. I'm just saying I don't know. But I love you too. I was the luckiest kid."

"No, Max is the luckiest kid. Now that I'm a rickety, senile old lady I've got enough money to spoil him like I couldn't with you all." She went outside. When I joined them a few minutes later, Max was hanging upside down on the monkey bars while she pretended to shoot lasers at him from her fingers. "Dad!" he screamed. "She's getting me!"

I am so lucky, I thought again. And every time I had this thought, it was so intense and clear that it felt like a revelation, even though I'd always known it.

The problem with epiphanies is that they can't sustain you forever. They are as fragile and ephemeral as the words in Charlotte's webs. After my dream about Alan and after that night spent praying in my car, I know that I felt clarity and assurance, and a sense that things would be all right. I felt loved. I remember that. And if I could snap my fingers and feel that way again five minutes from now, then I would snap my fingers, triple time. But I don't know how to bring those feelings back. And I also believe that I no longer *need* the comfort those feelings gave me. I get the same reassurance my family, from my friends, from my books, and my training.

That night, after Max was asleep and my mom had gone to bed, Janette asked if my mom and I had talked about anything interesting.

"I told her how I feel about the church right now," I said.

"Good," she said. "I'm sure that wasn't easy."

"It actually wasn't that bad."

She was quiet for a long time. Then: "Josh, would you do something for me?"

"Of course."

"I know it probably won't change anything, but would you be willing to talk to our bishop about how you feel, and just see if he has any suggestions?"

"Suggestions as far as what?"

"Well, I don't know. But I'd appreciate it if you'd be willing to go."

"Sure."

I didn't know our bishop well. I'd only had one other conversation with him, a "getting to know you" chat three or four years ago. This time, he put me right at ease by saying, "If I can help, tell me, but you don't owe me an explanation for anything."

Well, crap . . . he'd ruined all of the snappy answers I had come up with to refute the accusations and disappointment that he would aim at me. My anxiety and defensiveness fading, we talked.

I told him that my emotions are so chaotic that I can't even begin to trust them enough to draw conclusions about an objective reality, let alone use them to tell anyone else how they should live. I told him that I'm no longer sure of what we can know, but that I can't say I know things I don't anymore. I told him that when I go to church I sometimes envy those who seem so sure about everything, but not often.

I prepared for the castigation. Now he would say, "Hmm . . . What aren't you telling me?"

Instead, he said, "Josh, there's no magic answer. I can't make you feel anything you don't. Nobody can. I think you should keep trying, if you want to, and be more patient with yourself. We're all doing the best we can. If it's good for you, keep asking your questions, and let me know if I can help. I appreciate your honesty and I'm glad that you feel like you can talk to me about such difficult things. Do you have any other questions?"

"I don't think so. Wait—can I tell you a story?"

"Of course."

"When I was maybe twelve years old, we went to Disneyland. On that trip we went to the beach. I was really excited. So we got there and I ran toward the water, but when I got up to about my ankles, my body just, it's weird, but it just shut down. My heart rate went way up and I was cold and my stomach was flipping out. I backed out of the water and it faded. This happened every time I tried to go in, although I finally got up to my waist. I thought I'd probably just read too many books about sharks, but when I told my parents my dad said that when I was three, he and I had almost drowned in the ocean during another vacation. I was in his arms when he got caught in a tide and pulled out farther and faster than he realized. He said that a lifeguard pulled us out after we'd gone under. I don't remember this at all, but my mom said, 'I bet that's what's happening. You remember it.'"

"That's interesting."

"Yeah. And even though I can't remember it, it's obviously still in my head, although I have no problem going in the ocean now. That's kind of how church feels to me. Despite me telling you I don't know, and even with all of the arguments I could make about faith and reason, the fact is, I've been hearing this stuff every single day for most of my life, including my early years. It's all still in there, so while I can make a plausible case for doubt, I'm not totally free in my head, like there's a physical, gnawing fear of being cut off, or being wrong, or cast out, or whatever. Does that make any sense?"

He nodded. "Yes, and I can't really speak to that. It sounds to me like you're doing what you can do. I'm here to help if I can."

He was so kind and open that all I could do was hug him and say, "This didn't go at all how I pictured it."

Things don't always go this well for skeptics in the church.

There's a story in the Book of Mormon about a man named Korihor. Korihor goes around telling everyone that there's not going to be a Christ or Savior, that there's no such thing as sin, and that they should all start enjoying themselves more. He says that you can't really know things that you can't see. Some people listen to him and get up to all sorts of shenanigans, and others cast him out and ban him from their towns. He has a lengthy debate with a righteous man named Alma in a classic atheist-versus-believer smackdown. Korihor demands a sign. Alma says, "One sign, coming right up!" and Korihor, the poor bastard, is struck deaf and mute. Now he confesses that he always knew there was a God, but a devil had appeared to him and tricked him into doing his bidding.

Well, this contrition doesn't fly. Korihor, cursed and reviled, eventually becomes a beggar, and in a scene of breathtaking vagueness, he is "run down and trodden upon, even until he was dead," while among a group of people called the Zoramites. Holy crap!

I'm no Korihor. In terms of signs, I don't know what I would even ask for. I can't say that there's not a God. I can't say that there is. I can't say that I know the church is true. I can't say that I know it isn't. All I can say is that I don't know. And I don't know if it's possible to really know. Right now I have as little interest in creating skeptics as I do in creating believers. I have even less interest in being so skeptical and sneering that I am "trodden upon, even until I am dead."

That's a joke.

But truly, saying "I don't know" in this church is tricky. This isn't church that you only go to on holidays or weekends. This is all day, every day. It's a culture and a lifestyle. You demonstrate faith and devotion not only through your actions, but also with your thoughts. Sunday meetings are only part of it. Home teachers are supposed to visit families each month to share a message and see how the family's doing. If you're a man and you stop coming to church, you can expect a friendly visit or phone call from the elder's quorum presidency. If you say you don't know, then people *will know* that you don't know. You're not going to be set adrift while other church members know that you are struggling. That's something I love about the church. When I'm at church, I really feel like we're all in this life together and that we're responsible for helping one another. It's a wonderful reminder each week that there are groups of people out there that really care about one another. I could make one hundred phone calls right now and say, "Hey, I'm moving tonight and I haven't boxed anything up and it's going to be a ton of thankless work," and I'd probably get at least that many people to come help me.

When people tell me—when I'm at work, I have a face, or maybe a voice, that just says "confide"—that the church is a controlling, greedy, sinister monster that's only interested in brainwashing people and subjugating women, I say, "I don't know that church, but I can understand why you'd have a problem with the church's history." I know happy, generous people. I know my compassionate bishop. I don't see rubes and sheep. I'm way too ignorant and fallible and unsure to sneer at other people who are just trying to live the best way they know how. I see people who want the world to be better than it is and who are willing to work for it.

I just can't work at it in the same way they do anymore. I can't trust my emotions as confidently as they trust theirs. It sounds like a cop-out at this point to say, "Well, maybe I don't have the gift of belief," but maybe I don't. Maybe I never did. I can't remember. If there's a personal God, I have to believe that he knows my heart, and why I have to do what I'm doing right now. Why I have to live according to what makes sense to me, and not according to what is sacred to others.

Even though she says she's glad that we're now talking about it openly, my conversations with Janette aren't easy.

After my conversation with the bishop, Janette asked me how it had gone. I gave her the recap and tried again to summarize my doubts. She looked sadder and sadder and then said, "Josh, I won't stop believing for you."

In my mind, I'd said, "This concerns me, and this concerns me, and here's how I think about this, and here's why I'm not sure that this means what I thought it means," and what she heard was my attempt to persuade her to join me in a mad flight from faith. I was thinking out loud, but voicing my concerns was threatening and I've seen this many times: Wondering about the church can make someone feel like she's being attacked or that she's listening to something dangerous.

"I'm not asking you to," I said. "And, you know, I can't believe just to make things easier for you. It's not a choice I can make just like that. When I try to pray, or I try to read the scriptures, I get nothing. I don't feel anything. The things that used to work just aren't working. I don't know what else to say about that."

"Josh," she said. "It's a choice. You choose to believe, or you choose not to."

"But then you could just decide to believe anything and act like it was true."

"Yes. Maybe. But you can choose to believe something that feels right to you."

"That's exactly what I'm doing, because I'd expect you to lose respect for me if I just went through the motions, because that's what I've been doing, and *I've* lost respect for me. I have to step back for a while and see what I think without being in the middle of it."

"Okay," she said. "I can live with that. But what are we going to tell Max?"

"You know, *how* people think is so much more important to me than *what* they think. If you're okay with me telling Max how I think about things, and how I've gotten to the point I'm at now, then I'll feel like he's getting a chance to learn how to think. Once he knows how to think, he can decide what to think. I just want him to be aware that there are choices."

"And what do you expect me to tell him?"

"I just want you to be honest with him. We both just have to be honest with him. Tell him exactly what you feel and what you think. I will too. That kid has to have our support, whether he's faithful or not. I just want it to be his choice."

"So do you feel okay about everything? About us?"

I took her hands. "Yes. That might be the one thing I'm totally sure of. You and me. I'm lucky that I'm in a marriage where we can talk about this. We're both *willing* to talk about it."

"I feel the same way, and I don't think it needs to be a huge problem."

"Me either."

What I'll tell Max is that I love his mom, his grandparents, and his aunts and uncles and cousins more than anything. I'll tell him that they are my life, and they are a life worth living. When he asks what I believe, I'll tell him that I do believe in many of the tenets of the church:

Be kind and compassionate.

Serve others.

You are responsible for your actions and should be accountable for them, if only to yourself.

Don't be a dick.

Don't lie, kill, steal, or cheat.

Family is the greatest joy on earth.

Study the best books.

Be accountable to yourself.

I'll tell him that, as usual, Kurt Vonnegut said it best:

Tiger got to hunt,
Bird got to fly;
Man got to sit and wonder,
"Why, why, why?"
Tiger got to sleep,
Bird got to land;
Man got to tell himself he understand.

That's from *Cat's Cradle.*

I'll tell him that I was the luckiest, happiest kid in the world. I will tell him that there are no words I can use to describe how much I love my parents, and how grateful I will always be for them.

When he asks Janette what she believes, she will tell him what she believes. Together, we'll try to make sense of our lives and move forward, together.

In the mission field, people who are open to hearing the message are called investigators. I suspect that I'll spend my entire life investigating. I'm open to listening, to reading, to studying the scriptures, and to pondering what is taught by this church, or any other.

Investigator is a title I proudly accept. If it was good enough for Encyclopedia Brown, it's good enough for me.

It's taken thirty-five years, but I feel like I can finally breathe.

CHAPTER 13

616.042—Abnormalities, Human
165—Fallacies, Logic
305.891—Highland Games—Social Aspects

One evening Max and I were watching TV. I looked over at him, hoping to catch him smiling, which he does during every second of any episode of *Curious George*. I sneaked out my finger to tickle him, then stopped.

Max saw me watching. "What, Daddy?" he asked. He wore an orange T-shirt that said "Tough Guy" over the number 36. His blond hair was shaggier than I liked because cutting his hair was always a battle. His lips were redder than usual from the ICEE I bought for him on the way home from the library. I would say that he was the skinniest kid I'd ever seen, but that wouldn't be true; I'd seen pictures of myself at his age. We could have been twins.

Max smiled at me, the way I once smiled at my dad as we sat on another forgotten couch in front of an older television. The smile stopped me from saying, "You're blinking your eyes a lot more than you need to be. Why are you doing that?" As I watched, his lip curled a little bit and he did it more and more.

"What's wrong, Daddy?"

No.

No, not this.

Not for him.

Not for my son.

I kissed his forehead, went to my room, and closed the door. I got on my knees, laced my fingers together, and closed my eyes, but the words wouldn't come.

The door opened. "Josh? Are you okay?" Janette put a hand on the back of my neck.

"He's blinking!" I said, in a hysterical tone that would have been better suited to a phrase like, "He's on fire!" "He's blinking way too much. He's blinking. He's—"

"I know," she said. "I know. But—"

"I can't talk about this right now. I can't."

"Okay," she said. "Okay." She left.

I was still kneeling. I closed my eyes again. I tried to figure out what to say, and who to say it to. I stayed on my knees for a long time.

But nothing came.

There were no words.

When there were no words, I tried listening.

I heard nothing but my own pulse in the stillness.

In the climbing-disaster documentary *Touching the Void,** climber Joe Simpson recounts the thoughts he had while trapped, dangling with a broken leg deep inside a black crevasse within the Peruvian Andes's Siula Grande mountain. He had no reason to think he'd survive:

> I was totally convinced that I was on my own, that no one was coming to get me. I was brought up as a devout Catholic. I'd long since stopped believing in God. I al-

---

* Adapted from a brilliant book by the same name.

ways wondered if things really hit the fan, whether I would, under pressure, turn round and say a few Hail Marys and say, "Get me out of here." It never once occurred to me. It meant that I really don't believe and I really do think that when you die, that's it, there's no afterlife.

My situation certainly wasn't as grave as his, but I didn't feel any more capable of asking for help than he had.

The next morning, before the library opened, I was carrying a stack of books to the shelves and enjoying the quiet.

Misty sat on the desk, leaning back, legs crossed, a sharp, cruel-looking shoe dangling from one foot. She startled me so badly that the books fell from my hands, breaking the spine of the largest. I hadn't felt her in months, although I knew she'd been been spying on Max.

If you had stumbled across my story that day while making your rounds, it might have been titled:

So Your Ex Is Back?

How to Feel Desperate and Terrified

So You Thought You Were Riding Off Into the Sunset?

Maybe she hadn't seen me. She couldn't be here. She couldn't. I hurried past her into the staff room and snapped my name tag onto my shirt with as much authority as possible, but it's hard to do it impressively. *Click.* The sound was nothing compared to my teeth as they snapped together, my tongue escaping just in time. My neck knotted. I couldn't catch my breath.

Maybe I'd imagined her. Maybe I was trapped in a dream. Maybe if I stayed in the back and hid under the lunch table she wouldn't find me. Maybe if I just went home. Maybe—

I screamed. The effort grated my throat. Misty had snuck up behind me, slinking in without an access card, somehow slithering beneath the door. I clapped my hands over my mouth and hustled out to the reference desk. The only chance was to stay ahead of her, make her chase me. Maybe I could lead her off a cliff. My shift was about to start. As patrons flowed from the elevators, Misty sat next to me and pinched my cheeks with my own fingers until they were hot and sweat bloomed on my face. She bit the knuckle of my right thumb until it bled. She curled my toes until they ached with hyperflexion and the ends of the toenails began to roll back from the effort. I kept her quiet but couldn't remove the hooks she jabbed into every part of my vulnerable body.

The Longest Day
How to Eat Lunch Without Spilling All Your Food

I took a long break to lift in the library's fitness room. I locked the door. In the middle of a barbell jerk, my neck tightened as Misty grabbed it. I yelled, my head twisting to the right. I was able to catch the bar and lower it to the ground without falling or breaking the floor. There was no sanctuary here.

What to Do When the Custodian Appears and Asks You What in the World Is Happening? (Spanish Edition)

I had a meeting after lunch. I chewed my mouth to hot, electric ribbons and sweated myself into a disgusting mess.

Five o'clock. Finally. In the underground parking garage Misty's voice echoed in the cavernous room. She darted between the pillars, leaping out to poke and prod me.

Self-Defense for Dummies

In my truck I leaned my head on the steering wheel and forced the first full breath of the day through my lungs. It was the worst day I'd had in over a year. But I'd done it. I'd worked my shift with Misty hectoring and abusing me every minute. I'd done my work. I was exhausted and terrified. Misty wanted my son and now I'd revved back up into a wild state.

But I'd defied her. I had survived on pure spite.

That night I took Max to the park. While Janette read on a bench, we flew a beagle-shaped kite as the setting sun glared like the eye of Sauron. I watched him for signs of tics, but there was nothing. If a kite flyer can get "in the zone," Max was in it. Janette came and sat on my lap. I kissed her neck and let my head rest on her shoulder. "Today was awful," I said.

"What happened?"

"Tics."

"Mommy, look!"

She waved at Max. "I see you! There's a lot going on. It's not that surprising, is it?"

"Probably not. But I really thought I was done with this. Maybe it'll just be today."

"Anything I can do?"

"No. Believe me, I'd ask. Hey! Max, no!" He'd seen a moth in the early evening and was chasing it as the kite sailed away on the wind.

One day when I was four years old, I went outside to play with friends who lived down the street. I held a fearsome whip made of rope. My dad made it for me when I told him about the dog at the end of the street that always barked at me from behind its fence. That whip made me feel safe, even though I never hit anything fiercer than a pile of leaves with it.

But before I reached the dog I saw something on the sidewalk. I looked down. My eyes widened. I screamed! Lying there in vivid, moist, grotesque bas-relief, was a moth.

The moth had bright purple wings. The wings had vivid yellow streaks in them, like fingers. Its body was a dark brown, and two dark feelers extended from its head. Nothing too extraordinary about any of that. But I kid you not, from wingtip to wingtip that moth must have been a foot across. It was enormous. It was gorgeous and horrific.

I ran into the house, grabbed my mom's hand, and dragged her outside as I babbled and exclaimed.

I took Mom to the spot, pointed at the ground, and, of course . . . there was nothing there. I sputtered and protested and told her what had happened, but I couldn't reproduce it. I had no proof for her. No way to show her what I'd seen.

Mom could have reacted in a lot of different ways. She could have said:

"No, you didn't."

"Stop telling stories."

"It's not nice to lie."

"I don't have time for this."

Mom could have said a lot of things. Instead, she looked at the spot where the moth had been, she looked at me, she put her hand on my shoulder, she looked at the sky, and she said, "Hmm . . . Where do you think it went next?"

It was the right question, at the right time, from the right teacher. There was only one possible result: I couldn't help but wonder.

That's been good and bad. I think just about everything is interesting. However, I've not been able to stop wondering about things even when I want to, or especially when I want to.

Like the night after we flew the kite and Max chased the moth. I thought, *He was perfect, but part of you is in him. You did this to him. Now he's broken. What's going to happen to him? What are you going to do?*

"*Joooo-osh*," said Janette as I shifted yet again, causing the mattress liner to slip off the corner with an obnoxious *thwap*. "Calm *down*. It's going to be fine. *He's* going to be fine and so are you."

"But what if he can't handle school? What if he can't work?"

"What if he can't? Then we'll do what we need to do. It's not happening right now."

"What if he blames me? It's my fault."

"He won't. And even if he does, he'd be wrong. And it would be *our* fault. But this is totally irrational. You don't know if he's got it. Even if he does, you know it might not be as bad as yours. It could stop when he's five, or ten, or tonight."

I hoped so.

I hope so.

Janette was right; nobody knows better than I that if Max has Tourette's, there's no guarantee that it will be anything like my case. Maybe he'll never do more than blink. Maybe he'll stop blinking when he's five and that will be the end of this piece of his story. Maybe, like my own case, he won't really have trouble until later. Maybe he'll have a case so much worse than mine that they'll rename the disorder after him.

I can't know. But I can't stop wondering, either, especially now that my own tics have erupted again, worse than ever. I have to admit that I don't know as much about Misty as I thought I did.

She came back because of new and potent stresses that overwhelmed my system: first, Max's tics. Then I learned that a dear friend had breast cancer. My sister Megan was having new and horrible health challenges of her own. I thought I'd throttled Misty. Now Misty was back to throttling me.

I did what had worked before. I tested out my exercises. I tried to move better and rid myself of extra tension. Nothing helped. And every time a previous solution failed to bring relief, there was the stress of thinking, "Well, if you can't figure this out, how are you going to help Max?" This fed the stress, and around and around it went.

I didn't know what else to try. When I told Adam, he said, "That sucks, man, I'm sorry. Any idea why it's bad again?"

There was too much to say, and he'd already heard most of it. "I think I'm just too busy. I can't free up any space in my head. I'm a little embarrassed, honestly. I really thought I was cured."

"Yeah, I know, but it's fun to be wrong. It just means you can learn something. Can I help?"

"I don't think so. I'm still doing everything you taught me. It's just not working right now. I'll figure it out." I didn't sound confident.

"All right. Tell me if I can help. Don't be one of these proud douche bags who thinks he has to do everything himself or he's weak."

And he hung up.

What I didn't tell Adam—because I wanted to figure out the problems without his help—was that I was injuring myself constantly and there were few movements I could try without pain. Misty was constantly forcing me to tense my body, contracting the muscles all at once, as hard as I could. Normally this just wore me out, but if it happened when I was in the wrong physical position, it actually damaged me. These new mega-combo tics were showing up more often. For instance, imagine that you're standing on my left and suddenly the back of my left hand slaps your stomach—my arm has rotated out at a right angle. (I wasn't hitting people, that's just the motion.) That wasn't a new tic, but now, once my arm was rotated away from body, my elbow and bicep tendons were in a vulnerable position. And that's when I was contracting the hardest, once it got to that point. The tendons would scream and the muscles would grate over the bones and suddenly I wouldn't be able to do any pushing or pulling for a week.

There were equivalent pains in my legs, hips, neck, ankles, and jaw.

One by one, the movements that had once been beneficial to me were being taken away. Movements didn't test well—increase my range of motion—if they hurt, and now everything hurt.

I had gotten myself up to a 590-pound dead lift, a 375-

pound squat, and a 350-pound bench press.* Now I couldn't lift half of those numbers without pain. And the most maddening thing was that it wasn't pain from pulling nearly 600 pounds off the ground! It was pain from stupid tics!

But the numbers were never the point. Progress was the point. Dan John—a legendary track-and-field coach and dear friend—is fond of saying, "The goal is to keep the goal the goal." Meaning, don't get distracted. But Dan was used to having guys tell him, "I want to bench press five hundred pounds," but when he'd tell them to bench more often to improve the bench press, they'd say, "Well, someone on the internet said that the key to benching more is to press light kettlebells really, really fast. Shouldn't I be doing that?"

I just wanted my weightlifting numbers to go up consistently, to be stronger than the day before. I didn't care what the numbers were. And now, because of the pain, my ability to get stronger every day was in jeopardy.

I talked to my dad on the phone a couple of days later. "What does Adam say about it all?" he asked.

"He says don't be a proud douche bag. That's about it."

He laughed. "That's probably always good advice. Do you want to know what I think?"

"Sure."

"Well, let me ask you something first. Are you still lifting?"

"Not like I was. No. I mean, I do a little, I just haven't had the urge. Now that it's not helping as much."

---

* Now, this makes me stronger than people who don't train, and I'm at the high end of the intermediate level, but these numbers would get me laughed out of a powerlifting gym. There are guys in my weight class who can double my numbers, or more.

"Yeah, I can see that, but you need to do it. We've all seen it. You've seen it. Now why aren't you doing it?"

"I'm too tired."

"No, you're not. Why aren't you doing it?"

"I'm too busy."

"Ha! Are you going to answer me?"

Nope. I really don't know why it was so hard for me to admit that the tics were hurting me, but it was. "Dad, it's not helping like it used to. It's actually making it *worse*. And that's scary because I've got nothing else to try."

"Oh, so you feel *better* if you don't do it? So you try *nothing*?"

"No. I just . . . I'm tired of this. I want to know why it's happening again."

"Forget about knowing why and get back at it. If you're tired of what you're doing, do something else, but do something. Hike up your skirt, sonny."

I did it. Literally.

That night I played around online before going to bed. On Facebook, I saw a picture of a man wearing a kilt, mid-spin, preparing to heave a massive weight on a chain.

I Googled "getting started in Highland Games."

The next day I ordered a kilt and sent a check for twenty-five dollars to the liaison for the Highland Games in Payson, Utah. I had two months to prepare and no idea what to do. This is what constitutes due diligence in my decision-making process.

The Highland Games are contests of ancient Scottish athletic events. Most of them involve throwing weights, stones, logs, or sheaves of straw for distance or height. I had no experience with any of them and the techniques I watched online felt impossibly clumsy when I tried them, so I decided to go it alone this first time.

I spent the next two months throwing things in my backyard. Kettlebells, stones, chains, forty-five-pound plates, logs, and whatever else I could find. Throwing was totally different from anything else I had tried. It required fast, explosive movement. And little by little, to my great surprise, the tics began to let go of me again.*

One night when I got home from work I asked Janette to come talk to me in the backyard while I threw. It was dark.

I spun once, released the twenty-five-pound kettlebell, and knew it had gone wrong. It was too dark to see where it was going to land.

It landed on the roof with a fantastic crash. Janette was not pleased. But other than that night she was completely supportive. On the morning of the competition she said:

"Spin around. Let me see how pretty you are."

"No," I said. "Let's just go."

"Come on. Twirl!"

I gave her one small twirl because I knew she'd never stop. The gray-green-and-black kilt that hung to just above my knees flared out, then settled onto my thighs again. It cost seventy dollars from Sportkilt.com.

Janette, Max, and I got in the car and drove sixty miles to the Payson Scottish Festival. A Highland Games is like a combination of a track meet and a fair. When we arrived at the park, we wended our way through a series of booths, vendors, bagpipe bands, and concession stands before finding the grass field where the throwers competed.

Everyone but me seemed to be eating funnel cake, which is kind of like a spongy French fry with powdered sugar.

"Should we get Max a funnel cake?" I said.

Janette snorted. "I'll get you some when you're done."

---

* My theory is that if I do any lift for too long, the involved musculature gets too rigid, and rigidity is strongly associated to my tics. All of the heavy, slow lifting I'd been doing had tightened me up more than I realized. Moving a weight quickly through a safe range of motion—throwing—was loosening the tissue back up.

On the field, a group of men in kilts stretched, warmed up, yelled, and grunted as they threw the odd-shaped weights. I checked in, got my T-shirt (purchased with my registration fee), and tried to look like I knew what I was doing as I walked onto the field and introduced myself. I'd registered for the C class, the lowliest of the three amateur divisions. My goals: to not place last in every event and to find people who could teach me some technique.

The first event for C class was called "weight for height," or "weight over the bar." Here's how it works: The group agrees on what the starting height will be. A bar on a pole-vault-type apparatus is set to that height. Then each competitor, swinging a weight on a handle—forty-two pounds for our division—tries to throw it over the bar with one hand. If you clear the bar, you advance to the next round. If you miss, you get two more attempts at that height. If you miss those attempts, you have to watch everyone else continue while you sit there and wonder what might have been.

I was surprised that I won the event. Thousands of reps swinging a kettlebell and ripping heavy weights off the ground, not to mention my height, had given me an advantage. I faced the cheering crowd—seated on bleachers ten feet away—and took a bow. When I stood, I convulsed briefly, all at once, as if shocked. I clucked my tongue and let out a mild "Woo!" before rejoining my group.

Misty had followed us.

"That's my dad!" shouted Max from the bleachers.

That settled it. I wanted to win.

For the next seven hours, I threw with my group. I'd expected a group of big, strutting Scots with haggis dripping from their beards, everyone hoping the others would mess up, or scratch, or fall down, so that they could win instead. But everyone was encouraging. I was surprised a couple of times when athletes from the top class approached to give pointers to me and the other newbies. One man said that I'd do better if I wore cleats that would dig into the grass, and then insisted that I go get his extra set out of his car.

Everyone cheered. Everyone helped. Everyone improved.

Max and Janette disappeared a few times so that he could go play on the playground. Once when he reappeared he had a plateful of funnel cake for me. I sat on the grass with him during lunch and as we watched a flock of birds eat some spilled popcorn, Max blinked his eyes constantly, rapidly.

"Max, do you have something in your eye?" I asked, annoyed at my accelerating heartbeat.

"No, I'm good," he said.

"He's fine," said Janette. "You heard him."

I threw hammers. I pitched a burlap sack full of straw over a bar. I tried to toss the caber, an eighteen-foot metal pole for our class, and failed miserably. I heaved stones for distance. And finally, at the end of the day, it was time for the weight-for-distance event.

Picture a bowling ball on a twelve-inch length of chain. Your goal is to throw it as far as you can. The problem is that the bowling ball weighs forty-two pounds if you're in the C class, and fifty-six pounds for everyone else. No matter how awkward you think this sounds, it's more awkward than that. All day I'd been watching the other classes attempting this event. I'd seen people fall down and get flat out dragged from the box as the weight threw them, not the other way around. No other event had generated more grunting and screaming from the athletes.

When it was my turn, I looked at the crowd. Max stood on the other side of the yellow "caution" tape, but now he had put on my shoes, Converse Chuck Taylors that were twelve sizes too big for him. "Throw it far!" he yelled.

I tried, but somehow, when the weight spun around me, it tore off my kilt and dragged me three feet outside of the throwing zone. I had shorts on underneath, but still . . . the goal was not to tear off your kilt and scratch and get a distance of not even one inch. I'd seen guys eighty pounds lighter than I was throwing this weight for incredible distances. How were they doing it?

I wasn't sure I understood the scoring system, but I knew I had more second-place finishes in the events than anyone else in my group. I thought I could still place if I could get at least one substantial throw.

The next time up, I managed to keep my skirt on and get a decent throw in. I focused on being smooth, not trying to horse it up and muscle it out there.

"You made that look easy," one of my group members said. "It's nice to see someone with that much control."

I screamed and bit my tongue.

He stepped back. "What was that? Are you okay?"

"Yes, I'm fine," I said. "And thank you." And that was it.

"So how'd you get into this?" he asked, gesturing at the field.

There was no short explanation for that one, so I just said, "A friend thought I would like it."

"You're a strong guy," he said. "Do you work in construction or something?"

"I'm a librarian."

"Oh. Wait, what—like in a library?"

Then it was my final throw of the day. I blew Max a kiss, walked to the throwing zone, and hefted the weight. The chain clinked as it grew taut. I got low, dropping into a more powerful position. I tried to ignore the noisy crowd, the droning of the bagpipe bands, and to feel nothing but the pressure of the weight in my hand. To feel the brief control I had over my body. Then I realized my lips were moving, that I was actually speaking. I started laughing way harder than made sense to anyone else, stood up straight, set the weight down, and asked, "Am I allowed to reset?"

"Yes," said the judge.

Janette shouted, "What's so funny?"

I raised my palms and shook them at her: *It doesn't matter.*

I noticed that Max was holding one of my shoelaces in his hand. He had taken it out of my shoe and Janette had tied it around a rock. He was ready to throw.

Janette never asked me what I'd been laughing about. But if she had, I'd have told her that in the seconds before that throw, I'd caught myself praying.

Oh please oh please help me help me help me.

It wasn't directed to anyone in particular, but I was pleading for help, praying for a way to win.

I dropped into a crouch, spun, and threw, with a scream that had nothing to do with Misty. The weight soared from my hands, beyond my reach, up and up as the crowd cheered, and as I watched its trajectory, my arms outstretched to the sky, I could only hope that I'd done enough.

ACKNOWLEDGMENTS

When I finished reading the final version of this book, I thought, "This is a really weird story." The blame must lie with me, but I'd be remiss if I didn't provide a list of the other guilty parties.

First, my wife, Janette. I'll never be able to say what you mean to me well enough, but I'll show you.

My son, Max. Keep asking. I'll do my best to help you find answers.

Mom and Dad. People involved in the editing of this book kept saying, "It's just so refreshing to see someone write *lovingly* about their parents." What else could I have done? And you're still coming to my games after thirty-five years.

Megan, Kyle, Lindsey, and Sydnee. I'm proud to be your big brother and uncle.

My in-laws. I got just as lucky with all of you as I did with my own family.

Spencer Throssell. Thanks for the call. I missed you.

Adam T. Glass, man of one thousand scowls. You gave me my best shot at a normal life, which is all I ever wanted. Keep that claw hammer close.

My agent, Lisa DiMona, who loved the tree that oinks. It took four years, but we got there. I just realized that I still owe you 1,500 bucks.

My deadlifting editor, Megan Newman, who held me to a standard I didn't know I was capable of. And who stopped me from including something highly inappropriate about bonobos. Megan, did you ever suspect that sometimes I wrote crap just to annoy you and get your fiery reaction?

My publisher, William "the Legend" Shinker, who promised that my book cover would incorporate a kettlebell, a temple, and Mitt Romney. And who then backed out like a chicken.

Lisa Johnson, you probably don't know it, but you put me at ease during that first meeting when I was terrified that my tics were going to wreck the book deal.

Gigi Campo, who understands casual references to *Never Give an Inch*.

Beth Parker and Lindsay Gordon, who helped people find this story.

Frankie Faires, who understands pain and desperation. Come down from the mountaintop, you brilliant weirdo—people need to know about you.

All the children with Tourette's who have written to me. You're stronger than you think. Keep marching forward.

For the parents of children with Tourette's. They'll be fine. And if you ever think I can help you with anything, please ask.

The staff and patrons of the Salt Lake City Public Library.

The inimitable editor Betsy Rapoport, who once looked into my eyes and said, "Well, excuse my effrontery, bitch." I love you. No joke.

Readers of my blog.

Seth Godin, who, after seeing one of my tics, said: "Wow! This is like writer's block that you can see!" You were under no obligation to change my life, but I'm glad you did.

Chuck Palahniuk. "Wow, you should write," said your letter. I did. Thanks for the power panda and the switchblade comb.

Every author, reader, and librarian.

And finally, a very special thank-you to Stephen King. Your books gave me some close calls, but I'd read them all again. In fact, I'm going to start right now.